The British Library Studies in the History of the Book

A POTENCIE OF LIFE
Books in Society

A
POTENCIE OF LIFE

Books in Society

THE CLARK LECTURES
1986-1987

Edited by
NICOLAS BARKER

THE BRITISH LIBRARY
and
OAK KNOLL PRESS

© 1993, 2001 The Contributors

First published in 1993 by
The British Library

This paperback edition published in 2001 by
The British Library
96 Euston Road
London NW1 2DB
and
Oak Knoll Press
310 Delaware Street
New Castle
DE 19720

Cataloguing in Publication Data
A CIP Record for this book is available
from both The British Library and
the Library of Congress

ISBN 0 7123 4720 8 (BL)
ISBN 1 58456 054 1 (Oak Knoll)

Designed by John Trevitt
Typeset in Linotype Ehrhardt
by Norman Tilley Graphics, Northampton
Printed in England by
St Edmundsbury Press, Bury St Edmunds

CONTENTS

NOTE

The texts of Stan Nelson, 'The Growth of Typefounding as an Independent Trade', and G. Thomas Tanselle, 'The Nature of Texts', both originally part of the series, have been omitted here, for different reasons. Nelson's words were integrated with a practical display of the technique of manual typefounding which made his lecture perhaps the most memorable and certainly the most visually exciting event of the series, but also defeated reduction into mere words. Tanselle's text, which he generously gave only a short while after he had delivered it as the third of his A. S. W. Rosenbach Lectures in Bibliography at the University of Philadelphia, has been published by the University of Pennsylvania Press (*A Rationale of Textual Criticism*, 1989), and it seemed otiose, as well as trespassing too far on the Rosenbach Fellowships' liberality, to reprint it here.

INTRODUCTION

Nicolas Barker

'Books are not absolutely dead things but doe contain a potencie of life in them to be as active as the soule was whose progeny they are; nay they do preserve as in a violl the purest efficacie and extraction of that living intellect that bred them.' Milton's words are so familiar that we tend to take them for granted without pondering their meaning, and in particular the force they had when they were written, some time before 1644, when they were published. The relaxation of the regulation of the press and the ensuing flood of new books and pamphlets had roused popular attention to the potential power of the press, 'a potencie of life' indeed. But in 1644 it was again under threat; the events of the next five years, leading to the defeat of the monarchy that had sought to restrict the press, were unknown: the new-found freedom might be easily lost, as it was, temporarily and never completely, at the Restoration. Hence Milton's desire to define, as well as plead: to explain what was at stake, not merely to demand the preservation of the new liberty of speech. Books, he saw, were independent of their authors. A man might move a crowd by a speech; the words, set in print, might move a nation. But, beyond this, the words, as preserved in the form of a book, had an added potency, a power to move or influence people in ways the author had not imagined, perhaps long after he was dead. The book itself was, in this sense, animate.

What is more, Milton's concept of this animation extended beyond the text, a single thing, to embrace all the copies of it that might be made by other hands than the author's, scrivener's or printer's. All these had a further life that extended to their use by other authors and all the readers to whom they came, directly in their original form or in the indirect form of quotation or even unconscious adaptation in the hands of others. 'I know they are as lively, and as vigorously productive, as those fabulous Dragons teeth; and being sown up and down, may chance to spring up armed men.'

Areopagitica itself presents a curious instance of this. It was almost a century before it formally achieved a second edition, but the dragon's teeth sprang up with vengeance just after Milton's death when the licensing procedure finally got its quietus. The architect of its destruction was the eccentric deist Charles Blount. His attack was mounted in 1679 in *A just vindication of learning, and the liberties of the press*; he celebrated its success in *Reasons humbly offered for the liberty of unlisenced printing* (1695). In both these works Blount quoted in extenso and without more acknowledgement than an indirect reference from *Areopagitica*. What is more, the acknowledged second edition in 1738 was itself occasioned by another *cause célèbre*, the case of John Peter Zenger, set out in *A brief narrative of the trial of John Peter Zenger, printer of the New York Weekly Journal* (1736). Zenger's position as the publisher of a newspaper sponsored and largely written by those opposed to the increasingly autocratic administration of Governor William Cosby is a median point: he was the successor of the printers who defied Stuart censorship, the predecessor of Wilkes's coadjutors in *The North Briton*. The vitality of the press was dependent on the nourishment it got from the past: *Areopagitica* lived on, and still lives on.

What more explanation is needed of a book that seeks to describe this process – that is, the process of nourishment, the mutual and interdependent exchange between the press and the society that feeds and depends upon it? The historic reasons for it are set out in the first part of this book, and I will not enlarge on them here. But the facts set out there, and the questions which they raised, had already set me thinking, well before the director of the William Andrews Clark Library, Professor Norman Thrower, did me the honour of inviting me to be the Library's Visiting Professor in 1986-7. All this had been a matter of discussion between Professor Thomas R. Adams and me since 1984 when he addressed the problems that we had been discussing in a lecture in the then Clark series. From the text of that address grew not only the survey of the market for maritime manuals, a case-study of the impact of social need upon manufacture with implications outside its special field, which now appears on pp. 145-77 here, but also the first essay, which was not part of the Clark lecture series but its manifesto.

'A New Model for the Study of the Book' is a true collaboration. It has passed through many drafts between its two authors so often that we have long forgotten which of us wrote which words. Its point of departure was the rift that we sensed growing between historians and bibliographers on the essence of a subject which, paradoxically, both sides had just discovered to be of crucial interest to the other. We are, both of us, the sons of historians; we were born and brought up, as well as spending most of our lives, in an academic environment. We are no strangers to the misunderstandings, even feuds, as well as the quirks and absurdities, that can grow up in the common pursuit of learning and the truth. But the importance of this particular movement, as exemplified in Robert Darnton's stimulating and innovative 'What is the History of the Book?', first published in 1982, was too great to be allowed to take the normal course by which, in the gradual accretion of question and answer, theoretical as well as practical problems of historiography are resolved. Janus-like, looking both back and forward, at once addressing both historians and bibliographers, we have tried to set the balance of this discussion in what we conceive to be its true position. The facts remain, as they must be, undisputed: only the fulcrum has moved.

This statement, as it stood in 1986, was sent to each of those whom I invited to take part in the 1986-7 Clark lecture series. Each of the lecturers had a part, carefully chosen and discussed with them, in what was planned from the first as an integrated approach to the problem. I was delighted, but not surprised, by the sympathy and the imaginative grasp with which they seized the topic and by their own response to it, which exceeded my best hopes. Again, I will not elaborate on this here, since their texts are the best demonstration of it. I need only point out here that the combined approach was at once chronological and thematic: Richard Rouse and Lotte Hellinga dealt with the all-important subjects of the book before printing and the transition from manuscript to print as the normal form of the book, but both within the general context of the society of their time span. G. Thomas Tanselle, on the other hand, explored the nature of the text, as evinced in the formal structure of the book – a relatively modern theme, in content. Mirjam Foot, Stan Nelson and John Bidwell pursued other themes: bookbinding, typefounding and the paper trade, the last also introducing the all-important topic of money and capital, the often forgotten *sine qua non* in the life of books. Each of these, too, had a chronological base, stretching into modern times. Bliss Carnochan and Thomas Adams both happened to deal with an eighteenth-century context, but both addressed themes: the growth of authorship as a trade or vocation, and the interaction of its operating manuals with the practice of navigation, the sinews of trade. I initiated the series with some reflections on libraries, at once repositories for the preservation of books and the human experience that they cumulate, and temples to that learning.

All this took place in the William Andrews Clark Library itself, which provided not merely an ideal *endroit*, itself a monument, in both senses of the word, to the theme we were trying to put across. Montana copper provided the means, the complex base of North American culture provided the inspiration, and William Andrews Clark himself the initiative, for the collection of a library of books which provided me with the means of exploring and defining the theme. The beautiful building that he put up, at once the creation of an amalgam of past elegances, contemporary Angelino taste at a time of unsophisticated but rich efflorescence, and a strong sense that outward and inward form should reflect its contents and their needs, became my home for a year, and left an impact on our work that I cannot easily compute.

Equally, I cannot count, but only acknowledge the debt I owe, all the kindness I received from my colleagues there, Professor Thrower, Thomas Wright, Monica Savic, Carol Briggs, Beverley Onley, Pat McCloskey, Carol Sommer, Simon Varey and other visitors and users of the Library, and, above all, John Bidwell, a tower of strength in matters practical as well as scholarly, to whom the series owes more than can ever be apparent. I must also gratefully acknowledge the help of the friends I made at the University Reference Library at UCLA, which became a second home in Los Angeles, notably David Zeidberg and James Davis. Mary and Richard Rouse, also colleagues at UCLA, enhanced my stay, not only by a contribution which, if delivered by Richard, was (I quickly saw) joint work, but by generous hospitality and always stimulating converse. I can only guess at my further debt to the support and advocacy of Franklin Murphy, formerly Chancellor of the University, Robert Vosper, formerly University Librarian, and Jacob Zeitlin, alas no more now, but whose red barn on La Cienega Boulevard was the hub of the book-life of the whole Los Angeles community for so many years.

I cannot end without expressing a final word of thanks to my contributors, who, as I have said earlier, rose to a challenge, the challenge of expressing their own individual themes within the framework of a coordinated scheme. I like to think that they shared the ideals that provoked Tom Adams and me to begin our quest. Their response is not something I shall ever forget: its result I now leave you to enjoy. The curtain draws back; by the time it falls, I hope you will have a truer picture of the impact of the book on society, and society on the book.

A NEW MODEL FOR
THE STUDY OF THE BOOK

Thomas R. Adams and Nicolas Barker

I

'The History of the Book' has become a catch-phrase, adapted and half translated from the French. It is almost 30 years since *L'apparition du livre*, by Lucien Febvre and H.-J. Martin, from which the phrase stems, was published.[1] It is time to take stock of what has happened to bibliography as a science in that period; to consider the longer period during which 'bibliography' (in the modern sense) has addressed itself to the history of books; and finally, taking the longest period of all, the two millennia during which the book has developed in western Europe, to attempt a model for the study of books considered as historic artifacts and as a function of social history.

L'apparition du livre applied the comprehensive view of social history given currency by *Annales*.[2] Unlike the German school, who saw the manufacture and trade in books as a matter for straightforward chronicle (admirably represented in English by S. H. Steinberg's *Five Centuries*[3]), Febvre (who with Marc Bloch founded *Annales*) and Martin were concerned primarily with the impact of the invention of printing on society. 'Le livre, ce ferment' had dynamically changed society: to understand the change, it was necessary to understand how the new technology worked and how the new commerce had grown; but it was also necessary to understand how it had permeated and changed habits and ways of thought, communications and the structure of society. The use of maps and graphic diagrams, the visual aids of *Annales*-istic demography, made the presentation of this thesis more vivid and intelligible.

The seed thus sown by Febvre and Martin among historians has been slow to germinate. One important off-shoot has been Elizabeth Eisenstein's *The Printing Press as an Agent of Change*.[4] Its thesis – that large movements, the 'Renaissance' or the 'Reformation', were not so much

5

influences on the press as products of it – is a critique of history, rather than a work of primary research; as such it has been misunderstood by bibliographers, who have seen its dependence on secondary sources as a weakness. No such criticism could be made of Robert Darnton's *The Business of Enlightenment*,[5] based on the still-preserved archives of the Société Typographique de Neuchâtel, but he too has been concerned with the larger issues of the press as agent or product of the Enlightenment.

The bibliographer, his field of study thus unexpectedly dragged into the limelight by academic historians, has reacted to exposure on the wider stage with mingled fascination and alarm.[6] Both are evinced by the proceedings of several conferences, at Boston,[7] Wolfenbüttel,[8] Athens,[9] Paris,[10] Geneva,[11] and at Worcester,[12] where bibliographers and historians have gathered together, not so much to resolve their differences as to explore a common path forwards. The task of blazing a trail has been approached with much enthusiasm but not a little misunderstanding. Some sort of chart would clearly help.

Why, it may be asked, should any difference exist between bibliographers and historians? A century ago bibliographers and archaeologists occupied very similar positions in the scholarly world; both would have been called 'antiquaries'. A century later, archaeology has become an accepted independent academic discipline and course of study, with departments in most universities: bibliography still hovers on the sidelines of academe. There are two primary reasons for this. First, too many books survive from all periods, compared with any other kind of artifact, from cathedrals to pins, for them to be easily susceptible of 'archaeological' treatment. However numerous, the archaeologist classifies all objects of study as unique: the bibliographer's catalogue entry still treats all the hundreds or thousands of extant copies of a book as a single entity. Secondly, in bibliography there is no line dividing the dead past from the living present. Many – most – books are still living tools, kept in libraries for use. The passage of time alters the context of use, but does not isolate the book, as an object is in a museum. Archaeologists may handle such objects, curators display them to the public. The bibliographer may treat some books in this way. But for a librarian the prime duty is to make books available to all those who wish to use them.

Bibliography meant first writing, then the listing of books. From this it grew and came to include distinguishing one book from another, or different editions of the same book, the arranging books in order, by author, title, subject, place or date. Latterly, characterized diversely as 'analytical' or 'descriptive' bibliography, it has come to be treated as an ancillary discipline, in service to the higher goal of establishing an accurate text. Increasing sophistication has shown diminishing returns, in this respect. Hinman's *The Printing and Proof-Reading of the First Folio of Shakespeare*[13] was a major landmark in understanding early-seventeenth-century English printing house practices; it did not, as was first hoped when Hinman began comparing all the copies of the First Folio in the Folger Library, add substantially to the solution of the problem of an authoritative Shakespearean text. The mass of ancillary evidence thus amassed, however, led to a further change of direction summarized in D. F. McKenzie's celebrated statement, 'The essential task of the bibliographer is to establish the facts of transmission for a particular text, and he will use *all* relevant evidence to determine the bibliographical truth.'[14] Thus the activities of literary bibliographers shifted focus from the purity of the text to its transmission. Participants in the Boston 1980 meeting of the Rare Book and Manuscripts Section of the Association of College and Research Libraries at Boston have now taken this process still further in 'A Statement on the History of the Book'.[15] In the preamble they say that the 'history of the book' means 'all aspects of the history of production, publication and distribution, from the stage of authorship on through to the impact of books on readers and, ultimately, on society'. It is in the insertion of the word 'ultimately' that we see the influence of social historians emerging. The statement would have been just as strong an assertion of the importance of the history of the book without it. With it, bibliography again becomes ancillary to social history, again a 'hand-maiden' to another discipline.

In the largest sense, every discipline is, in certain respects, the hand-maiden of others. Is the study of books to be doomed to perpetual servitude to all others? Like jurisprudence, it demands a knowledge of all things human and divine, since the subjects of books are equally diverse. If ever there was a subject (in modern academic jargon) 'interdisciplinary', it is the study of books, since they are the most important and (next to coins) numerous of human artifacts; they are vital witnesses to the progress of civilization. The subject is important enough to be recognized as something that stands by itself. Like many 'new' areas of study, for example anthropology, it does not fit into a conventional academic framework. It does not apply a specific discipline (such as history or physics) to all events, but all disciplines to specific events, in this case books. How then to define its scope, its true function?

7

To answer this question, let us reverse the historian's point of view and consider, not the impact of the book on society, but that of society on the book. What did people imagine a book was? What was it for? The modern tendency is to assume that a book was what it is now, a tool. It is difficult to recognize how recent a concept this is, the creation of mechanical multiplication, five centuries old but still new. In one sense, a real and practical sense, it was not new in the fifteenth century. Multiple copying of texts, by a variety of means, had existed for at least two millennia: what was new was an abrupt change of scale, of volume. Books possess an earlier, greater, power, as the vehicle of knowledge or inspiration that outlives the time in which they were first conceived or written. It was a form of magic. We still acknowledge this when we say 'I couldn't put it down.' But this was not solely a factor of the text. The physical form of the book was equally important. A book can exercise its power by its outward or inward appearance, by its impressive strength and durability, by its size, large or small. Now, when all except large picture-books are easy to handle, we forget the importance of size: a ponderous folio was impressive, but so equally was the miniature book. A large book might indicate the power it exercised over those who handled it; a small book indicated the power of its owner over the book. Holy Writ or the law set on a great lectern was a monument to all who beheld it: a pocket-book of hours or account book added its virtues to the owner wherever he or she went.

To us, the miracle of the Stonyhurst Gospel is its beauty and (even more) the fact of its survival from the seventh century to our time. But the shape, script and binding, as well as the text, are witness to the power attributed to it when it was first created, as a mobile supplement to the miraculous tomb of St Cuthbert. Its power was acknowledged again when with other relics it was disinterred at the Translation of Saint Cuthbert's bones to the High Altar at Durham in 1104. Ellinger, Abbot of Tegernsee in the eleventh century when he had a series of near identical gospel-books and psalters made for use in his own abbey and its dependent houses, was not evincing an early interest in fascimile reproductions nor just ensuring uniformity of liturgical practice; each book was to be an image of divine authority.[16] Vespasiano da Bisticci's memoirs explain the figure cut in the world by his fifteenth-century customers who demanded the grand books he supplied. The beautifully written and illuminated copies of the works of the great jurists that

Cardinal Oliviero Caraffa acquired and commissioned in the sixteenth century were not just for reading, but were part of the outward and visible splendour of his court and the canon law dispensed in it.[17] The pile of books on the coffee table today impresses on you the wealth and cultivation of the owner.

The capacity to multiply books did not diminish this power, nor society's appreciation of it, but changed it. Abbot Tritheim, asking whether the mere quantity of paper copies would prove an effective a substitute for the known durability of vellum,[18] guessed the change; but the need for the permanence of the individual copy typifies the power as well as utility of the book, not just the text. This is the 'rough magic' that Prospero abjured when 'deeper than did ever plummet sound, I'll drown my book':[19] the book meant more than the text, preserved memorially or in another text. This is why 'books are not absolutely dead things, but so contain a potency of life in them to be as active as that soul was whose progeny they are'.[20] Pope, who took so much care with the presentation of his works in print, knew why:

> Yes, I am proud, I must be proud to see
> men not afraid of God, afraid of me.[21]

Voltaire, who took equal pains to assert the power of his works, knew the force of retention: 'Le secret d'ennuyer est ... de toute dire.'[22] The power of books is not just what strikes the eye, but what may be latent, to be disclosed in the future.

This latent power is vastly magnified by the multiplicity of copies. The successive editions of *The Pilgrim's Progress* show its growth from popular tract to classic; the changes of format, from popular chap-book in the eighteenth century to the pocket classic to edition-de-luxe, to canonical status as an 'Oxford English Text', are equally revealing of the way it has woven itself into the national, now international, consciousness. Cross-fertilization ensues, in a way that the most interdisciplinary studies can hardly capture. How much did *On The Origin of Species* owe to the acknowledged influence of Lyell's *Principles of Geology*, and how much to the copy of Milton that went everywhere with Darwin on the voyage of the *Beagle*?[23] How potent was the influence of *On the Origin of Species* on the novels of George Eliot?[24]

These are questions that cannot just be answered by matching words and texts. The author's intention, the process by which it was converted into a text, the form in which the text was published, its reception, dissemination, the anatomy of its survival – all this can be related to books, vast but not infinite in number, and the supporting evidence that explain their existence and movements. The relation of intention to reception is a special aspect of this, which we consider below (see Appendix).

III

The fact that historians have begun to take a serious interest in the book as such is a step forward of major importance. On the other hand, there are pitfalls ahead. Overwhelmed and bemused as they have every right to be with the volume of secondary writing on the subject (let alone that of primary material), it is not surprising that historians should seek to impose some kind of order, a framework, so that the subject can be treated systematically. But, like all scholars, they have already spent all their professional life with books and so bring to the subject unconscious assumptions about the book derived from that experience. This has unexpected advantages, like M. Jourdain's discovery that all his life he has been speaking prose.[25] It also has disadvantages: the scholar who buries himself in the large secondary literature on the whale fisheries could well write a book on the assumption that a whale is a fish. Unfortunately a patronizing tone has appeared in some of the writings that have thus far appeared suggesting that the work thus far done isn't 'real' or important history.[26] No one questions the need of social historians to construct a framework which they believe will serve as the most effective way of arriving at their goals. When books and their history fall within this framework, the social historian must indeed make judgements and choices about those aspects that are most significant for their purpose. But that is social history: they are not writing the history of the book.

All this is not to say that social historians cannot make important contributions to it. Indeed, they are particularly well placed to do so. The history of the book has all too long suffered from fragmentation. Too many bibliographers have been content to dig their own small patch, without surveying the whole landscape beyond. There is a need for integration. The most significant recent contribution is Robert Darnton's model 'The communication circuit', which he offers as a possible framework for absorbing and interpreting the masses of information we have on the 'fate of books'.[27] It is a schematic structure that is well adapted to the needs of the history of the book in general, allowing as it does for the interplay between external forces and the various processes through which the book goes. The word 'publisher' is anachronistic,

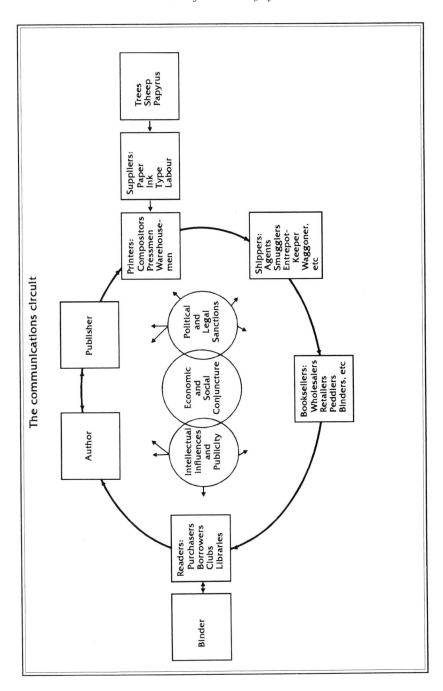

The communications circuit

except for the last century, and conceals a tissue of complex relationships between the roles of patron, printer, stationer and bookseller. The 'bookbinder' is oddly placed, outside the circle in which he more often forms a link between printer and bookseller. The interposition of the shipper as a major factor seems odd: lines of communication, by sea or land, were certainly an important factor, and the necessity for barter explains some odd book-movements, but the shipper (as opposed to the wholesaler) merely provided a service, as he would for any other commodity.

However, from the point of view of serving the history of the book, the weakness of Darnton's scheme is that it deals with people, rather than the book. It is concerned with the history of communication. The principal emphasis is placed on the people who participate in the process through which the book went in providing a means of communication. For the purpose of the social historian is is a useful approach. For those who are concerned with the total significance of books (especially the printed book) it has limitations. To begin with, it ignores the sheer randomness, the speculative uncertainty of the book trade. Especially in the early day of print, those who made or sold books had no precise idea what would sell where, or how to reach that market. Books often took longer to sell, and travelled far further, than conventional lines of communication and trade would suggest.

If the printed book is an artifact that in its creation, dissemination and continued existence has had a profound influence on the history of the world, it is an influence that we still do not wholly comprehend. We have to remember that the printed book was preceded by, and long overlapped with, the manuscript book. (*The Character of a Trimmer*, written late in 1684, began to circulate in manuscript early in the new year; only in 1688, after its work was done and as the Glorious Revolution imminent, did it reach print, and in a form so corrupt as to show that many scriveners had copied and recopied the text before it reached the printer who ultimately printed it.)[28] Now the printed book in turn is being superseded by the electronic book, as print superseded the manuscript. However, for a period of roughly five hundred years the printed book reigned supreme, as a method of recording, communicating and storing all that people put on paper: knowledge, ideas, persuasion (political or religious), diversions, etc. Its influence on one or more of these areas touched almost every aspect of what we call western civilization, in ways we have still to discover.

Now comes the troublesome question of whether the term 'printed book' is really precise enough. It conjures up an image of the codex, the bound volume of printed and folded sheets sewn along the folds and usually (but not always) put between two covered boards. It takes only a moment's thought to realize that printing was used for a great deal more than producing that kind of artifact. The most obvious are broadsides and other similar printed ephemera. In the early days of the planning of the *The Eighteenth Century Short Title Catalogue* it was suggested that ephemera be omitted. This proposal was dropped when it was pointed out that that would leave out John Dunlap's broadside of the *Declaration of Independence*, the earliest official version of that document. For purposes of brevity the terms 'Printed Book' or just 'Book' will be used here, as no doubt it will in future writing on the subject. However, in the interests of clarity somewhat more precise definition should be made at this point.

The term we propose is an awkward one: bibliographical document. By this is meant something printed or written in multiple copies that its agent, be it author, stationer, printer or publisher, or any combination thereof, produces for public consumption. This can include anything from a multi-volume set to a slip of paper. The controlling factor is that the document was designed to perform a specific function, either private or public. Thus an issue of a newspaper, or magazine, or a fascicle of a book in parts, are bibliographical documents. Proofs of books, printed blank forms to be filled in, playbills, proclamations, printed pictures, business cards, even matchbox covers are all documents. The size of the audience addressed is not a factor; rather it is the fact that the agent's intention involves the process of duplication, so that more than one person can have access to what is on the paper. This need and intention was one of the important elements that led to the invention of printing, and the development of printing had an equally important (but not exclusive) reciprocal influence on the process, and, while not ignoring the existence of manuscripts or documents, it is to the printed biblio-graphical document that we now direct our attention.

The artifact and its uses thus defined, what kind of structure can we create that will encompass all aspects of the subject in such a way that the work of those who specialize in one part of the field will not be lost to those who work in other parts, for whom it might have some bearing? The structure, or model, now to be put forward owes its inspiration to that offered by Darnton: that is, a circle of connected elements which are influenced, or can be influenced, by the forces placed in the centre. But since our theme is the book rather than the people involved in its

13

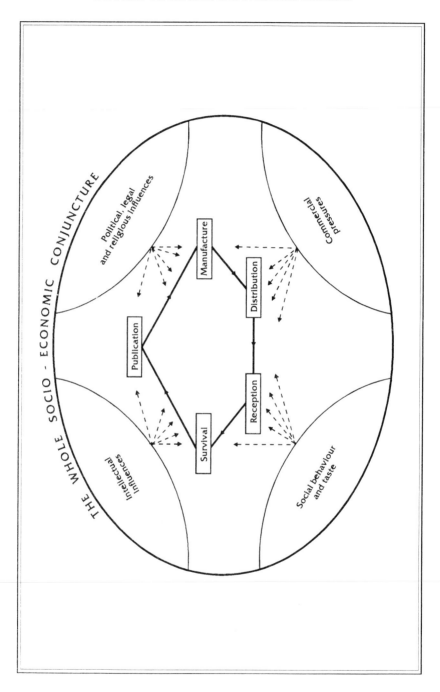

movements, the order of Darnton's elements and forces is inverted. The cycle of the book becomes the centre: the indirect forces are seen outside it, looking and pressing inwards. Instead of the six groups of people who make the 'Communications Network' operation we have five events in the life of a book – publishing, manufacturing, distribution, reception and survival – whose sequence constitutes a system of communication and can in turn precipitate other cycles. Instead of overlapping circles of influence in the centre, indicating intellectual, socio-economic, and official pressures, there are four separate zones, enlarging the scope of outside influences, on the periphery of the circle, each influencing two or more of its stages, depending on individual circumstance. Secondary groups such as the 'binder' or 'shipper' have been omitted, because they are subsumed in one of the five categories. The text is the reason for the cycle of the book: its transmission depends on its ability to set off new cycles.

What follows is a preliminary attempt to expand the concept. The only testing it has received is a group of eighteenth-century English maritime books published by the firm of Mount and Page, a promising field since the books were long-lasting and reflected market acceptance to an unusual degree.[29] These books addressed a comparatively small but well-defined audience. Their publishers depended on a few titles that required reprint after reprint, many of which are extremely scarce today. Besides books, they were also the leading chart publishers, as well as being stationers. Much of their success undoubtedly depended on a special relationship with the maritime establishment, particularly Trinity House. From this, we may infer that the most important force represented here was commercial. Other forces, political, social and intellectual, also played their part, if less directly: the growth of England's maritime power, the vogue for 'projectors', the new zest for science and technology, the accurate measurement of time and distance and cartography itself, are all background influences. And so Mount and Page's books passed through the five stages, just like any other book, and the firm prospered. Indeed, it survives today (1993) under a different name as a printing house.

IV. PUBLISHING

Publishing is the name we have given to the point of departure, the initial decision to multiply a text or image for distribution. To understand it we have to balance the many factors taken into account in the decision to publish a particular book at a particular time. There are four parties to the transaction, any of whom might be identical with each other: author, patron (or financier), manufacturer and distributor. The factors in their decision can be grouped under four headings: creation, communication, profit, preservation. Creation is the desire to present a text, whether written recently or long ago, in a particular physical form. Communication is the intention to make it known and available to others. Profit is the need for the enterprise to make a return, which may be commercial (revenue from sales), indirectly commercial (an advertisement or prospectus), or non-commercial (the promotion of religion or a political cause or the enforcement of law). Preservation is to ensure its continued existence through the creation of multiple copies. Usually, but not always, all four factors were at work. The many variations in publishing practice comes through the amount of emphasis placed on each of the factors in any given instance.

The most familiar kind of publishing is commercial. Here the profit is a surplus of revenue over expenditures after costs are met. Although their business is also communication, what there publishers choose to communicate is contingent on the health of their business. If, on occasion, a publisher may be willing to publish something in which he has a particular interest, whether it shows a profit or not, any loss must be made up somewhere else. The function of the patron is to obviate this need by meeting the costs in advance: manufacturer and distributor will require at least a guarantee before embarking on a doubtfully saleable book. The influence of preservation varies with the opinions and wishes of the publishers. There are some works that at the outset are intended to be lasting. This is reflected in the way the book is made. Others are felt to be transitory, and this too is indicated in the way they are manufactured. Likewise some publishers take pride in the design of their books, while for others anything that is serviceable will do. An author, printer or publisher may be prepared to invest extra time and money to achieve a splendid form, hoping that others will share their view. In the end, if the venture is a commercial one, the cost must still be met, and the business as a whole must prosper.

Not all people who publish do so expecting a profit. We tend to think of publishing as an enterprise invariably commercial, but how many books published in the last five hundred years paid for themselves through sales and how many were financed in part or wholly in some other way? We do not know, but there were and are those whose primary consideration is communication. Here the burden of cost falls on the author or patron. Ecclesiastical bodies financed the printing of several substantial early books, an important factor when the new mass book trade was in its infancy. Gibbon published the first volume of *The Decline and Fall* on commission (i.e. at his own risk); from the second volume on, success assured, publication was financed by Cadell and Strahan, a commercial partnership.[30] Much of the poetry published in the nineteenth and twentieth centuries was done in this fashion, Walt Whitman's *Leaves of Grass* being a notable example.[31] Another recent example of a 'commission' book turning best-seller is Irma S. Rombauer's *The Joy of Cooking*, 1931.[32] In general, commercial publishers cannot afford to be adventurous; a good deal of what is published represents a willingness by someone else to make an investment.

A more prominent, although often forgotten or ignored, kind of publication is undertaken by corporate entities: the role of the church has been noted; the state, its rulers and officials, and commerce in all its forms have an interest in publishing. In general, their decision to sponsor a publication is based on the desire to satisfy non-commercial advantage (e.g. political control, religious orthodoxy or advertisement), profit, in an immediate sense, being a secondary or negligible consideration. These other gains are real enough to the sponsors, even if, as in the case of university presses, their object is something as altruistic as the promotion of scholarship.

The desire to publish for the purposes of preservation does not occupy a prominent place today, but it bulked larger in the decision to publish in the early days of printing. It led, in the case of the many editions of the classics published in the 1470s, to the first major publishing error, over-production.[33] Still, the rescue of Greek texts was an important factor twenty years later in Aldus's program.[34] More recently, the concept of preservation has become involved with that of restoration, the re-creation of the author's original intention. It was a desire to preserve that motivated the William Blake Trust and the Trianon Press to produce the facsimiles of Blake's illuminated books, as well as to give wider currency to works not otherwise easily available. Microform publication can fulfil the simpler task of giving new life to a unique or fragile original.

Like preservation, the desire to create a particular kind of book does not usually play a primary role in the publishing decision but, directly or indirectly, it has its place. The author's original intention, in so far as it is reflected in the form in which his manuscript is prepared, has an initial influence. Typographical design and layout, binding and paper, can play a more than passing part in how a book is received, and how it performs the function for which it was created. It was a primary part of Gutenberg's partnership to give the texts that were now multiplied by printing, the Bible, Donatus's grammar, indulgences, a form that in each case matched the most universally accepted manuscript exemplars. This process led to a new impulse towards standardization, an improvement (it came to be seen) on the variable forms that preceded it. The creation or popularization of small formats was an idea important in itself, greater than the sum of all the many copies it brought into existence. Portability was a major gear-change: it facilitated the movement of books singly, whereas before wholesale distribution was the rule. A small book could be carried wherever its owner (and his successors) went, a point often made to Aldus by his correspondents: once a heavy folio reached its first destination, by manufacture on the spot or transport through the book trade, it tended to stay there. Portability made the Elzevir 24mos so successful. It was a fundamental part of the publishing decision, as it was with Penguin Books in 1935 and Pocket Books in 1939.[35] The end product of the decision to publish is a physical object, and the reasons why a particular form is chosen is an essential element in the process.

The decision to publish, not the creation of a text, is, then, the first step in the creation of a book. The nature of the text and, in some but not all instances, the intention of the author are factors in this decision, but other forces control it that have little to do with the intrinsic merit of the text.

V. MANUFACTURING

Manufacturing is primarily a matter of technology and economics. Chronologically it comes first because it was the development of the central technology, printing, that made possible the existence of the object under discussion, but the economics of the technology make it dependent on the decision to publish. The need of the printer, papermaker and binder to make a profit on their investment is a major factor in that decision, quite apart from the commercial considerations involved in publishing. The extent to which the commercial press in Venice in the fifteenth century was dependent on the non-commercial needs of German monastic houses is another typical factor, as is the desire of an author or his patron to promulgate his work, or the requirements of state or church. Besides major enterprises, a consortium set up to print a great book or a series of books, or the small but growing number of printers with established premises, equipment and work-force, there were many smaller, based on the production and sale of a single book, paid for by author or a patron. In all this diverse and experimental activity, external influence, whether a fixed economy or state or ecclesiastical control, played little part.

The history of the technology of printing already has a large literature, but more is still to be discovered. For instance, it is often said that the printing press of 1800 was essentially the same as the printing press of 1500, yet the enormous growth in the number of books, the size of editions, the creation and development of types and formats, all brought about significant alterations, not only in the structure of the press, but also in compositional techniques, the employment of craftsmen, and industrial procedures generally, between the sixteenth and eighteenth centuries. The bare facts of the mechanical revolution of the nineteenth century are well known: the power press, stereotype plates, machine casting and composition, and illustration procedures. The broader issues remain neglected: how are these mechanical innovations related to those of earlier, industrial 'projectors', Arkwright or Jacquard, and to the general history of technology, and what questions posed by the economic pressure on manual production did mechanization answer?

Another dimension to the subject that has received a good deal of attention but in comparative isolation is type design and typographical layout. That is the process that determined how the printed page was to appear to the eye of the reader, a process that married technology with aesthetics. Even further from the centre of the subject is the whole area of illustration. The wood-block and engraved plate and other methods of reproducing images not made up of letters of the alphabet not only developed along with movable type, but became an integral part of the process we call printing. The vast majority of printed illustrations, including maps, in the last five hundred years have been issued as parts of printed books. This element has generally been discussed purely in terms of its aesthetic or subject content: its importance as a force in the communication process and as a factor in increasing its commercial effectiveness has been generally neglected.

The manufacture of paper and ink likewise have their own histories about which a good deal is known, particularly the former. The technology of both had to keep pace with that of the development of printing technology. Paper in particular underwent dramatic changes to meet the demands of the nineteenth century. These changes in turn had important consequences on the whole matter of survival, since they called in question the future of our record of the past. To a lesser extent ink has gone through the same process. The combination of paper and ink through the impact of metal type in the printing press creates an object with distinct visual and tactile qualities. These vary from place to place and time to time, as each country or locality developed its own style. A knowledgeable person can open any book from any period and, quite aside from its language, tell at a glance roughly where and when it was printed. This appreciation of the physical dimensions of the cultural and economic evidence implicit in any copy of a book deserves more attention as an aspect of the impact of printing.

For a long time binding was considered something apart from printing in the process of book-making. Right up to the twentieth century, it was always possible to buy a set of unbound sheets from the printer or publisher, to be bound at the cost of the purchaser (a fact emphasized in Darnton's diagram). But long before the invention of printing there were connections between stationers and binders, and in the fifteenth century it must have been as easy to buy a printed book bound or unbound. While some purchasers of books continued to commission their own binding, or even employ their own binder, the ordinary buyer increasingly expected a bound book, either properly bound or in a temporary protective wrapper. Not until the nineteenth century was binding automatically integrated into the process through which the book went on the way to the ultimate purchaser. Its original purpose was protection but from the earliest days it took on an additional symbolic function. The history of the subject thus takes place on two different levels. The first has to do with structure, the manner in which the folded sheets were attached to each other so that a protective covering could be attached. This process could be summarized as one of progressive simplification, in the interest of volume, speed and cost, with a parallel decline in durability. The second was the outward appearance of that cover. Jewels and gold, or finely embroidered cloth, as well as leather, might enhance the medieval book. Decorated leather, then cloth and now paper (another progressive decline in durability) have since been used.

Beginning with a printed label, the binding was increasingly used to advertise a book. In Anglo-American publishing this took the form, comparatively early, of colour printing and intaglio impressions of designs on thick paper boards. Now in the manufacture of the modern paperback the cover often costs as much as the text within it. The dust-jacket, which began simply as a protective cover for the book and the elegant decorative binding beneath it, has evolved into a vital instrument in publicizing and selling the book, so much so that collectors of modern books attach as much importance to its condition as to that of the rest of the book. The jacket and its close relation, the paperback cover, have reduced the binding proper to insignificance.

Structure and decoration are basic factors in understanding reception, function, influence and survival of books. One of the present writers discovered Anthony Powell's Dance to the Music of Time because of the attractive covers of the Fontana paperback edition. Frequently-used reference books are expected to have sturdier bindings than a romantic novel. A famous book of which most surviving copies of the first edition seem to be in mint condition raises questions about the extent of its influence when first published. Most of the eighteenth-century English pamphlets that have survived are, or were at one time, bound in volumes of pamphlets. Thus, the esteem in which the book has been held both in general and in particular cases can, in part, be traced through the way it was assembled and decorated. There are many social implications here, which extend beyond the book itself, not the least of which are the rise and fall of the library in the design of houses, and the architecture of modern institutional libraries, with the rise and fall of the monumental main reading-room. The place that books had in the social values of the time is expressed in the frame built to hold them. Besides its decorative function, the external appearance of the book has, with the advent of trade binding, become a function of distribution.

Throughout the whole manufacturing process the historian must take into account the essential ingredient that made it all happen, labour, particularly the place and function of labour in a new technology. The degree of literacy required to carry out the tasks and its effect on both social and economic forces have often been written about, but their interaction remains to be calculated. This involves more than counting each step in the process, how it was carried out and how it changed over time as all aspects of bookmaking (paper making, manufacture of ink, manufacture of type, setting of type, operation of the press and binding) grew from manual to mechanical operation. How these operations were brought into harmony and co-ordinated to produce a physical object – the book – is a further dimension. To appreciate how all these different kinds of labour functioned it is necessary to go beyond the economic and social status of each group and find out how each operates separately and collectively as a part of the larger society of which they were a part. The person who determined how a page was to be set, while part of the same unit as the person who operated the press, required different mechanical and intellectual skills, was paid differently, and had a different relation to the author or publisher whose text was being printed.

Labour, in one form or another, played a role in all the other aspects of the history of the book, publishing, distribution, reception and survival, but only in manufacturing does it have an overt effect, the product of its special skill. Capital, by contrast, came from a variety of sources, related to a wider and less specialized spectrum of economic progress. The emergence of an industry with a specialist work-force and supported by capital investment presents the socio-economic historian with a wealth of facts recorded in conventional form: that is, in chronicles, archives, and earlier historical writings. The history of the manufacture of books has its own story that parallels, has links with, yet remains quite separate from, that of other individual developments. The rise and fall of Robert Hoe and Company, whose printing presses were shipped all over the world from its red-brick factory on the East River in New York, the rise and fall of the red-brick mills of the Amoskeag Company on the Merrimack River in Manchester, New Hampshire, McCorquodale's quarter-mile-long printing machine room in Wolverton, and John Player & Son's industrial palace at Nottingham have much in common. Yet in detail the story of every business is different. The similarities and differences such as this must be taken into account in any study of the book and society.

VI. DISTRIBUTION

With distribution, the history of the book begins its dynamic phase: without it the book cannot perform its essential function, to communicate. On the most fundamental level it consists of four elements: the initial impetus, the consequent moving of books, the destination, both intentional and unintentional, and the momentum that carried the process along, which may last a long or a short time and move fast or slow.

In its simplest form the process of moving consists of moving a book or shipment of books from one place to another. It can be as straightforward as buying a book, or borrowing it, and taking it home; at the other end of the scale, it must allow for the complex financial, logistic and legal factors involved in smuggling forbidden books into a country and subsequently circulating them there. Among the people who might be involved are the bookseller, the shipper, the propagandist, or a librarian. The transportation can be across the street, within a city or country, across a border or across an ocean or sea. The vehicle can be a single person on foot, a cart or a ship. The consignment can go unwrapped, in a parcel, in barrels or cartons. The form in which the books are sent can be fully bound, folded but unbound, or in sheets. The financial cost can consist of cartage, shipping costs, customs duties, insurance, warehousing and bribes. It may be based on money or credit, or the first consignment may have a matching return, involving barter. An awareness of the presence or absence of these forces can in certain circumstances add to an understand of the role the book has played in particular circumstances.

Movement is sometimes illusory. A student of American thought who writes on the impact of *The Education of Henry Adams* on American readers between 1907 and 1918 is likely to be misled. '1907' is the date of the first edition, and the only date given in the bibliography of the *Literary History of The United States* (1948). But the first printing was private and intended for a few friends so that they could comment. It was not until 1918 when Houghton Mifflin brought out the first trade edition that there was any significant movement of the book. The first edition was not distributed in the sense of being originally designed for that purpose.[36]

The forces that set the process of distribution in motion are probably those that chiefly interest the historian. The most obvious is the desire to communicate, but the motive can take a variety of forms: to amuse, to instruct, to convince, are among the most frequent. There is also the desire to recoup and improve on the investment, to gain storage space or to make a gift. All of these involve a variety of mixed motives. Indeed it is the mixture that helps determine the nature and extent of the distribution. Equally important is the lack or limited efficacy of some or all of the normal resources for distribution. If we are to understand the impact or role of any book in society this negative factor must be taken into equal consideration with the positive factors.

A subtle and little-explored aspect of the question is the underlying force that leads a person to believe that what he or she has to say can be of interest to others. A strong sense of purpose or duty are possibilities that come most immediately to mind. These motives do not necessarily have to be the author's own, as is evinced by the careers of two New England poets as far apart in time as Edward Taylor (1664?-1729) and Emily Dickinson (1830-1886).[37] In both cases the motives that set off the forces of distribution came from a source other than the writer. The century between their lives saw the emergence of the professional writer, an important epoch in the history of authorship. But in the earlier phase contemporaries of Taylor, like Cotton Mather and Michael Wigglesworth, found (and Mather sought) print as a vehicle for publishing their works. There is also the special case of authors like Spinoza, who wrote for a publication that was denied him (yet his works found their way to the market). At every period, some authors have sought publication, while others have had it thrust upon them.[38]

Another negative factor that deserves more attention than it has received is the effect of national barriers, or the extent to which the books of one country were or were not distributed in others. Parochialism, language customs and censorship are the most obvious blockages. Holland and Switzerland at various times were successful at marketing books beyond their own borders, while the bookfairs of Germany and elsewhere played a vital role in making the book trade an international affair. Distribution in Europe after the rise of nation states deserves more attention. To what extent did the late unification of Germany and Italy make them different from England and France? How is the book trade altered by different economic circumstances, such as the gold of Spain which imported books for cash, while elsewhere barter, by exchange of books or other commodities, was the rule?[39] The early universality of Latin is another factor: its collapse brought about a new market for translations.[40] Did some kinds of books, such as scientific works, cross boundaries more readily than others? To what extent was distribution dependent on overseas trade, however unselective, such as the liturgical output of the Plantin Press,[41] the books in Spanish that Antonio de Salamanca had printed in Rome,[42] the English books that Thomas Osborne in London sent to Isaac Norris in Philadelphia, or the books imported or printed by Mathew Carey in Philadelphia that Parson Weems peddled in the southern states?[43]

There is one further factor that may influence distribution, official control or censorship. The range of what might or might not be legally printed or distributed has varied greatly in modern societies. The effectiveness and range of the control exercised by the church and state has considerably influenced the publication of many different kinds of books in many ways, from their content and forms to the means by which they reached their readers. Absolute rulers aimed at absolute control of publications, as did the post-Tridentine Catholic church, even if they could not wholly prevent infiltrations from outside or public and private divulgation inside their own territories.[44] The character and effectiveness of a publication must, at any particular time or place, be judged in relation to the nature and effectiveness of official control. At the same time, the moral and political climate of the time may affect censorship no less effectively because it is indirect or commercial in its operation.

The most immediate destination of a book, once it is published, is that intended, the audiences to which the author and publisher addressed it; identifying those audiences is usually our first concern. The evidence that points to the intended audience includes the nature of the text, the size of the edition, the typographical format, the points of distribution, the reviews and advertisements. Of equal importance is the unintended audience: that is, the people to whom the publication found its way, unanticipated by the author and publisher. This can happen either by direct purchase or through a secondary distribution system. The latter can take various forms: it may come about through subsequent gift or loan of copies by the first acquirer, or through unauthorized reprints or translations, either in the place of origin or in other cities or countries. Libraries are an all-pervasive and continuous element in secondary distribution. There is also the second-hand market for books, which pre-dates printing and has only recently detached itself completely from the new-book market. It also involves the fragmentation of the work as originally published, through the reprinting of sections, acknowledged or un-acknowledged, in other writings; and, finally, its assimilation, con-sciously or unconsciously, into a wider area, as phrases find their way into the language, ideas into knowledge.

Distribution during the period immediately following publication is only the first part of the subject. There is also the matter of how the copies of a book which have survived until today reached their present resting place. It is here that an understanding of the second-hand-book trade becomes important. People who buy second-hand books may do so for other reasons than those that impel people to buy new books; because they find the price attractive, whether less or more than it was originally; because they have already read them, rather than to read them for the first time; or not to read them at all, but to preserve them as historic or aesthetic artifacts. But they buy books and that activity is as much a part of the history of the book as the other. Here we find ourselves involved in the history not only of the second-hand and antiquarian book trade, but also in the history of building libraries, of private collecting and of the concept of 'classics', the selection and revival of works that have survived (that is, have a continuing usefulness and vitality) from a remote past.

Finally there is the nature of the movement and momentum that carries a book through its life cycle. The movement is initiated by the desires of the author and publisher when they launched the book on its way. The momentum is provided by the desire of others to possess the book. Again the most obvious of these desires is the wish to read the book, but to do so one must possess the object. Further, the desire to possess a book does not necessarily mean a desire to read it. Immediate reading is only one of the purposes for which people buy books. They may buy books to read later, an intention not always fulfilled, or for reference. But they may also buy a book because their position or function (or their view of that) demands it. Reasons for acquisition may be altruistic: so that the family, or community, whose needs and wishes may differ from the owners, may benefit from what he acquires. Books may be bought just as furniture, to garnish a room; that too is use expressing status. Finally, there is the power conveyed by the book itself, an incalculable, inarticulate, but none the less potent factor in the mixture of motives that makes people want books. There is more to the possession of books than mere utility.

One question, then, that immediately comes to mind when visiting a large private library, with shelf upon shelf of books whose matching or harmonious bindings present an impressive array, is how many of these were read by the owner when purchased or by others, or even read at all. Indeed the survival of a book is linked directly to the frequency with which it has been used. Movement, like everything else in our culture, is not a continuous process. In the case of books, once they have completed their first cycle and are either destroyed or have ended up in some resting place such as a library, their next movement is often the result of something other than the desire to read. External forces, the breaking up of estates, new building, wars, politico-religious disruptions such as the dissolution of monasteries or revolutions, are what send books off on their next journey to other homes, sometimes through the second-hand and antiquarian market, to other collectors, some to come to rest again in an institutional library, where, by now, they may be treated as treasures and kept in a rare-book room.

But even here, where to most historians the book seems to stop, its active life over, it goes on. Depending on the policy of the library of the attitude of its users, a rare-book room can be a barrier or an aid to further use. The balance between use and preservation changes, but continues. References to the rare-book room are apt to be derogatory, implying that it stands in the way of writing history. Such irritation lacks any recognition that without the protected survival of old books it might be difficult, and in some cases impossible, to write that history in the first place. But it also proves the power of the book, its continued vitality, else why the irritation? The astute librarian, treading the line between use and preservation, will observe this power and develop scholarly skills and activities beyond the routine functions of librarianship to ensure that effective distribution, in a new sense, continues.

Distribution is an important part of the historian's concern in understanding the text as text. The number of reprintings, or lack of reprintings, immediately after publication are factors that enable us to determine the extent to which the author and publisher succeeded in achieving their immediate goals. Later reprintings and revivals, subsequent changes in the form of the book or the style of author or imprint, tell us something about the long-range impact of the text. They may come in response to new movements or a revival of interest in the text, or they may be a mechanical repetition, an enshrinement of the text: the form of publication shows whether the temperature is hot or cold, whether the work is warming to new life or freezing to death; the number and location of surviving copies is a different but equally important index.

Distribution, then, includes more than simply getting a book or text from one person to another. It also includes the extent, in time and space, to which that process takes place. It also helps to define the area or areas that were affected by the act of publication. It is a densely woven network about which we still know comparatively little.

VII. RECEPTION

Unlike the three previous themes reception is, initially, a passive thing, and for many of the recipients it remains mute since they leave no direct record of their reactions, if any. The problem of penetrating a reader's mind – to say nothing of groups of readers – makes this one of the most difficult aspects of the history of the book, and 'reception theory' has become an important branch of modern critical theory (see below, Appendix). But, however difficult to achieve, understanding reception is most important if we are to evaluate what impact the book has had. There is a certain amount of direct documentation, but to a large extent it is necessary to turn to indirect evidence. The evidence can be broken down into four groups: direct documentation, popularity, influence and use.

Direct documentation consists of two kinds, published and private responses. The public responses consist primarily of reviews and answers or commentaries which are published. In addition there is the border area of public oral responses, speeches, conversations and the like, which are reported and published at second hand. While all this evidence is direct evidence, it is, in general, evidence of a particular person's response. On occasion, of course, a commentator will endeavour to report the general response to a piece of writing, or a body of writing, but here again it is the evidence of only one person. All this is only an immediate response. Later assessment, in a historical context, of the individual work or a body of work, while in a larger sense reception, is primarily a study of reception not reception itself.

The popularity of a work can be measured in a number of ways; the most obvious is the number of times it was reprinted and the number of copies printed.[45] This may include not only the whole text but adaptations of it for various purposes and translations. It is here that the techniques of analytical bibliography come into play because of the importance – particularly in the era of hand-set type – of complex and deceptive evidence: corrections during the press-run; all the sheets of a single press-run deceptively issued with different edition statements attempting to suggest popularity, or the closely allied practice of substituting a new title-page on an old impression; close imitation in resetting for reasons of convenience or piratical deception, or even to conform with legal requirements.

Extensive reprinting of a text cannot be taken as a direct measure of popularity: it is at best an indication. What we really need to know is how many of the copies were actually read? What happened to the copies printed? What levels and areas of the reading public did they reach, and to what extent did copies not reach a reading public at all? Were they all sold by one bookseller, were they circulated through an elaborate chain from wholesaler to hawker, were they remaindered or simply given away? If remaindered, how many remained unsold and were scrapped, how many survived to attain a new distribution as valuable old books, and how many went directly to library shelves, there to remain undisturbed for many years? The number of editions and copies is, needless to say, but one measure. There is also the important question of how many people read or heard read a particular copy, and this in turn involved circulating libraries and their lending practices, the availability of printed matter in public places such as coffee houses, barber shops and railway waiting rooms, the extent to which private owners lent their books, and the number of copies available in proportion to the population of a particular community. How many books owed their popularity not to being read at all, but simply talked about? What influence did the title-page, often separately printed as a poster, have? Still another measure of popularity is the proportion of survival. This is an area which has received little attention but we must not forget that there were books that had a popularity, short or long, so intense that most or all of the copies have disappeared. Perhaps the most obvious are practical works with little 'literary' merit such as schoolbooks and manuals, but it must also be remembered that novels and plays now considered serious were once considered to be not worth preserving.

Popularity is but one, and in some sense the least important, aspect of response. There is the larger question of influence: that is the extent to which it can be demonstrated that the publication of a work made a recognizable or measurable difference in what happened after publication. Did the author or publisher see concrete results and, further, was the result what had been hoped for or was it something else? Was a poet's reputation enhanced by extolling an unpopular cause, or was he condemned as a crank? Did an instruction manual make it clear how to operate a computer or was the prospective user confused? These are short-range questions. The poet's work may be rediscovered later, indeed he may have been resigned to that in the first place. Time and events may vindicate him. The technical language of the manual may be ahead of its time, and future users find it lucid as understanding of the computer becomes widespread. Looking at the extent to which the act of publishing achieved its intended goals is only one criterion of reception and, in larger terms, a comparatively small aspect of the subject. The larger one is made up of the results that go beyond the original intention. One of the frequently neglected results of a decision to publish is the loss of control over what happens next. On the simplest level the major difference between a letter and a printed book is that to a large extent the audience for a letter can be controlled, while the audience for a printed book is beyond the control of those who originated it.

What then is the nature of the influence of distribution when it goes beyond its initial objectives, and how does it manifest itself? How can we see it and assess it?

The frequency with which a text was reprinted in some form or other during the years following its initial appearance is a starting point for gauging its indirect influence. This is particularly true of a work that lies dormant for a long period of time only to be revived when another set of circumstances calls for a new printing. There was only one edition of *Areopagitica* in 1644: it signified but did not initiate a change in public attitude. Although reprinted anonymously and digested as someone else's work in 1688,[46] the next acknowledged edition was not printed until 1750, at the same time as the London edition of the trial of John Peter Zenger appeared. Herrick's *Hesperides* (1648) achieved its second edition in Bristol in 1810. But this does not mean that either work ceased to be read or did not have an underground life paraphrased or quoted in other works.[47] While authors usually hope that their writing will have a timeless appeal, they cannot control the future, so that this kind of later dissemination is the result of forces that are quite different from those that controlled initial publication. A much more elusive, and in many ways a more important and less understood, aspect of reception is the way that the ideas, and even the actual wording of those ideas, are picked up and used with or without acknowledgment by later writers for a variety of purposes, some having nothing to do with the original intention of the author and publisher. It is worth noting that an early attempt to bring this secondary use under control was made by the Cambridge bookseller, John Bartlett, to whom Harvard professors turned when trying to identify a quotation. His *Familiar Quotations* came out in 1855.

A change of language can effect even more startling transformation: the translator may do his work to fulfil needs differing from those that produced the text in the original language. When Joel Barlow, the Hartford Wit, in 1792, translated Brissot de Warville's *Nouveau voyage dans les Etats-Unis de l'Amérique* as *New Travels in the United States of America*, he turned it into a Federalist tract by alteration, omission and addition.[48] It is this dimension of reception that has received the smallest amount of attention.[49] It is elusive, but the process of tracing a text and its influence through other publications is a vital aspect of the role that printing and the book have played and it can only be done with a full awareness of who received what books and in turn produced what books derived in part from that experience.

There is also the question of literacy, an increasingly fashionable but rather ill-defined area of study. Who could read or write seems a simple question. Reading, however, is not easily distinguished from memorial repetition. A book may be used for show, or a prompt, rather than actual reading. To be able to sign your name does not prove that you can write. A signature does not mean that the same hand could write other words. Writing and reading are separate activities: the ability to write tells us nothing about the frequency or ease with which a writer could also read. But the diffusion of books is dependent on literacy. Where and how did people obtain them, at what price, and what were the physical circumstances under which they read them? All these questions are essential elements in assessing reception.

There are other questions, more remote but not less important. What was the influence of physical circumstances on reading? What role did illumination play? Did the variation in hours of daylight at different

latitudes have any effect on patterns of reading? How did the improvement of artificial lighting, or the development of reading glasses, affect
readers' habits? As the amount and complexity of reading material
increased, what happened to the speed and thoroughness with which
people read? Is not literacy relative and the study of it useful only in a
specific context? The audience for Pope's poetry probably includes few
ordinary tradesmen or master mariners. Yet to be successful the first
had to be able to do accurate bookkeeping and the second to use the
mathematical and astronomical tables necessary to navigating across the
open ocean. In fact, the whole development of science depended as much
on mathematical literacy as it did on the use of words. There is a further
dimension to literacy, too, namely the impact of visual images as a form of
human communication. These were manufactured by analogous processes (paper and the rolling press) and distributed by similar routes as were
books and verbal documents. The links between the two were aptly
demonstrated by William M. Ivins, *Prints and Visual Communication* (New
York, 1953).

If, then, our understanding of reception is episodic and scattered, the
width and extent of available evidence should encourage, not discourage,
further research. Scarcity of documentation presents the historian with
a challenge, not a limitation. Still, imagination and determination are
required to identify and interpret the sources. Archaeology recreates the
way people lived from what is dug out of the ground, on the land or in the
sea. For later culture, including our own, it supplements documentation.
McKenzie's summons to 'use *all* relevant evidence' has a special force
for those who try to calculate the reception of the book. We cannot fully
grasp it unless we take into account that there had to be a physical
confrontation before reception could take place.

VIII. SURVIVAL

The idea that survival should be treated as a separate element in the
history of the book is unconventional. Yet, if we start with the premise
that the book as a physical object is the point of departure, then evidence
that the object existed is essential. The most conclusive such evidence is
the survival of a copy or at least a fragment of a copy. The circumstances
under which this survival took place then becomes as important a part of
understanding the subject as are the circumstances which brought it into
existence in the first place. Some books owe their survival to secondary
causes, by being used as binder's waste or box linings. Like old

newspapers found at the bottom of long unopened trunks in the attic, these survivals have a curious fascination. In addition, there are also those books for which we have only circumstantial evidence of their existence. This is true of the first works printed in Latin America and in what is now the United States.[50] They present a somewhat difficult problem, but must be taken into consideration if we are to gain a full understanding of the role the book has played.

There are three stages in the life of books that have survived. The first includes its creation and initial reception: this is the period during which it is used to perform the function for which it was brought into existence. The second is the period during which it comes to rest without any use or at least intensive use. It is during this period that it is in the most danger of disappearing. If circumstances are right then it will survive until the third period. This is when it is discovered that it is a book desirable as an object, either in its own right or because of the text it contains. It documents the age that brought it into existence and thus enters the world of collecting and scholarly research.

The main factors that determine whether or not a book survives the first stage also fall under three heads: the physical form in which a text survives (and without which it cannot survive), the size of the printing and its subsequent popularity. In varying degrees each of these can work for or against survival. It is a general truism that big books tend to survive better than small books. A weighty set of folio volumes sewn on sturdy cords and firmly attached to wooden boards covered in pigskin is more resistant to wear and tear than a broadside. The development of the readable octavo or small format that can be slipped into one's pocket insured a greater use of books and theoretically a greater rate of disappearance. But this was balanced by longer press runs, and also by the instinct to preserve, implicit in the idea of the book as a symbol of status, inherent in the text or, latterly, explicit in the notion of the book as something old. The possession of books thus became important to many levels of society, and the publisher and the bookseller were able to supply them all at appropriate prices. A more practical factor in the relationship between format and survival is the materials from which the book is made. It may be that Abbot Tritheim was right. If we take the Gutenberg Bible as the starting point, book-making has been going downhill ever since, with alarming rapidity as manufacture becomes more and more mechanized. A hard-cover book no longer necessarily means a more durable book. Even with the best of intentions, printers and binders during the last half of the nineteenth and first part of this century have produced, under the pressure of industrialization, books that have deteriorated with alarming rapidity. Out of this has grown an entirely new dimension to the history of the book which will have to be taken into account when posterity comes to study our own time, that is conservation.

It might be supposed that there would be a direct relationship between the size of printing and the survival rate but in fact in almost every case this is modified by popularity. If a book is printed in a large number of copies it is because it is anticipated that there will be a demand for it. If demand is thus keen, then the likelihood that copies will be read to pieces increases. Other books acquire 'classic' status: if not printed in such large numbers, they are never out of print, and the physical form with which successive ages have ensured their immortality is an important index of their status and survival. The relationship between the number of surviving copies and the extent to which a book may have been read is under-explored and open to misinterpretation. This is equally true of classics, which may survive because they were prized but not read, and of books that were intensively used, such as children's books, schoolbooks, handbooks, and manuals which have a poor survival rate.[51] It can be argued that the latter played as large a role in the development of society as classics and literary works in general. Certainly we know a good deal less about how they functioned and what they achieved; the evidence still lies buried.

Popularity as a factor tends to operate positively on the text and negatively on the book. That is, a popular work tends to get reprinted, while the use that goes with popularity tends to reduce the number of surviving copies, at least of the earlier printings. This is, however, only a tendency and applies primarily to texts for which there is a continuing demand over a period of time. There is the equally familiar phenomenon of the book whose first editions seem to have survived in larger numbers than later ones. Charles Darwin's *On the Origin of the Species*, 1859, was, until the growth of the history of science as a popular field of collecting, a comparatively easy book to buy. On the other hand, cheap reprints that came out at the time of the Scopes trial in 1925 are a good deal more difficult to find on the antiquarian market.[52] This paradox reflects the fact that some books start as scholarly works, with the status of classics (and are therefore preserved), and only later achieve the popularity which destroys more copies than it keeps.

Although we know what the most obvious forces are that bring about the destruction of books during the initial stage of their existence, we have not yet found out enough about how they operate to use their

33

evidence on a large scale in order to understand survival. This is not to say that the evidence is not there to be discovered: there are enough individual cases where a full enough story is known to give some notion of the process of survival. Works by Copernicus, Galileo, Audubon and Darwin have all been studied, with interesting and in some cases revolutionary results.[53]

The second stage in the process is that period following a book's initial popularity when it comes to rest, usually on a bookshelf. If this bookshelf is part of a library, the chances of its contents' survival are considerably greater than those of the books in a corner cupboard that serves as a catch-all. This security is increased if the library has a stable existence and those responsible for it view the books as a collection to be preserved rather than as a mere accumulation. If the books are felt to be a coherent entity with a collective significance, casual or deliberate depletion is less likely. Indeed the history of this period of survival is an important part of the history of book collecting and libraries, although a part that has not received as much attention as the more conventional approach which concerns itself with the deliberate building of collections and the active service functions of a library.

Institutional libraries are obviously the most stable. Libraries associated with the state, the church and universities are not only much more likely to have a longer life than private collections; they also tend to absorb both private collections and individual books, particularly if assisted by a system of copyright deposit or an active policy of acquiring older books. Non-institutional collections have also played a vital role, but because many of them are private less information about them is readily available. The most prominent are libraries formed by the wealthy, noble or otherwise, for whom the gathering of a library was as important a statement of their social and economic status as their collections of paintings, tapestries and the great mansions built to house them. We should not forget those wealthy collectors who form collections with the deliberate intention of handing them over to an institution which otherwise could not have afforded them. But these are only one end of the scale of which the other is the humble home in which a copy of the Bible constitutes the centre-piece of a handful of books kept on a shelf, traditionally by the fireplace. In between there is the artisan, business-man or teacher who has around him books, manuals and treatises which help or are essential in his work. Different socio-economic classes use and preserve books for different reasons, in different quantities and in different ways. (The fate of *Pilgrim's Progress* is a case in point.) Similarly, there are those for whom the act of reading is an essential part of living, a group which has always constituted only a relatively small segment of the population. Such reading can be for anything from simple entertainment to a conscious effort to broaden knowledge or improve education. The collections that result are primarily the product of the reading interests involved. Their survival, when it happens, is usually the result of salutary neglect. A person or an institution may, for whatever reason, go through a period of buying and reading everything available about an historical figure such as Napoleon, Franklin D. Roosevelt or Winston Churchill and bring together a respectable group of books on the subject. But when that interest ends the books may find themselves relegated to the back room. Perhaps the greatest threat to them is posterity's need for the space they occupy for other purposes. This is as true of the avid reader of paperback detective stories as of a research library with deaccessioning policies.

Perhaps the biggest single factor favouring the survival of books during this middle period lies in the nature of the book itself. It is an object that certain kinds of people like to possess. In the process, they develop special attitudes toward it. For some, like Milton, the destruction of a book is a crime.[54] On the other hand, oddly enough, the failure to return a borrowed book or even stealing a book (except from a bookstore) is considered less of a misdeed than the same treatment of other kinds of personal property. The sense in which the text is detachable from the book allows the borrower to feel that if he fails to return the book itself he has not wholly stolen it.

The desire to preserve books is ingrained in all sorts of people but in none so important as the bookseller, particularly the second-hand bookseller. The most familiar manifestation of books, not protected by lying quietly on library shelves, is the second-hand book store, usually in a low-rent area with low overhead, which the owner has packed with thousands of books as a result of almost indiscriminate buying of whole libraries and collections. It can be argued that this is basically a business and that like any other commodity books are a means of making a living. However, except in some of the more sophisticated parts of the antiquarian trade, few second-hand booksellers make more than at best a comfortable living.

More recent trends, resulting from the changing role and character of the book, and in the United States a tax ruling that makes it difficult for publishers to maintain a large stock of books in print, have and will continue to bring about changes in the older patterns. The increasing cost of space makes difficult the preservation of large numbers of books, in gross or singly, for both publishers and booksellers. But the growth and spread of the second-hand and antiquarian book trade throughout the world testifies to the continued fascination that books as physical objects still hold for a great many people. For confirmation one need only attend one of the many antiquarian book fairs that flourish nowadays.

It is during the middle period that most of the destruction of books occurs. Unless they find their way to a collection, library or dedicated second-hand bookseller their chances of survival are slim. Even then the forces of neglect, indifference and ignorance cause the disappearance of many volumes. The conditions under which books are kept, whether in the industrially polluted north or the pest-ridden tropics, have resulted in deterioration, even before the use of wood pulp instead of rags built decay into the very material of book production. Preoccupation with other responsibilities has led many librarians and others to regard out-of-date or little-used books as an unnecessary burden, just as it has made them blind to or unable to cope with the historical importance of certain kinds of material, such as official publications or ephemera. Such errors in judgment are not confined to librarians: there was a bookseller whose enthusiasm for F. Scott Fitzgerald led him to develop a fine stock of his books only to unload it just before the Fitzgerald revival; the sale of the Harmsworth Collection took place as the nadir of old book prices; Mervyn Peake's books, now in great demand, spent many years on the remainder book stalls.

The final stage in the life of a book is when it becomes desirable in the world of book collecting, a world in which the tangible qualities of the book are considered as important as its contents. Some books never have to go through the first two stages but enter the collecting world almost as soon as they are published. The modern press book is perhaps the best example, but the price of Audubon's *Birds of America*, 1827-38, began to increase immediately after its publication; if it were possible, a detailed study of the resale value of the Gutenberg Bible might produce some interesting results. Beyond this are the forces of fashion and the march of intellect, and, most important, the lapse of time itself that little by little brings books or groups of books in to the arena of desirability, whether to be read as texts or preserved as artifacts. This distinction is hard to pin-point. The interests of a great innovative collector can make certain subjects widely collected by his imitators. New fields of scholarly interest can flush out material that would otherwise be neglected. Makers of bibliographies document the importance of whole groups of books that previously were treated with contempt or indifference. Pollard and Redgrave's *Short Title Catalogue* made *all* books printed in England or English before 1641 collectable as did Charles Evans's *American Bibliography* for books printed in what is now the United States before 1801. Lawrence E. Romaine's *A Guide to American Trade Catalogs, 1744-1900* (1960) awoke a new interest in the printed relics of economic and industrial history. All these forces interact, lubricated by the antiquarian bookseller, so that there is a steady advance in the epoch before which it can be said any book is a rare book. 'Rarity' itself is a misleading concept; books become 'rare' not because they are scarce, but because commercial forces, following those of intellectual fashion, give them a new value as a commodity. Initially it was the year 1500. Today it has passed the year 1800 and is moving through the nineteenth century, so that it is at least safe to say that by the year 2000 it will be the year 1900 (the work just beginning on the *Nineteenth Century Short Title Catalogue* would seem to insure this).

The multiple forces which have worked and still work to allow books to survive for us to study so that we can have a 'history of the book' at all are little understood, or rather their interaction within themselves and with the other factors which must be taken into account is little understood. This is in part because of the great emphasis that has been placed on the inter-relationship between the text and the book with the emphasis on the text. The function of the book as text, as a vehicle carrying information within it, is obvious, but the information that it provides by virtue of its mere survival and the existence is not less important because less obvious. The loss due to non-survival, even less measurable, cannot be left out of this equation.

Completing the circuit – the return from survival to publication – is the fuel of the dynamics of the book. A majority of the books in the libraries of the world are reprints not the original edition. Remember that unless a prototype has survived no decision can be made to republish and thus start the process all over again under different circumstances. The large reprint and microform industry now testifies to the continuing importance of republication in the history of the book, a factor that dominated the circuit in the era of the invention of printing. Indeed the success of the first major microform publication, the microfilm of all the books and broadsides listed in STC published by University Microfilms International, had its origins in a need for survival. The decision by the British Museum to allow the company to bring its cameras into the Library in the 1940s was a result of a concern for their preservation in wartime. The other advantages of microform, such as saving space, which later became important were secondary then if they were considered at all.

An equally obvious publication that results from survival is the whole body of scholarly writing made possible because a copy or copies of books long forgotten are rediscovered when the progress of research gets around to asking for them. Libraries, like museums, are always amused, if mildly irritated, when a scholar makes headlines with an announcement that a lost book or manuscript has been 'discovered' in a collection when the curator knew it was there all the time. It is too often forgotten that before a question can properly be answered it must be properly asked. Survival is not merely a physical fact, but the degree to which that fact is known.

IX

After so extensive an exploration of the ramification, the outer fringes, of the book circuit, it may seem equally otiose to close the circle by pointing to the link between survival and publishing, or to explore the outer edges of the circle, the external forces that exert influence on the circuit. We will therefore be as brief as may be.

'Tout s'achève en Sorbonne', wrote Valéry: everything ends up as a PhD thesis.[55] So books, whether viewed as intellectual instruments or social documents, continue to exist because more books are written about them and thus depend on them. Valéry's pessimism might be countered with the analogy of the coral reef. Survival is a cumulative process.

The four external forces could be divided into many more (or less) categories: it is in the nature of such exercises in social anatomy that there is no right scheme. All schemes have some truth, and all are equally open to dangers of over-simplification. Our pattern has only the merit of following the sequence of the book circuit. Ideas for books, whether for printing something new or reprinting something old, spring from the intellectual climate of their time and influence the decision to publish. Sanctions imposed by society, cross-linked with the intellectual climate, moderate that decision and have a marked impact on both manufacturing and distribution. Commercial pressures, the ease and cost of communications, bias both manufacturing and distribution, and have their own influence on the media of reception. The changing tastes and habits of society, which set their mark on reception, thus reach back to distribution and on to survival, and simultaneously link with the march of intellect and new decisions to publish that it engenders.

It is only in theory, in the simple context of a diagram, that these forces can be disentangled from each other, or from the special circumstances of the creation and survival of books. However, the existence of such a framework may have a purpose now. The passage of the old bibliography to the new history of the book is not simple: it is accompanied by an abrupt change from a reductionist to a maximalist philosophy. At the same time, there has been an enormous increase in secondary source material, only incidentally caused by the increase in the scope of the subject; antiquaries will always go on digging.

Our scheme is designed to encompass all the topics that would properly be included in the history of the book. It is a framework designed to fit the vast and sprawling mass of source material in such a way as to introduce to it those who are not familiar with all aspects of the subject so that it can be explored without the threat of straying outside familiar territory. What we offer is a map. It is a map not unlike Isidore of Seville's seventh-century map of the inhabited world which placed Jerusalem in the centre as a sort of prime meridian, and located other known geographical features, such as the Nile and the Mediterranean, schematically, suggesting relationships rather than exact locations. The medieval world-map was a synthesis designed to show what was known and perceived about the growing welter of facts and myths relating to the geography of the earth. It is a staging-point in the process that has only recently culminated in the mapping of the world from direct observation by satellite. Our scheme for the study of the book is likewise intended only as a point of departure, a brief for a map that can encompass what we know and perceive. Fuller knowledge of the circumstances and the passage of time will change the pattern. The book will shift from its central position as other form of communication grow in importance. But for two millennia its place has been pivotal and its prominence will continue for some time to come. So Jerusalem continued to serve as a prime meridian on some world maps until the middle of the fifteenth century, not to be finally displaced until the discovery of the New World revolutionized geography.

A map cannot save the traveller from all dangers that may beset his path. It may save him from some; it also offers him the promising opportunity of pointing out its errors when he returns home, safe and sound.

THOMAS R. ADAMS and NICOLAS BARKER

NOTES

1 Lucien Febvre and Henri-Jean Martin, *L'Apparition du Livre*, Paris, 1958; in English as *The Coming of the Book; The Impact of Printing, 1450-1800*, trans. David Gerard, London, 1976.

2 For an early assessment see Wallace Kirsop, 'Literary History and Book Trade History: the Lessons of *L'Apparition du livre*', *Australian Journal of French Studies*, 1979, 16, pp. 488-535.

3 S. H. Steinberg, *Five Hundred Years of Printing*, Harmondsworth, 1955, 2nd ed. 1961.

4 Elizabeth L. Eisenstein, *The Printing Press as an Agent of Change: Communications and cultural transformations in early-modern Europe*, Cambridge, 1979. For a condensation see her *The Printing Revolution in early modern Europe*, Cambridge, 1983.

5 Robert Darnton, *The Business of Enlightenment: A Publishing History of the Encyclopédie 1775-1800*, Cambridge, Mass., 1979.

6 The most prominent expression is to be found in the reviews of Eisenstein's *The Printing Press as an Agent of Change*; see particularly Paul Needham in *Fine Print*, 1980, 6, pp. 23-5, 32-5. For an assessment of her achievements and failures by an historian see Anthony T. Grafton, 'The Importance of being Printed', *Journal of Interdisciplinary History*, 1980, 11, pp. 256-86. *The Advent of Printing: Historians of Science Respond to Elizabeth Eisenstein's 'The Printing Press as an Agent of Change'*, ed. Peter F. McNally, Montreal: Graduate School of Library and Information Studies, 1987, includes a list of all the reviews of the work up to the time of publication.

7 *Books and Society in History*, Papers of the Association of College and Research Libraries Rare Books and Manuscript Preconference, 24-28 June 1980, ed. Kenneth E. Carpenter, New York and London, 1983.

8 *Buch und Buchandel in Europa im achtzehnten Jahrhundret: the Book and Book Trade in Eighteenth-Century Europe*, proceedings of the Fifth Wolfenbütteler Symposium, 1-3 November 1977, ed. Giles Barber and Bernard Fabian, Hamburg, 1981.

9 *Le Livre dans les Sociétés Pré-Industrielles*, Colloque International du Centre de Recherches Néohelléniques, Athens, 1982.

10 *La Bibliographie Matérielle*, Giles Barber, Nicolas Barker, Jean-Daniel Candaux, Nina Catach, H. Gaston Hall, Allan Holland, Wallace Kirsop, Paule Koch, Roger Laufer, Henri-Jean Martin, Jeroom Vercruysse, Ian R. Willison, présentée par Roger Laufer, Table ronde organisée pour CNRS par Jacques Petit sous l'égide du CNRS-GRECO n°1 (Groupement de Recherche sur Textes Modernes) tenue à la Bibliothèque Nationale à Paris les 17 et 18 mai 1979, Paris, 1983.

11 *Actes du colloque international sur l'histoire de l'imprimerie à Genève*, ed. Jean-Daniel Candaux and Bernard Lescaze, 27-30 avril 1978, Geneva, Société d'histoire et d'archéologie, 1980.

12 *Printing and Society in Early America*, ed. William L. Joyce, David D. Hall, Richard D. Brown and John Hench, Worcester, Mass., 1983 (the papers of a conference held October 1980).

13 Charlton Hinman, *The Printing and Proof-Reading of the First Folio of Shakespeare*, Oxford, 1963.

14 D. F. McKenzie, 'Printers of the Mind; Some Notes on Bibliographical Theories and Printing House Practices', *Studies in Bibliography*, 1969, 22, p. 75.

15 *Books and Society in History*, pp. xi-xii.

16 Christine Elisabeth Eder, 'Die Schule des Klosters Tegernsee im frühen Mittelatter im Spiegel der Tegernseer Handschriften', *Studien und Mitteilungen zur Geschichte des Benediktiner-Ordens*, 1972, 71, pp. 6-135.

17 Diana Norman, 'The Library of Cardinal Oliviero Caraffa', *The Book Collector*, 1987, XXXVI, pp. 354-71, 471-90.

18 Letter to Abt Gerlach von Deutz (1492), quoted by W. Wattenbach, *Das Schriftwesen im Mittelalter*, 3rd edn, Leipzig, 1896, p. 452.

19 Shakespeare, *The Tempest*, Act V, Scene 1.

20 Milton, *Areopagitica*, ed. K. M. Lea, Oxford, 1973, p. 6.

21 *Epistles and Satires of Horace Imitated* (1737-8), epilogue, dialogue, 2:197-8.

22 *Sept Discours en vers sur l'homme*, VI. Sur la nature de l'homme, ll. 174-5.

23 Gillian Beer, *Darwin's Plots: Evolutionary Narrative in Darwin, George Eliot and Nineteenth-Century Fiction*, London, 1983, p. 87.

24 Ibid., pp. 149-235.

25 Molière, *Le Bourgeois Gentilhomme*, Act II, Scene 4.

26 R. Darnton, 'Reading, Writing, and Publishing in Eighteenth-Century France: A Case Study in the Sociology of Literature', *Daedalus*, Winter, 1971, pp. 214-56; id., 'What is the History of Books?', and E. L. Eisenstein, 'From Scriptoria to Printing Shops: Evolution and Revolution in the Fifteenth-Century Book Trade', *Books and Society in History*, ed. K. E. Carpenter, New York, 1983, pp. 3-42.

27 Robert Darnton, 'What is the History of Books?' *Daedalus*, 1982, 111, pp. 65-83, reprinted with slight alterations in *Books and Society in History*, pp. 3-26.

28 *The Works of George Savile, Marquis of Halifax*, ed. Mark Brown, Oxford, 1989, I, pp. 33-5, 61-8.

29 T. R. Adams, 'Mount & Page: Publishers of Eighteenth-Century Maritime Books', *infra*, pp. 145-77.

30 N. Barker, 'A Note on the Bibliography of Gibbon, 1776-1802', *The Library*, 5th series, 1963, 18, pp. 40-50.

31 Gay Wilson Allen, *The Solitary Singer: A Critical Biography of Walt Whitman*, New York, 1967, pp. 147-51.

32 There is no imprint on the title-page. The verso reads 'St. Louis: A. C. Clayton Printing Co. 1931'. It was not until 1936 that Bobbs-Merrill of Indianapolis took it on as a trade publication.

33 Rudolf Hirsch, *Printing, Selling and Reading, 1450-1550*, 2nd edn, Wiesbaden, 1974, pp. 27-40.

34 M. Lowry, *The World of Aldus Manutius*, Oxford, 1979, pp. 79-82, 229-49. N. Barker, *Aldus Manutius and the Development of Greek Script and Type in the 15th Century*, Sandy Hook, Conn., 1985.

35 Thomas L. Bonn, 'The First Pocket Book', *Printing History*, 1983, pp. 3-14. Sir William Emrys Williams, *The Penguin Story, 1935-1956*, Harmondsworth, 1956.

36 See the 'Editor's Preface' by Henry Cabot Lodge in the 1918 edition.

37 The first piece of Edward Taylor's poetry to be printed appeared in an article by

Thomas H. Johnson in the *New England Quarterly*, 1937, 10, pp. 290-322. He also edited the first collected works, *The Poetical Works of Edward Taylor*, New York, 1939. Five of Emily Dickinson's poems were printed during her lifetime but without her consent. The first collection of her work to appear in print was *Poems by Emily Dickinson*, ed. Mabel Loomis Todd and T. W. Higginson, Boston, Mass. 1890.

38 A. van der Linde, *Benedictus de Spinoza: Bibliographie*, The Hague, 1871. W. Schmidt-Biggeman, *Baruch de Spinoza, 1677-1977: his work and its reception:* [Exhibition held at Herzog August Bibliothek in Wolfenbüttel, 21 Feb. – 30 Apr. 1977, ed. with an introduction, trans. from the German by Rand Hensen], Baarn, 1977.

39 R. M. Kingdom, 'The Plantin Breviaries: a case-study in the 16th century business operations of a publishing house', *Bibliothèque de l'humanisme*, 1960, 22, pp. 133-9.

40 Steinberg, *Five Hundred Years of Printing*, pp. 117-27.

41 Colin Clair, *Christopher Plantin*, London, 1960, pp. 87-104.

42 Sir Henry Thomas, 'Antonio [Martinez] de Salamanca, printer of *La Celestina*, *c.* 1525', *The Library*, 5th series, 1953, 8, pp. 45-50. F. J. Norton, *Italian Printers, 1501-20*, London, 1958, pp. 101-2.

43 M. E. Korey, *The Books of Isaac Norris (1702-1766) at Dickinson College*, Carlisle, Penna., 1976, pp. 4-6.

44 A. L. Haight, *Banned Books*, New York, 1955.

45 Figures are apt to be misleading, if only because the exceptional is more frequently cited than the normal. The latter was commonly 200-500 copies in the first century of printing, rising to 500-1000 by the 18th century and 1000-3000 after the Industrial Revolution. Ficino's translation of Plato (1491), with an edition of 3000, Gibbon's *Decline and Fall of the Roman Empire* (1776-88), also 3000 in the first printing of the later volumes, Mrs Henry Wood's *East Lynne* (1861), 500,000 copies by 1900 and Mrs Humphrey Ward's *Robert Elsmere* (1888) 70,500 copies of the first three printings, were all exceptional.

46 On Blount's *A Just Vindication of Learning and of the Liberties of the Press*, London, 1693, and *Reasons humbly offered for the Liberty of Unlicensed Printing*, London, 1693, see Macaulay's *History of England* (ch. 19) and Robert Birley, *Printing and Democracy*, London, Monotype Corporation, 1964, pp. 22-4. The first edition of *Areopagitica* is by no means a scarce book. The standard authorities, NUC, Wing and the RLIN and OCLC networks list twenty-five copies in libraries in the United States. Wing lists five copies in the British Isles, the maximum number it will list. There is little doubt that there are a great many more. It appeared regularly in Anglo-American auctions until the mid 1960s, when seventeenth-century English books in general began to be in short supply. From 1902 to 1965 it was sold at auction only slightly less than once every year. Many more copies passed through the book trade during those years. To what extent, then, were these copies actually read at the time of publication?

47 John Sparrow, 'George Herbert and John Donne among the Moravians', Martha Winburn England and John Sparrow, *Hymns Unbidden*, New York, 1966, pp. 1-28.

48 J. P. Brissot de Warville, *New Travels*, ed. Durand Echeverria, Cambridge, Mass., 1964, p. xxvii.
49 But see Kenneth E. Carpenter, 'The Bibliographical Description of Translations', *Papers of the Bibliographical Society of America*, 76, 3, pp. 253-71, which offers new hope here.
50 *Rare Americana: A Selection of One Hundred & One Books, Maps & Prints NOT IN The John Carter Brown Library*, Providence, RI, The Associates of the John Carter Brown Library, 1974, nos. 10 & 41. The recent announcement of the discovery of copy of *The Oath of a Freeman* is not accepted by the authors. See 'A Scandal in America', *The Book Collector*, 1987, XXXVI, pp. 449–70, 1988, XXXVII.
51 T. R. Adams, 'Mount and Page: Publishers of Eighteenth-Century Maritime Books', *infra*, pp. 145-77.
52 In addition to the two standard editions: Oxford, Oxford University Press, and New York, D. Appleton, which appeared in 1925, there were two inexpensive printings: London, Watts for the Rationalist Press Association no. 530, and New York, A. L. Burt, no. 514, Home Library, New Pocket Editions of Standard Classics. No copies of the latter two appear in *The National Union Catalog of Pre-1956 Imprints*. See R. B. Freeman, *The Works of Charles Darwin, An Annotated Bibliographical Handlist*, 2nd edn, Folkstone, 1977.
53 Owen Gingerich has now located over 550 copies of the two sixteenth-century editions of *De Revolutionibus* (1543 and 1566); Robert Westman has discovered 151 copies of the first edition of Galileo's *Dialoghi* (1632) and 58 of the second (1635); Fries has listed all surviving copies of Audubon's *Birds of America*; Freeman's work on Darwin, though extensive, remains unpublished. See O. Gingerich, *Journal for the History of Astronomy* XII (1981), pp. 53-4, and letter in *Papers of the Bibliographical Society of America*, LXXVI, 1982, pp. 473-6, and 'In Quest of Copernicus', *AB Bookman's Weekly*, 19 December 1988, pp. 2447-53; R. Westman, 'The Reception of Galileo's "Dialogues": a Partial World Census of Extant Copies', *Novità Celesti e Crisi del Sapere: Atti del Convegno di Studi Galileiani, Annali dell' Istituto e Museo di Storia della Scienza*, Monografia, VII (1983), pp. 329-71; Waldermar H. Fries, *The Double Elephant Folio: the Story of Andubon's Birds of America*, Chicago, 1973; Richard Broke Freeman, *Charles Darwin: a Companion*, Folkestone & Hamden, 1978, pp. 220-1 (see also *The Book Collector*, XVI, 1968, pp. 340-4).
54 Milton, *Areopagitica*, p. 6.
55 Paul Valéry, *Variété* II, Paris, 1930, 50-2 ('Oraison funèbre d'une fable'); quoted by R. Birley, *Sunk Without Trace*, London, 1962, pp. 207-8.

ACKNOWLEDGEMENT

The figure 'The Communications Circuit' is reprinted by permission of *Daedalus*, Journal of the American Academy of Arts and Sciences, from the issue entitled 'Representations and Realities', Summer 1982, Vol. 111, no. 3, p. 68.

THE COMMERCIAL PRODUCTION OF MANUSCRIPT BOOKS IN LATE-THIRTEENTH- AND EARLY-FOURTEENTH-CENTURY PARIS

R. H. ROUSE AND M. A. ROUSE

THE CITY OF PARIS, in the thirteenth century, was the first place and time north of the Alps to have a flourishing commercial trade in the production and sale of books. We must understand, of course, that a trade in books in the era before print differed from the printed-book trade. A manuscript-book producer did not make a number of books and attempt to sell them; rather, he was commissioned by a buyer to make a specific book, and did so – the sale came first, as usual in a 'bespoke' trade. Paris in the course of the thirteenth century became the first city in western Europe large enough, and with a sufficient concentration of the wealthy literate, to support a good number of people who earned their livelihoods by producing manuscripts to order, on this bespoke basis.

The reputation of the Paris book trade was widespread, even south of the Alps. At the beginning of the fourteenth century Dante, in the *Commedia*, mentions 'Oderisi ... leading light of that art which, at Paris, they call illumination' – implying that the thought of decorated manuscripts was inevitably coupled with Paris.[1] And even by the middle of the thirteenth century Odofredus, teacher of Roman law in Bologna (d. 1265), casually alludes to it, in an anecdote illustrating the fact that a father must know when to forbid certain expenditures: With only 200 pounds per year to support his whole family, a father gave his son the choice of studying at either Paris or Bologna, saying, ' "I shall send you 100 pounds a year." But what did the boy do? He promptly went off to Paris, where he had his books made with little apes and letters of gold!'[2] – a reference to fancy manuscripts of the Paris commercial trade, with their gold-leaf initials and with apes and other animals in their margins.

Our best information about the trade, aside from very rare indirect references of this sort, consists of the surviving manuscripts themselves. Using these as their evidence, art historians in recent years have pointed out the existence of many commercial workshops or *ateliers* that operated in Paris in the middle years of the thirteenth century. The late Robert Branner, in particular, singled out on the basis of painting styles some fifteen or more different shops dating from 'the reign of St Louis', i.e. 1226-1270.[3] Later scholars have disagreed with Branner's specific classification of manuscripts, but none disputes his fundamental assumption – that the making of books was a group enterprise, which frequently involved not merely a master and his apprentices, but rather the collaboration of two (or even three?) different shops, in the production of a single book. The researches of François Avril, Joan Diamond, and others, on Parisian manuscripts dating from these years and on into the first decades of the fourteenth century, confirm Branner's findings for the mid-thirteenth, that book-producers shared out their jobs – because these scholars have found repeated instances where two or more artists alternated, or otherwise shared, in the illumination of a single manuscript.[4]

The practical logistics of this shared production continue to elude us: Why did they work together, and how was it arranged, and who planned out and supervised the actual task, and where was it done? – all the tangible details that would make this world live for us. A major drawback is the lack of real names and locations. For all the thirteenth century, and on into the beginning of the fourteenth, the art historians have to deal with shadowy workshops dubbed after their best-known manuscript or the idiosyncrasy of an artist – the Workshop of the Master of the Long Hands, or the British Library MS Additional Atelier, or the like. By sheer luck, this frustrating veil of anonymity is temporarily swept aside at the end of the thirteenth century, in the records of a special royal tax. Coupled with the records of bookmen whose names appear in fourteenth-century documents of the University of Paris, and with records of names in surviving thirteenth- and fourteenth-century manuscripts, the tax lists for the first time give us a precise roll-call of the makers of books in Paris.

The tax in question was the *taille* of the 1290s imposed by King Philip the Fair (1285-1314), called the *maltôte* by contemporaries. The *taille*'s rate was one penny in the pound on all commercial transactions, i.e. a sales tax of 0.4%.[5] Naturally, the merchant community detested it. Small though it seems to us, this was the first indirect tax in French history, and the collecting of it bid fair to be an expensive nuisance. Therefore, the city of Paris (in common with several smaller cities of the realm) agreed with the king's financial officers simply to pay a fixed sum of 100,000 *livres tournois* in a series of eight instalments, beginning in 1292. Unfortunately, the *taille* records for two of the instalments have been lost. The manuscript record for 1292 survives as a separate volume at the Bibliothèque Nationale, while the books for each of the years 1296-1300, bound together, are presently in the Archives Nationales of France.[6]

The total sum was apportioned among all the members of the city's commercial community. The amount of the tax was further divided parish by parish and, within each parish, street by street and shop by shop; and the rolls record the name, the occupation and the tax of each shop-keeper. Although the discreet muscle behind the collection was provided by royal sergeants and bailiffs, the amount of each merchant's tax was determined by a commission of neighbours; and the amount was roughly proportionate to the merchant's business income (rather than to property value, or inherited wealth, for example).

Consequently, the surviving books of the *taille* (1292, 1296, 1297, 1298, 1299, 1300) show us who the bookmen or *libraires* were, and where they were, and how much their businesses were worth in comparison with their neighbours'.

In any given year, the number of bookmen or *libraires* numbered about thirty, give or take a half-dozen; together with members of related trades (parchment-sellers, illuminators, binders) they were located in two concentrations:[7] (1) Roughly half the total number were installed on the Left Bank, dispersed among the streets that housed the colleges, halls, and teaching centres of the University of Paris (the Sorbonne, the Dominican priory of St-Jacques, the church of Ste-Geneviève up the hill, the central meeting hall of the Mathurins, etc.). These *libraires* must have been particularly (though not exclusively) caught up in serving the needs of the students and masters in the schools. On the entire Right Bank, in contrast, there is only one *libraire* in all the surviving *taille* rolls, situated just beside the Louvre whence his principal business must have come. (2) The rest of the *libraires* of Paris, again about half the total, were squeezed on to one short street on the Ile de la Cité, the Rue neuve Notre Dame, as concentrated as one can imagine.

This neighbourhood, within easy reach of the cathedral church of Notre Dame and the palaces of king and bishop, had already been touted in mid-century, in one of the earliest commercial book advertisements; at the end of a lawbook in Old French, dating from around 1250, the colophon says, 'Here ends Justinian's *Code* in French, complete and unabridged, sold by Herneis *le romanceeur*. Whoever wants a similar book, let them come to him and he will give them good advice – regarding this book, and all others. He resides at Paris, in front of Notre Dame' (Giessen, Universitätsbibl., MS 945, fol. 269v).[8] His nickname 'le romanceeur' means that Herneis was specifically known for producing books in the vernacular, rather than books in Latin – such as the Justinian. To say that he was located 'in front of Notre Dame' probably meant that he had his shop on the street itself, rather than on the medieval *parvis*, the raised paved square west of the cathedral. Certainly by 1292, the year of the first *taille* book, all *libraires* on the Ile had their businesses along the Rue neuve. And, as Herneis's advertisement implies, this segment of the Paris booktrade concentrated on vernacular books – books in French for wealthy noblemen and noblewomen – more than on books in Latin (Bibles, theology, schoolbooks) for wealthy prelates or for masters and students.

The Rue neuve Notre Dame is one of those Parisian streets that no longer exist; it was incorporated into the modern parvis of the cathedral over a hundred years ago. In the thirteenth century, the Rue neuve ran eastward from the main north–south road across the Ile, called the Marché Palu (now the Rue de la Cité), to the *parvis* Notre Dame. It was literally a 'rue neuve', a new street, because Bishop Maurice de Sully had had the street cut through the hodge-podge of roads and passageways *c.* 1165, to allow transport of the stone for the construction of Notre Dame Cathedral. It was the first rectilinear, or straight, street built in Paris since the Romans had laid out the Rue St-Jacques.[9] The street was only about ninety yards long on its north side, perhaps a hundred yards on the south. For a comparative notion of its size, consider that the whole length of the Rue neuve would fit inside the nave of the cathedral of Notre Dame, without upsetting the high altar or overflowing into the side aisles. Short as it was, the Rue neuve ran through two parishes. The western two-thirds belonged to the parish of Ste-Geneviève-la-petite (so called to distinguish it from the large Ste-Geneviève-du-mont, on the Left Bank). A portion of the shop frontage on the north side of the Rue neuve was taken up by this church. The eastern third of the Rue neuve, the end toward the cathedral, belonged to the parish of St Christofle; part of its southern frontage was taken up by the *Hôtel-Dieu*, the principal charitable hospital/hospice of the city. Two, or possibly three, little passageways or *ruelles* entered the street on its north side; one would exaggerate in saying their presence created four city blocks, but that is a useful image.

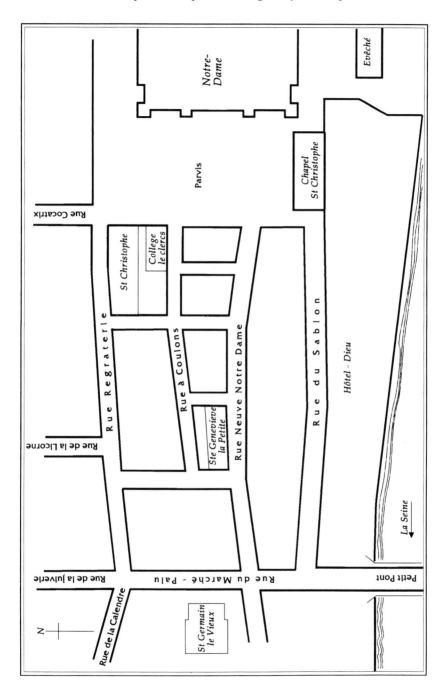

With the aid of these landmarks, we can in many instances locate the members of the book trade in the 1290s almost to their very shop doors.[10] For example, in the parish of Ste-Geneviève-la-petite, on the north side along with the parish church, were located Giles of Soissons, who was both *libraire* and book-binder, and Jehan de Laigni, illuminator of books; by 1298 Jehan had been succeeded by his widow Ameline de Berron, who was both illuminator and *libraire*. Thomas de Saint-Paul, *libraire*, was there until at least 1300 (the last *taille* book), and by 1316 university records show a *libraire* named Jean de Saint-Paul (but no longer any Thomas) on the Rue neuve, presumably Thomas's son or nephew who had succeeded him as proprietor; Jean continues in the shop until at least 1323. Raoul le genne Breton, *libraire*, is called Raoul le genne (= *le jeune*, the younger) to distinguish him from Raoul le vieil Breton, *libraire*, whose shop was on the opposite side of the street – probably these were father and son.

On the south side of the street in this parish were still more book people. In 1292 we find the *libraire* Alain le jeune (in this instance, we cannot answer the question 'younger than whom?'); and in the next surviving *taille* book (1296), and for some years thereafter, this shop is taxed in the name of his successor 'Julienne, widow of Alain the younger, *libraire*'; but by 1300 Julienne has given up the book trade and is living with a kinsman, a stonemason, outside the gate of St-Victor – perhaps she was elderly by then. Another family business is that of Dame Aaliz à lescurel ('at [the Sign of?] the Squirrel'), likewise on the south side of the street in the parish of Ste-Geneviève-la-petite. Added to her entry in the tax book is the mention of 'Fortin, her son', from 1292 to 1298. But in 1299 and 1300 the main entry is that of 'Sire Fortin de lescurel, *libraire*', with the addition 'Dame Aaliz de lescurel, his mother'. Obviously, control of the book business has passed from mother to son. (The significance of their titles – *Sire* Fortin, *Dame* Aaliz – is not clear.) The shop of Nicolas d'Estampes, *libraire*, likely represents yet another family of bookmen; the name of Nicolas alone is attached to the shop in the *taille* book of 1292, the names jointly of Nicolas d'Estampes and Robert d'Estampes, *libraires*, in 1296, and thereafter – beginning in 1297 – the tax is charged to Robert alone. Still on the south side of the Rue neuve, in this same parish, is the shop of Jehan de St-Pere-aux-bues, *libraire* (his ungainly name indicates that he came all the way from the parish of St-Pere-aux-bues – two hundred yards distant, on the northeast side of the Ile); that of Robert de l'Ile-Adam, *libraire*; and Mestre Raoul le Breton, *libraire* – who, beginning with the 1296 *taille* book, is called

Raoul le vieil Breton, to distinguish him from his younger namesake, probably his son, across the street on the north side. There was also the shop of Hervi le parcheminier. Finally, on this south side of the street in the parish of Ste-Geneviève-la-petite, there was by 1297 a Thomas le Normant, *libraire*, who in 1316 took an oath as a stationer for the University of Paris. By 1323 (long after the *taille* records cease), Geoffroy 'dictus le Norman' swears an oath, in company with Thomas, as a *libraire* on the Rue neuve, no doubt a younger kinsman (son, nephew, younger brother); and in 1342 it is Jean 'dictus le Normant' who appears on the University records, the successor of Thomas and Geoffroy whose shop was doubtless still on this same spot. (Geoffroy's and Jean's soubriquet, *dictus le Normant,* 'called "the Norman"', implies that this has become a family name, instead of an indication that their home was in Normandy.)

The portion of the Rue neuve that fell within the bounds of the parish of St-Christofle was a good deal shorter than that in the parish of Ste-Geneviève-la-petite, but even so there were several *libraires.* On the north side were Guerin l'englois, *libraire,* and 'son gendre' – his son-in-law, not important enough to be named, but earning enough to be taxed; by 1297 the nameless son-in-law has been replaced in the tax rolls by Guerin's daughter Bourge (widowed, very likely); also on this side of the street are Jehan Blondel, *libraire,* and Nicolas *le libraire* with 'Colart his son'. On the shorter south side of Rue neuve in the parish of St-Christofle were shops of two more *libraires,* Agnien and Poncet.

In addition to these shops, there are two other *libraires* whose shops were on the Rue neuve in the 1290s but whose parish, or whose side of the street, is unknown – Colin de la Lande and Gude de Biaune.

The book trade was not the sole commerce on the Rue neuve, of course. Others (from both parishes and both sides of the street) included two doctors, three poultry dealers, a couple of mercers, several (six or seven) notaries, a tailor, a seller of spices, and now and then a lawyer (i.e. some years one is there, some years not). But certainly we are right in regarding this as 'the street of bookmen', with its fifteen or twenty different establishments of either *libraires* or related trades. Moreover, we are right to think of this as a centre of the production of vernacular books for wealthy laymen and -women. We want to emphasize, of course, that the concentration of bookmen on the Rue neuve, and their production of manuscripts written in the vernacular, did not suddenly begin in 1292 – rather, it was the *taille* which suddenly began in 1292, giving us records for the first time of what was obviously already a well-established community. Nevertheless – with this *caveat* well fixed in mind – we can note that the large-scale production of vernacular texts for an audience of lay readers does not antedate the records by any great period. Some of the most popular products of the trade, in fact, were not written (or, in some instances, not translated from the Latin) until the second half of the thirteenth century;[11] and most of the surviving manuscripts that came out of this trade date from the end of the thirteenth century or later.

Robert Branner, relying mainly on deduction from the state of the surviving manuscripts, said, 'The physical proximity of the ateliers in the decades following 1230 ... seems to be directly reflected in their increasing collaboration on "in-house" jobs.'[12] Now that we have seen the reality of how many *libraires* worked, cheek by jowl, as contemporaries on the Rue neuve Notre Dame, the notion of collaborative production seems not just plausible but likely. There is a problem, though: Branner was talking about the illuminators on the Left Bank, while we have given all our attention to the *libraires* on the Ile. It is time now to confront the question, just what was a *libraire*, in the late thirteenth and early fourteenth centuries?[13] The etymology of the word will not help in the slightest, for it simply means 'person having to do with books'. For help with this matter, we turn to a different sort of record, the archives of the University of Paris.

For the well-being of the university, the availability of books was absolutely essential – enough books, affordable books, books containing a minimum of scribal error. In the controlled economy of medieval Paris, it was a natural step that the university, with royal blessing, should therefore take over the regulation of the city's trade in books. All the *libraires* of Paris, in a body, had to swear an oath of observance of the university's regulations, every two years or at the university's pleasure. Beginning in 1316 (forty years after the first such oath), the *libraires'* names are attached to the oaths, at times with street addresses as well.[14] Besides these corporate or group oaths, each *libraire* also had to take an individual oath – perhaps on the occasion of buying or inheriting his or her shop. A meaningful proportion of these oaths, of both sorts, survive, which gives us names from the early fourteenth century. Besides providing names, the regulations also define one aspect of the 'office' (as the university called it) of *libraire*: the service that *libraires* rendered to the university was primarily the sale of used books; the *libraires* swore to deal honestly with masters and students – swore not to underpay when they bought, not to overcharge when they sold – the rate of their profit was fixed at a little under 2%.[15] Moreover, a small cadre (four? five?) from among the *libraires*, the university stationers, were made responsible for renting out copies of useful texts, one quire at a time, to enable students and masters to make their own copies; the university regulated the fees for this also.[16]

We can see at once that none of this sounds lucrative enough to have enticed so many members into the trade – ones whose business, moreover, was doing well enough to have been taxed. The key to this seeming enigma is that the university regulations ignore the *libraires'* dealings with extranei, 'outsiders': provided they met their university obligations, the *libraires* were otherwise free to serve anyone they pleased. And it was here, in the free commercial market, that the *libraires* conducted their most lucrative trade.

In particular, three figures from the university's records demonstrate what the Rue neuve *libraires* did, and how they worked, and – a fascinating part of the story – for whom. Geoffroy de St-Léger and Thomas de Maubeuge both swore their individual oaths to the university on the same day, 26 November 1316,[17] and they appear again on the corporate university oaths of 1316 and 1323; Richard de Montbaston, perhaps younger than they, took his oath in 1338; all three were located 'in vico novo', on the Rue neuve.[18]

According to the records, Geoffroy de St-Léger in 1332 sold a four-volume *Speculum historiale* to the lawyer Gérard de Montaigu for the large sum of 40 pounds.[19] More intriguing is the appearance of the name of Geoffroy de St-Léger ('C'est Geoffroi de S. Ligier') or the initial G. beside numerous illustrations in a surviving manuscript of Guiart des Moulins's *Bible historiale* (Paris, Bibl. Ste-Geneviève, MS 22) – an Old French adaptation of the popular Latin Bible history (*Historia scholastica*) by Peter Comestor.[20] François Avril has identified at least forty-seven manuscripts in which this same artist figures, either alone or in collaboration with other artists.[21]

This artist, known as the Master of *Fauvel* from the subject of his most famous illustrations, had evidently been hired by the *libraire* Geoffroy de St-Léger to illuminate these sheets of the *Bible historiale*, and the artist noted (as a reminder to himself), 'These are Geoffroy's' – to distinguish them from sheets or quires that he was painting for some other *libraire*. Amongst the other bookmen with whom the Fauvel Master collaborated between the years *c.* 1316 and 1337 were Geoffroy's contemporaries and neighbors on the rue Neuve, Thomas de Maubeuge and the husband-and-wife partnership of Richard and Jeanne de Montbaston.

As to the texts that the Fauvel Master illuminated, they have a notable uniformity. There are few books in Latin, including two missals, two collections of royal acts, and one collection of papal letters. The remainder are illustrated vernacular books, i.e. books for educated laymen and -women rather than for bishops or university masters. They include six copies of the *Bible historiale* (two of them are two-volume sets, besides), four copies of the *Grandes chroniques de France*, three of the *Roman de la rose*, two of Pierre Bersuire's *Ovide moralisé*, a half-dozen or more collections of tales from ancient history (*Roman des sept sages de Rome, Roman d'Alexandre, Histoire de Troie*, etc.), several elements of the Arthurian legend (*Lancelot, Arthur le restoré*, two copies of *Histoire du Graal et de Merlin*), travel and crusading stories, and the satirical *Roman de Fauvel*, among others. The patrons of these manuscripts included the chancellor of France, nobles such as Louis I duc de Bourbon, and two queens: Clémence of Hungary (second wife of Louis X) and Jeanne of Burgundy (wife of Philip VI).

The manuscripts epitomize the type of production that Joan Diamond has dubbed 'the vernacular style': (1) works written in the French language; (2) illustrations comprising a cycle of column-width miniatures that are simple in design and hackneyed in execution – a sort of assembly-line, interchangeable-parts level of illustration; and (3) a collaborative mode of production, which sees two or three or more *libraires* and/or illustrators working to make a single book.[22] The details of the collaboration are not known, but it is our assumption that a *libraire* who accepted an order for a specific book often turned to his neighbours on the Rue neuve for help in finishing the job within a reasonable amount of time. Doubtless he or she called upon certain colleagues more than on others, but it always remained a fluid association. If you like, you may think of it as Geoffroy being the main contractor who subcontracted to his neighbours on one occasion, just as (for the very next job, perhaps) his neighbour might be the main contractor for a book, subcontracting part of the job with Geoffroy.

Toward the end of his career, the Fauvel Master can be seen collaborating with Richard de Montbaston. Richard was evidently both *libraire* and artist. His name also appears on the corporate oath of the bookmen in 1342, but he is dead before 1353 – the date naturally makes one wonder if he was a plague victim. In 1353 Jeanne, 'widow of the deceased Richard de Montbaston', took her oath as *libraria et illuminatrix*, carrying on the family business.[23] Richard leaves his name on the pastedowns of an illustrated *Légende dorée* dated 1348 (BN fr. 241) – the wording is significant: 'Richard de Montbaston, *libraire*, residing at Paris on the Rue neuve Notre Dame, made this French *Legend* to be written....'[24] The force of the phrase 'fist escrire' (made, or caused, it to be written) implies that Richard was in this case the main contractor who parcelled out the work among his neighbours. The text in this manuscript – a French translation of the *Legenda aurea* made by Jean de Vignay (d. bef. 1350), whose patron was Jeanne de Burgundy, Philip VI's queen – is textually closer to the archetype (the original) than virtually any other surviving copy.[25] It is not known for whom Richard de Montbaston made this book; but it was already part of the French royal library when that collection was first recorded in 1518, which suggests that Montbaston's book was commissioned by a member of the court circle.

The illustrations of this *Légende dorée*, true to the 'vernacular style', are workmanlike and nothing more. They are surely Montbaston's own work. In other surviving manuscripts he can be seen working in collaboration with the Fauvel Master, including Arsenal MS 3481 (*Lancelot*), BN fr. 60 (*Roman de Thebes* and *Histoire de Troie*), BN fr. 22495 (*Roman de Godefroi de Bouillon et de Saladin*), dated 1337, and others.

Of the Fauvel Master's three named *libraire*-collaborators, Thomas de Maubeuge is the earliest we know. Like Geoffroy's and Richard's, Thomas's production was vernacular and his clientele noble or near-royal. The records for the county of Hainaut show that in 1323 Thomas sold a 'rommanch de Lorehens' to the count for thirteen pounds Parisian – almost twice the price of the horse that had been purchased for the trip from Hainaut to Paris.[26] In 1349, Thomas de Maubeuge sold a 'rommant de moralite sur la Bible' (doubtless Guiart des Moulins's *Bible historiale* again) to the future king John the Good.[27] One surviving manuscript, an illustrated *Grandes chroniques de France* dated 1318 (BN fr. 10132), is attributed to Thomas by its elaborate opening rubric: 'Ci commencent les chroniques des roys de France ... lesquelles Pierres Honnorez du Nuef Chastel en Normandie fist escrire et ordener en la maniere que elles sont, selonc l'ordenance des croniques de Saint Denis, a mestre Thomas de Maubuege, demorant en rue nueve Nostre Dame de Paris, l'an de grace Nostre Seingneur M.CCCXVIII' ('Here begin the chronicles of the kings of France ... which Pierre Honoré of Neufchatel in Normandy caused to be written and to be put in the present order – matching the order of the St-Denis chronicles – by Master Thomas de Maubeuge, residing on the Rue neuve Notre Dame in Paris, AD 1318').[28]

By now we have seen enough of them to suggest that such advertisements were an innovation of the commercial producers of vernacular books – prominent announcements, in red or in a display script, inserted in the manuscripts themselves, giving notice of the name and business address of the maker and inviting any who liked the book to come and buy more of the same. The earliest known example comes from Champagne, *c.* 1230 or 1240, at the time when production of vernacular books was beginning to shift from provincial centres to the capital. BN MS fr. 794, a collection of romances called the Guiot Anthology, has this colophon at the end of its first section (fol. 105): 'Cil qui lescrist Guioz a non / devant N're Dame del val / est ses ostex tot a estal.' ('The one who wrote this, Guiot by name, has his shop established in front of Notre Dame del Val [in Provins].')[29] We have noted similar colophons or rubrics in the Paris trade, advertising the work of Herneis *le romanceeur*, Richard de Montbaston, and Thomas de Maubeuge. This practice – no doubt more widespread that the surviving examples attest – fits well our image of this active body of tradesmen.

Thomas de Maubeuge's BN fr. 10132 is a large volume, containing at least thirty-one miniatures; save where they have been cropped, instructions to the artist survive in the margins. Perhaps Thomas himself was the illustrator as well as the producer of this manuscript (after the model of Richard and others). Whether or no, we can say at any rate that the illustrator of Thomas's chronicles collaborated with the Fauvel Master in several other manuscripts, including a *Roman de Graal* (BN fr. 9123) and another *Grandes chroniques* (Musée Goya at Castres, unnumbered).

Thomas de Maubeuge's most illustrious steady customer was Mahaut, countess of Artois in her own right and countess of Burgundy by marriage (d. 1329). Mahaut was daughter of Count Robert of Artois, who was nephew to King Louis IX, St Louis; Mahaut's daughter, Jeanne of Burgundy, was married to King Philip V (1316-1322), and her second daughter Blanche was (briefly) married to Philip's brother and successor Charles IV (1322-1328). As a chatelain of the haute noblesse she has left (fortunately for us) good account books of payments made. With her royal and near-royal connections, she will fittingly conclude our topic by exemplifying the audience which patronized the commercial book trade in vernacular texts.[30]

In 1305 Mahaut ordered (locally in Artois, it seems) a sumptuous *Grandes chroniques*, with 40 gold initials. In 1308 she paid 7*l.* 10*s.* for French books bought at Arras, a *Histoire de Troie* and a *Roman de Perceval*. In 1310 she paid 7*l.* for a *Roman de Tristan* bought for her at Arras. In 1312 at her castle of Hesdin (near Arras), she paid three local scribes to write and a local artist to 'illuminate, bind, and cover' a *Roman du grand Kan* (i.e. the voyage of Marco Polo). We might note here that the version of Polo's travels that circulated in northern France was written only in 1307, and that 1312 – early for a provincial copy of this text – was remarkably early for an illustrated copy.[31] (Mahaut's treasurer Thierry d'Hireçon, a kinsman, commissioned a copy for himself also, in 1315 at Arras.) By 1313, records show that Mahaut's book-buying extended to Paris, where she maintained a residence; in that year she purchased two books in French from Thomas de Maubeuge for 8 pounds, the *Voeux de Paon* and a *Vie des sains*.[32] In 1316, insurgents invaded her estates at Hesdin and carried off objects of value, which Mahaut listed in a claim to parlement after regaining the castle; they included 200 pounds' worth of books, all in the vernacular: 3 'romans de Tristan', one of which had been recovered; 1 'romans des fais d'outremer' (either William of Tyre or Oderic de Pordenone); 1 'romans des enfances Ogier'; 1 'romans del ordenance maistre Tancre' (law book in French of Maître Tancrede, jurisconsult); 1 'romans de Renart'; 1 'romans des coustumes de Normandie'; 1 'romans de la Violette petit' (by Gilbert de Montreuil); a 'Bible en romans' which madame had recovered (perhaps really a Bible, but more likely Guiart des Moulin's *Bible historiale*); a 'romans de la vie des Sains' and a 'romans de la vie du grant Kaan' – these last two, plus one of the Tristans, we have seen her buying.[33] In 1326 she bought a volume of 'heures dou Saint-Esprit et heures de la Crois', another of hours of the dead, and (in 1327) hours of St Louis, all from a certain Nicholas, *libraire* on the Rue neuve Notre Dame in Paris; whether these were in French or Latin we do not know. In 1327 she commissioned Thomas de Maubeuge to refurbish her chapel (stripped or damaged during the incursion of 1316) with a new missal and breviaries; and she bought from him two especially costly volumes, 'un romant contenant la vie des sains, les miracles Notre Dame, la vie des sains peres et plusieurs autres hystoires' – a replacement, perhaps, for the lost *Vie des sains* – for 80 pounds, and 'une Bible en francois' for the substantial sum of 100 pounds.[34]

Mahaut of Artois dispels some of our myths – about the vernacular book trade, and about the books sold to women of her class. She is not a demure lady who sits with her needlework and her lap dog, caressing her one pretty picture-book of prayers. For the most part, those of her books we have mentioned here are not at all 'coffee-table' books for display, with exquisite full-page illustration by the likes of Master Honoré or Jean Pucelle and with 'gold letters and little apes' (though indeed she had her share of those). This is a vigorous, sometimes belligerent, woman of affairs who reads, really reads. She has the wit to know what she likes, the industry to search out where they may be found, and the money to commission copies for her use. The commercial book trade on the Rue neuve Notre Dame made its livelihood from a whole class of the literate wealthy like Mahaut, providing attractively if not extraordinarily illustrated books in the vernacular; and the speed of production was increased by the sort of collaboration that was encouraged by the concentration of *libraires* on the Rue neuve.

NOTES

Reprinted, with substantive revisions, from *Medieval Book Production: Assessing the Evidence*, ed. L. L. Brownrigg, Los Altos Hills, Calif., 1990, pp. 103-115; by permission. *Paris Book Producers, 1200-1500* was the subject of the 1992 Lyell Lectures in Bibliography, which we are currently revising for publication.

1 ' "Oh!" diss'io lui "non se' tu Oderisi / l'onor d'Agobbio e l'onor di quell'arte / ch'alluminar chiamata e in Parisi?" ' *Purgatorio*, canto XI, ll. 79-81; granted, the demands of rhyme may have played a role here. Concerning Oderisi, see S. Bottari, 'Per la cultura di Oderisi da Gubbio e di Franco Bolognese', in *Dante e Bologna nei tempi di Dante*, Bologna, 1967, pp. 53-9.

2 ' "Vade Parisios vel Bononiam et mittam tibi annuatim centum libras." Iste quid fecit? Ivit Parisios et fecit libros suos babuinare de litteris aureis'; Odofredus, *Lectura super Codice*, Lyon, 1552, f. 226rb. Robert Branner, *Manuscript Painting in Paris During the Reign of Saint Louis: A Study of Styles*, Berkeley, 1977, p. 2, translates the passage '. . . had his books made to prattle with gold letters' – which solves a grammatical problem, but does violence to the meaning. See, for example, Albert Blaise, *Lexicon latinitatis medii aevi*, Corpus christianorum, continuatio mediaevalis, Turnholt, 1975, p. 88: '*babuino, -are*, orner de miniatures représentant des babouins (ou autres monstres)'.

3 Branner, *Manuscript Painting in Paris*, esp. app. 5, pp. 200-39.

4 See J. Diamond, 'Manufacture and Market in Parisian Book Illumination around 1300', in *Europäische Kunst um 1300*, Akten des XXV internationalen Kongresses für Kunstgeschichte 6.6, Vienna, 1986, pp. 101-10; F. Avril, 'A quand remontent les premiers ateliers d'enlumineurs laïcs à Paris?' in *Les dossiers de l'archéologie: Enluminure gothique*, 16, 1975, pp. 36-44; and see in particular M. Avril's contribution to *Le Roman de Fauvel in the Edition of Mesire Chaillou de Pesstain: A Reproduction in Facsimile of the Complete Manuscript, Paris, Bibliothèque Nationale, fonds français 146*, introduction by Edward H. Roesner, François Avril, and Nancy Freeman Regalado, New York, 1990, esp. pp. 42-48. We are grateful to M. Avril for allowing us to read his introduction in typescript.

5 For a concise explanation of the circumstances surrounding this levy see Jean Favier, *Philippe le Bel*, Paris, 1978, pp. 189-91. Karl Michaëlsson provides the

most thorough description of the mechanics of assessment and collection of the tax in Paris, in his introduction to the editions cited in the following note.

6 It is unclear why the two missing instalments covered a span of three years (1293-5), while the surviving instalments seem to have been annual. Three of the *taille* books have been edited: H. Géraud, ed., *Paris sous Philippe-le-Bel: ... Le rôle de la taille ... 1292*, Paris, 1837; Karl Michaëlsson, ed., *Le livre de la taille de Paris ... 1296*, Göteborgs Universitets Årsskrift 64 no. 4, Göteborg, 1958; and Michaëlsson, *Le livre de la taille de Paris ... 1297*, ibid. 67, no. 3, 1962. Michaëlsson had earlier edited the *taille* book of 1313, a special levy for the knighting of Philip the Fair's oldest son, in the same series, 57, no. 3, 1951; but by 1313 the members of the book trade had been exempted from the tax, and their names are absent from the street records. The records for the years 1298-1300 are available only in manuscript: Paris, Arch. Nat. KK 283.

7 For a list of all the *libraires* known by name to have worked in Paris between 1292 and 1353, with the documentation for each, see R. H. and M. A. Rouse, 'The Book Trade at the University of Paris, ca. 1250-ca.1350', in *La production du livre universitaire au moyen âge: exemplar et pecia*, ed. L. J. Bataillon, B. G. Guyot, and R. H. Rouse, Paris, 1988, pp. 40-114, esp. pp. 89-103. We shall publish a much fuller list, of all known members of the Parisian booktrade between 1200 and 1500 (*libraires*, illuminators, scribes, binders, parchmenters, and paper-sellers), in a study subsequent to the publication of the Lyell Lectures.

8 'Ici faut Code en romanz, et toutes les lois del code i sont. Explicit. Herneis le romanceeur le vendi. Et qui voudra avoir autel livre, si viegne a lui, il en aidera bien a conseillier, et de toz autres. Et si meint a Paris devant Nostre Dame.' The colophon was first printed in J. Valentino Adrian's *Catalogus codicum manuscriptorum Bibliothecae Academicae Gissensis*, Frankfurt-a.-M., 1840, p. 278; from there it has been cited in the secondary literature, most recently by Branner, *Manuscript Painting in Paris*, p. 2.

9 Concerning the history of the Rue neuve see J. Hillairet, *L'Ile de la Cité*, Paris, 1969, pp. 30-48, esp. 39-40. Information about the cross streets and about the location of the dividing line between the parishes comes principally from the *taille* books themselves. We have made use of two maps (modern attempts at the reconstruction of medieval Paris), namely the map that illustrates Géraud's edition of the *taille* book of 1292, and the map labelled 'Paris vers la fin du XIVe siècle' created by the SDCG-Laboratoire de cartographie thématique of the CNRS, copyright Paris 1975.

10 Although the records allow us to see whether a given shop was on the north side of the street or the south, and whether in this block or that, one cannot discern the precise sequence of shops from east to west, since the tax assessors did not report (or the recorders did not record) the shops in exactly the same order from one year to the next.

11 To take as examples works specifically mentioned in this article: the *Bible historiale*, Guiart des Moulins' popular adaptation/translation of the *Historia scholastica*, was completed in 1294; the version of Marco Polo that circulated in northern France dates from 1307; the French translation of the *Legenda aurea* was the work of Jean de Vignay, who flourished in the first half of the fourteenth century (d. before 1350).

12 Branner, *Manuscript Painting in Paris*, p. 15.

13 Although M.-C. Léonelli's 'Un libraire d'Avignon à l'époque du Grand Schisme,' *Bulletin philologique et historique du Comité des travaux historiques et scientifiques, 1977*, Paris, 1979, pp. 115-22, is set in a different place and at the end rather than the beginning of the fourteenth century, it is instructive to see the varied activities of her *libraire* – agent for third parties in the sale of second-hand books, assessor who evaluates the books of others for sale, parchment-seller, beadle of the university, contractor or overseer for the production of new books; his father also was a *libraire*, and his brother a scribe.

14 The various oaths are edited in the *Chartularium Universitatis Parisiensis* (hereafter CUP), ed. H. Denifle and E. Chatelain, 4 vols., Paris, 1889-97. The oldest surviving oath, that of 1275 (CUP no. 462, vol. 1, p. 532), does not record the names of those who took it, nor does the next, of 1302 (CUP no. 628, vol. 2, p. 9). In all the years before the Black Death, the only corporate oaths that provide the names of the *libraires* are those of 1316, 1323, and 1342 (CUP nos. 733, 824, and 1064, vol. 2, pp. 190, 273, and 530).

15 See CUP nos. 462 (AD 1275; vol. 1, p. 532), 628 (AD 1302; vol. 2, p. 97), and 1064 (AD 1342; vol. 2, p. 530). The rate specified was four deniers in the pound, or 1.7%.

16 For a description of the stationers' function, and recent bibligraphy, see Rouse and Rouse, 'Book Trade'.

17 Geoffroy's individual oath, CUP no. 732, vol. 2, pp. 188-9; Thomas's and Richard's, CUP no 732, vol. 2, p. 189n.

18 Thomas's and Geoffroy's address is given, e.g. in CUP no. 733: '... librariis infrascriptis, videlicet Thoma de Malbodio, ... [et] Gaufrido de Sancto Leodegario, in vico novo quoad presens commorante....' Richard's address, 'demourant a Paris en la rue neuve Nostre Dame', appears in BN MS fr. 241 discussed below.

19 Paul Delalain, *Etude sur le libraire parisien du XIIIe au XVe siècle*, Paris, 1891, p. xxxvii n. 1. See the forthcoming publication of the Lyell Lectures for a more precise examination of this 'sale'.

20 Samuel Berger, *La Bible française au moyen âge*, Paris, 1884, pp. 288, 376-7, first called attention to these annotations.

21 See *Roman de Fauvel*, intro. pp. 46-47. Our discussion here of the manuscripts that comprise this artist's oeuvre is based on M. Avril's work. For a discussion based on the manuscripts themselves, and for the early history of BN fr. 146, see the published Lyell Lectures.

22 See most recently her 'Manufacture and Market' cited above. Despite the obvious surface differences, there is an underlying similarity between the collaborative practices of the fourteenth-century commercial trade in Paris and the later London trade described by A. I. Doyle and M. B. Parkes, 'The Production of Copies of the *Canterbury Tales* and the *Confessio amantis* in the Early Fifteenth Century', in *Medieval Scribes, Manuscripts & Libraries: Essays Presented to N. R. Ker*, ed. M. B. Parkes and Andrew G. Watson, London, 1978, pp. 163-210.

23 Jeanne's individual oath, CUP no. 1179, vol. 2, p. 658n.

24 BN fr. 241, back pastedown: 'Richart de Monbaston libraire demourant a Paris

en la rue neuve Nostre Dame fist escrire ceste legende en francois, l'an de grace Nostre Nostre [*sic*] Seigneur mil.CCC.XLVIII.' The note on the front pastedown is almost identical.

25 We are grateful to Richard Hamer for having shared with us his findings regarding the place this manuscript occupies on the stemma of the *Légende dorée*.

26 Godefroy Ménilglaise, 'Etat des bijoux et joyaux achetés à Paris pour Marguerite et Jeanne de Hainaut en 1323,' *Annuaire – Bulletin de la Société de l'histoire de France*, 6, 1868, pp. 126-47 at 143-4; cf. 143 n. 4.

27 L. Delisle, *Cabinet des manuscrits*, 2, Paris, 1868, pp. 15-16 and n. 9.

28 We are grateful to Walter Cahn, who first drew our attention to this manuscript.

29 See Mario Roques, 'Le manuscrit fr. 794 de la Bibliothèque nationale et le scribe Guiot', *Romania*, 73, 1952, pp. 177-99, the colophon on 179; we are grateful to Terry Nixon for this reference.

30 Concerning Mahaut, see J.-M. Richard, *Une petite-nièce de saint Louis: Mahaut, comtesse d'Artois et de Bourgogne*, Paris, 1887; her books are the focus of ch. 8, pp. 99-106. John Benton called this book to our attention. For a more recent discussion of Mahaut, as both a patron of letters and a political force, see J. N. Hillgarth, *Ramon Lull and Lullism in Fourteenth-Century France*, Oxford, 1971, pp. 164-85.

31 For this information we are grateful to C. W. Dutschke, who is engaged in a study of the circulation of Marco Polo in manuscript.

32 Thomas's receipt survives; see Richard, *Une petite-nièce de saint Louis*, p. 102 n. 3.

33 Mahaut's claim has been printed; Le Roux de Lincy, 'Inventaires des biens meubles et immeubles de la comtesse Mahaut d'Artois pillés par l'armée de son neveu, en 1313'. *Bibliothèque de l'Ecole des chartes*, 3e sér., 3, 1852, pp. 53-79, booklist on 63.

34 See Richard, *Une petite-nièce de saint Louis*, p. 104 and n. 4.

THE CODEX IN THE FIFTEENTH CENTURY

Manuscript and Print

LOTTE HELLINGA

IN THE EARLY 1470s Werner Rolewinck, working in Cologne where he was a Carthusian monk, compiled his great World chronicle, the *Fasciculus Temporum*. Nearing the end of his work, he described events that belonged to the ten years between 1454 and 1464, well within his own lifetime: a disastrous earthquake in Naples, a comet, a miracle or two, and, as a more general phenomenon of the decade, he noted the rapid increase in ever finer inventions, and wrote: 'Et impressores librorum multiplicantur in terra'.[1] With these words, saying that printers increased and filled the earth, he echoed the first chapter of Genesis and implied that the advent of printing, and more specifically the creation of printers, was no less a divine creation than the Creation of Man, and that it could be associated with the Tree of Knowledge and perhaps even the Fall. Rolewinck's near-contemporary, Johannes Trithemius, described him as a very learned man, of great erudition and with a subtle mind,[2] and perhaps we may read some mild irony in Rolewinck's tone. The image of the Tree of Knowledge, however, was probably not far from the mind of the early printers. This tree may well be the basis for the emblematic significance of the many printers' devices in the form of a torn-off branch from which the shields identifying the printing house are suspended.[3] If this is so, it shows a vivid sense of the notion of the spread of knowledge, the dissemination of texts, and the role the new art of printing was playing in this in itself very natural process.

We should not lose sight of the perception of contemporaries while trying to come to grips with the vast quantity of fifteenth-century books that history has preserved to the present time. Modern approaches tend to seek models to direct our perception. This is in recognition of the fact that the material we deal with when studying books – not only fifteenth-century books – is diverse, complex, and may appear unstructured to the modern observer. Recording, cataloguing the material, is one way of

63

providing structures, but is not a fully adequate aid to the perception of, say, the impact of printing, or of the book as functioning in its own time. It is very much a phenomenon of our own time to strive after an understanding of function, the concept of the book as a form of communication and part of the texture of society. These are aspects to which we are all sensitive, living as we do in a time in the grip of the digital revolution in communication and its impact on a changing society.

It is therefore hardly surprising that the most developed and most recent of such models has the form of a circuit of communication. It was proposed by Robert Darnton as an answer to the *Annales* approach of the study of the book,[4] and recently modified by Adams and Barker who have revised the model, based on a view of the book which is wider than that of Darnton, who admitted to thinking mainly within the limitations of eighteenth-century French books. There is not much point in arguing about such models, since we all have to remember that they are merely there to help our perception, to help us find a key to what the past has to tell us. The communication circuit is certainly a useful model for understanding the function of the book at any one time from its conception to its distribution. That is an important aspect of what we loosely call *the* history of *the* book.

The material with which one works naturally dictates the form of any model. Since I work mainly with fifteenth-century material, I may be more aware of a phenomenon of very rapid growth and development. Many aspects of the communication function of print have to be inferred for fifteenth-century material, whereas they are more readily available for later periods. As an incunabulist I can therefore not entirely resist arguing that for the longer view, the study of the development of the printed book with all its social and intellectual implications, the old analogy with the life sciences should not be entirely sacrificed. Incunabulists have an early stake here, for it was that very great pioneer of incunable studies, Henry Bradshaw, who in the 1860s used the term 'natural history method' when he devised a system for the classification of types and printers.[5] But there is much more to such an analogy than the taxonomy of types alone, and much that is germane to other periods of book production. In the transmission of texts, and their survival in books, we can see a selection process at work that can be expressed in evolutionary terms, leading to a perception of the environment as a controlling factor in more than one sense.

There are advantages in drawing on the experience of scientific disciplines in dealing with problems of definition and context when we try to master large quantities of material. An analogy with the modern life sciences may also lead to an awareness that in books and other documents we are dealing with material that belongs to a living world, material with an awesome life-span compared with human life, but nevertheless finite in nature.

A text usually has a much longer life than any of the material vehicles in which it is presented. Re-creating a text, selecting it for renewed communication at any given time, always means presenting it in a new material structure. The nature of this structure is, as we all know, determined by time. In the fifteenth century this would usually get the form of a codex, produced either by a variety of procedures within the long scribal tradition, or by the brand-new art of multiplying books in print.

There are many misconceptions about the relation of manuscript codex and printed codex in the fifteenth century, when the transition in the form of production took place. I think that in the first place it is crucial to try to view the books through the eyes of contemporaries, to gauge how they perceived them.

Printed codices were greeted with astonishment, pride and enthusiasm as soon as they became available on the market, with a few rare but significant exceptions. But to most people these books were first and foremost *codices*, vehicles for text, whether they were printed or not. The amazement lay in the fact that you could have them 'good cheap', as William Caxton never tired of pointing out, in short, that people like Caxton himself and his readers could afford them at all.

In basic structure there was no difference with the manuscript codex. The material difference for the user lies in typography alone. The technical requirements of typography immediately introduced simplification in form, and all through the first half-century of printing we can see a relentless process of simplification of graphic form at work. This simplification consisted of a selection of those features of script that were essential for communication, and, conversely, the rejection of the endless variation in form and function that the writing hand can create. Written script forms can be ambiguous: there can be innumerable small distinctions in, say, the value of a capital as expressed by graphic means. In typography, on the contrary, such variation is impossible; once forms have become fixed in metal they force you to make decisions, either, for example, to be seen as a capital or a lower-case character, and nothing in between.[6] The often-heard observation that in the early years printed books imitated manuscripts fails to recognize a much more interesting phenomenon: a selection process of functional forms. It was the loss in subtlety and individuality that repelled some fastidious bookmen, as diverse as the Florentine bookseller Vespasiano da Bisticci and the Burgundian prelate Raffael de Mercatellis, who both eschewed printed books in favour of manuscripts.

It is also often heard that manuscripts and printed books were not distinguished by their users in the fifteenth century. This is again true – up to a point. There are contemporary catalogues and inventories that list both kinds of codices indiscriminately mixed; in such lists the codex, whether printed or manuscript, is primarily a vehicle for the text and a source of information. It is not as if in the fifteenth century people were blind to the difference between the two. They were quite keen to distinguish manuscripts and printed books as soon as current value was brought into play. Printed books were usually cheaper than manuscript codices, even when the latter were simple. In inventories drawn up for probate, or the few lists of books to be sold at public auction known in this period, a careful distinction is made between manuscript and printed books, as much as between bound and unbound books.[7] In the course of the first decades of printing, from the mid-fifties to the end of the fifteenth century, the printed book took over the function of the manuscript codex with accelerating speed. Naturally the two modes of production existed for a while side by side. By the middle of the 1480s, however, the production of manuscripts began to decline steeply. By the end of the century a codex produced in manuscript usually signalled a very particular message: 'I am something unique', it said, 'I am not an ordinary book, but I am made in a way that cannot be produced in print.' In this pattern belong the very colourfully illuminated codices of the late fifteenth and early sixteenth centuries, birds of paradise that are famous as vehicles of pictorial art more than as vehicles of texts. As texts they usually represent a terminal state in the tradition, for their luxurious form prevented them from serving the continuation of the tradition by being copied by a scribe or entrusted to the hands of a compositor.

In this paper I am mainly concerned with the function of the codex book in the transmission and dissemination of texts. Transmission is a process that takes place when one individual text – manuscript or print – is reproduced, either copied in manuscript or typeset and printed. Dissemination is usually thought of in terms of the distribution of a particular product (manuscript or print), but can also be thought of more loosely as the dissemination of a text to reach new markets – that is, widening a geographical area, or reaching more readers and possibly new classes of readers. In the course of this lecture I hope to observe with you something of transmission and of dissemination in that wider sense.

Textual transmission would appear to be a preoccupation of our own time, but in fact the idea of transmission in connection with creating texts was expressed from an early age on. An early example of such a representation is a well-known ivory ninth-century book cover which shows St Gregory the Great writing his work while three scribes are simultaneously multiplying his text by copying it.[8] This is almost an emblematic representation of 'dissemination', while in parallel 'transmission' was often depicted by the scribe copying from one or more sources. A different form of transmission is the *topos* of the teacher reading out from a book to pupils, who in their turn may be making notes about the text, but who, until printed books became a common commodity, were not likely to be seen with many books in their hands (see fig. 1).

The author at work is a representation that is found all through the Middle Ages in numerous examples, and had an *equally* emblematic as well as illustrative function. The author usually writes *his book*, a codex apparently completed and even bound, a form of iconographic anticipation that often seems to puzzle interpreters who tend to take this literally. Occasionally, however, a painter may depart from this convention. One such was Tomaso da Modena, who painted in 1352 in the Capitolo dei Domenicani in the church of S. Nicolò in Treviso a sequence of frescoes representing famous Dominicans, each sitting at a lectern and occupied with one or more books, either reading or writing. Tomaso painted them with remarkable variation and individual expression.[9] Perhaps as a device to introduce as much variation as possible, one of them, the twelfth-century preacher Giovanni da Schio, is represented while preparing to write. He inspects the tip of his pen, and on his desk in front of him is a sheet of vellum, with a few words ('Ave Maria'), waiting for continuation of work by the pen of the scribe, the sheet clearly showing lines dividing it into four pages (see fig. 2). It is a division that is familiar as page imposition in the printing process, but may not have been unknown in the production of manuscript codices. In the same way as later for printed books, the pages on the sheet were to be folded together, once they were all written, to form a quire of probably more than one sheet, on completion to be bound with other similar quires to form a codex. This meant that the assembled book had to be visualised and planned beforehand, in order to write the appropriate combination of pages on the sheet. A few such 'imposed' manuscript sheets have survived as witnesses of this procedure. It is not possible to say on what scale this

Fig. 1. Master with pupils, before the invention of printing. Collection of texts for higher education, written in the fourteenth century. The British Library, MS Burney 275, leaf 176 verso.

Fig. 2. Writing on a full sheet divided into pages: Tomaso da Modena, fresco in S. Nicolò, Treviso, painted in 1352, depicting Giovanni da Schio. From J. J. Berthier O.P., *Le chapitre de San Nicolò de Trevise: Peintures de Tommaso da Modena*, Rome, 1912.

method of producing codices was applied. It may have been one 'mode' of production that existed along with other methods, much as the *pecia* method was a mode of production to be applied in certain circumstances.[10] Tomaso is generally thought to have been an illuminator of books and connected with the booktrade in Bologna before he moved to Treviso. As a witness for scribal practice he must not be too easily dismissed.

When movable type was invented, and with it the process of producing multiple copies from one text 'written in metal', as they said in the fifteenth century, it was not necessary to introduce any innovation in the structure of the codex, by then a form of document with a standing of over a millennium. Nor was there any essential change in the concepts of its production: but what had until then possibly been an occasional method of production, writing on a whole unfolded sheet, became with the introduction of printing the *only* possible way.

Printing a book – or any other document – from metal types cannot be carried out without the use of a printing press, and a printing press means that sheets of paper or vellum have to be placed on the press, later to be folded. This, in its turn, means that the imposition of pages has to be determined in advance, in the same way as the sheet was divided which is still waiting for the writing of the scribe in Treviso.

In the last few years we have made some progress in understanding the development of the early press. The platen was small, the size of a folio page, and only one folio page, a half-sheet, was printed at a time. Even smaller presses were used to print quartos in half-sheets, one page at a time. But in the 1470s printing houses in Italy developed a press with moving carriage, allowing a full sheet with two folio pages or four quarto pages on each side to be printed at one time, in two pulls.[11] This improvement of the press had far-reaching consequences for the production of texts: two or more pages of text, one usually not following the other, had to be on the press at the same time to print sheets that were later folded together to form quires. Supplies of type were insufficient for compositors to set enough pages to complete a whole quire. Pages were therefore set in non-sequential order. In the fifteenth century, and later, this is common practice for books printed on two-pull presses. Since Charlton Hinman the most famous, and certainly the most thoroughly investigated, example is Shakespeare's First Folio.

In manuscript examples which survive after they were used in the printing house as *exemplar* for books on two-pull presses, we can observe that lines were counted off and marked in advance, and then, as typesetting went along, were marked again to record what had actually happened.[12] It was often difficult to make the text fit exactly as marked off in advance, and in early books 'seams' are often visible to the alert eye. On the other hand, compositors were artful, and did not need much experience to use all the means available to them to disguise any problems: variations in spelling, spacing and contraction or expansion of words, even mild adaptation of the text could be called in to produce well-balanced and seamlessly fitting pages of typesetting. It is therefore mainly a matter of the professional ambition of the compositor whether we can detect the problems he may have had with copy fitting. Whether easily detectable or not, copy-fitting problems did affect the typesetting of the text substantially; it is therefore always of importance to establish the order of typesetting if one is interested in establishing the transmission of the text in print.

For books printed in the twenty-odd years before the development of the two-pull press it is usually difficult to demonstrate in what order they were typeset and printed; even when printing one page at a time there may be advantages in completing (out of textual sequence) the sides of a sheet, and therefore in choosing not to work in the sequential order of the text. It is therefore not possible to predict the order of typesetting for the very earliest printed books. Findings so far indicate, however, that the text was often set sequentially, and that each sheet was therefore put on the press in at least four separate phases (more if there was also colour-printing). The order of composition of the very first printed book, Gutenberg's 42-line Bible, was shown by Paul Needham in a study based on the ink analysis instigated by Professor Richard Schwab.[13] A progressive sequence, with division of work over compositors and presses, had already been established at the beginning of this century by the German incunabulist Paul Schwenke. Dr Needham showed that the ink analysis confirmed and gave greater precision to the division of printer's copy for the Bible which had previously been surmised by Paul Schwenke, and hence to its production in relatively small sections. Linking the sections had sometimes given rise to difficulties in the printing house which can still be observed; within the sections the compositors worked (at least most of the time) in page order.[14]

I could establish a similar procedure for one of the first books printed in Italy. This is the Augustine *De Civitate Dei* printed in 1467 by the German printers Conrad Sweynheym and Arnold Pannartz at the Benedictine monastery of St Scolastica in Subiaco, the first press active in Italy.[15] Most histories of printing gloss Subiaco as 'near Rome'. 'Near

Rome', I can tell you from personal experience, is well beyond Tivoli, a two-hour increasingly scenic bus-ride followed by a brisk walk up the mountain. Once there, however, one can be rewarded, not only by the unforgettable serenity of an ancient monastery, but by having side by side one of the books printed by this deeply intriguing press, and the manuscript that was used as *examplar* by the compositors. The manuscript, a modestly decorated codex that is perhaps some twenty years older than the printed book, is full of corrections and notes written to prepare it for printing. Evidently it was read critically and with great care to improve the text. The compositors handled the manuscript also with respect, although we can plainly see marks and annotations made before they set type, and also the marks and notes they made as they went along, as they finished each page.

In two sections of the book we find sequences of notes that seem to have been made by two distinct compositors. They are unique in the history of printing: many of the sections are marked with letters and figures which correspond to pages in the printed book, as we can understand on the basis of other (later) examples of printers' copy. But in sections of this manuscript a number of pages are in addition marked with an indication of a day of the week in abbreviated form, followed by the letters a.p. or p.p. for *ante prandium* or *post prandium*, 'before lunch' or 'after lunch'. To be able to relate the work of a compositor to an actual time sequence is rare indeed. Actual time is usually the one factor that eludes us in the production of an early printed book, until such times that printers' archives or correspondence provide external information. Here we appear to see, however, that for these two compositors time did not matter very much; or it seems not to have been a pressing factor. They worked at great and irregular intervals, as for example in quire [g], where notes were made relating to nine out of its twenty pages, in this order:

> Wednesday before lunch,
> Saturday before lunch,
> Tuesday before lunch,
> Monday after lunch,
> Monday after lunch,
> Thursday after lunch,
> Monday after lunch,
> Monday after lunch,
> Thursday after lunch.

We can infer from the relation of cast-off pages to actually typeset pages that the compositors went through the book in textual order, page after page. We must therefore conclude that one compositor worked on quire [g] for at least four weeks, possibly more, but never more than two half-days a week. Would he have been a monk, taught by the more experienced printers Sweynheym and Pannartz by whose names the press is known? At some stage in their learning process someone, at least, must have told them not to relate the record of the stints they had done to the time-clocks in their stomachs, nor to any time at all, but to the book they were engaged on making. Others, or even the compositor himself, should after an interval be able to resume work at the right place in the text of the *exemplar*, and continue typesetting in full awareness what page in the quire of the printed book it was going to occupy. This was necessary for the correct positioning of the page on the sheet, even when printing took place one page at a time. That is the significance of these marks, which were as necessary with small units of one page at a time, as later when the larger unit of the whole outer or inner sheet went to press at the same time. For one-page printing they were perhaps even more necessary, because the procedure offered less chance for self-correction before it was too late. So someone in the Subiaco monastery must have taken the aspirant compositors aside, and pointed out that it did not matter *when* they set their pages, but that it was vital to record *what* they had done. Elsewhere in the Subiaco manuscript we find notes designating pages within quires, just such notes as are familiar from slightly later *exemplaria* used in printing houses.

Important evidence has come to light to support this thought, and its implications go well beyond the explanation of the notes in the St Augustine manuscript. This evidence is presented in a letter addressed to the abbot of Gottweig (near Melk) which is now preserved in the Abbey of Melk. It was written in 1471 by a Benedictine monk named Benedict Zwink of Ettal, who for many years resided in the abbey of St Specus which adjoins the monastery of St Scolastica near Subiaco; there he was known as Benedictus de Bavaria. Zwink wrote in connection with plans to extend the Benedictine congregations of Bursfeld and Melk to include those who observed the rules of Subiaco and Montecassino. Unity of liturgy was an important objective in these plans, and to that end agreement about the divine service should be obtained. 'Since it might be difficult for all monasteries to compare and edit breviaries,' writes Benedictus, 'it will be easy to produce 100 or 200 copies on the presses, just as we have also produced 200 copies of St Augustine's De Civitate Dei in the form of type as enclosed. In the monastery of St Specus we can make use of this technique to the full, for we have the equipment and the people [who know how to use it]. If we could form part of this religious union [the extended congregation], all books, whatever the number required, could be printed and distributed to all monasteries which in their turn would have joined the congregation, with the equipment which is available on the spot, and with the help of five brethren who could be instructed in this technique ...'.[16] There is no trace in the form of a printed breviary, or further correspondence, to show that anything has come of the suggestions made by Benedictus. In the absence of any surviving printed materials we must surmise that the daily tasks in the monastery (which may account for the many days not covered by the apprentices' notes) overcame the less immediate duty to serve the unifying and missionary power of the printing press: the typographical equipment at Subiaco decayed unused. The letter of Benedictus shows, at least, an early awareness of the power of the press in communication and in unifying those separated by great physical distance. The traces of apprenticeship within the monastic confines, taken in combination with Benedictus's letter, suggest that the establishment of a press in Subiaco may have been more connected with plans for monastic reform than is evident from what it produced, or from what survives of its production.

It is only rarely that we can compare a printed book with a manuscript that had served as printer's copy. So far less than twenty have been recognized as having served in this function.[17] Sometimes the marks are very unobtrusive, and we can expect that more will be found as interest in tracing these relationships between documents of the fifteenth century is growing. The few instances that have been studied have greatly helped our understanding of the procedures underlying the transmission of texts either from one medium to the other – the manuscript codex to the printed codex – or from printed book to printed book. A printed book would be treated in exactly the same way as a manuscript codex, re-formatted and marked up accordingly, unless the printer chose to make an exact replica of his printed exemplar by using the same type or type-size and producing a page-for-page or even a line-for-line reprint. Although this procedure was quite common in the fifteenth century, the number of instances is far exceeded by the quantity of books produced by the more tortuous procedure of calculating and casting-off copy.

It has often been said that once a text appeared in print its further tradition would be one of successive editions, each reprinting the text of its predecessor.[18] Such logic is far from reality. I should like to look with you in some detail at an example that includes transmission from edition to edition, but also the dissemination of a text over most of the reading world. It is a book that first appeared in print a few years after the Subiaco St Augustine, of which some thirty editions printed in the fifteenth century are known to survive. The text is the collection of *Facetiae*, or jests, collected by an almost contemporary author, Poggio Bracciolini.[19]

A first glance at a *stemma* of its line of descendance (see fig. 4) shows that what we see here is not at all a straightforward tradition. Yet there is logic in it which we can begin to understand when we know a little more of the text at the time it began to appear in print. One of the charms of this text is that the author himself provided ample information about its origin. Poggio Bracciolini's fame as a humanist scholar is based on his discoveries in the first half of the fifteenth century of early manuscripts of important classical texts in Switzerland and France. He travelled widely as apostolic secretary, and in that function made a network of friends and acquaintances, and also enemies. In the 1430s Poggio wrote down the stories and anecdotes, many of them quite improper, that were swapped in the ambiance of the apostolic secretariat, in what he called the *bugiale*, or *Officina Mendicatorum*, the lie-factory. Poggio was interested not only

Fig. 3. An early example of a printed book to be read whenever you had a moment to yourself: Pseudo-Augustinus, *Soliloquia*. [Cologne, Arnold ther Hoernen, 1471-72]. in-16°. The British Library, IA.3136.

in Latin as the language of classical Antiquity, but equally in Latin as a living language. His experience as apostolic secretary and his many travels had convinced him of the practical necessity of Latin as a *lingua franca* to be used in speech as well as in writing, unencumbered by the pedantic rules invented by grammarians. His collection of jests was a conscious attempt to use Latin in the fast throw-away manner usually associated with the contemporary use of vernacular language, either in discourse or in literature. His chosen literary *genre* straddles both aspects of language to perfection.

His free use of Latin brought him in conflict with grammarians, and one of them, Lorenzo Valla, insulted him by making disparaging remarks about the quality of his Latin. Poggio responded in 1452 in a series of *Invectiva in Laurentium Vallam*, in which, in the full flow of outraged rhetoric he claimed: 'My Facetiae were circulated all through Italy, France, Spain, Germany and England, read by all such who understand Latin, and approved by all men of letters.' The date 1452 means of course that we can just, but only just, be certain that Poggio's text had this international circulation in manuscript, not in print.

When printing did arrive, however, Poggio's claim met even fuller justification, as you can see by the wide spread of places of printing in the *stemma*. The popularity of the text diminished somewhat in the 1480s, when translations into Italian began to appear, thus totally defeating Poggio's purpose. But the Latin version was still reprinted a number of times, and the tradition in print found its apogee in Poggio's collected works, printed in Basle in 1538, which is the text used as authority by all modern scholarship. We can be quite certain that more editions were printed than now survive. Almost all the presently known editions of the text are extremely rare: they were small quarto books, many of them not particularly well printed; in the sixteenth century the text was placed on the *Index Librorum prohibitorum* because of its disrespect to the clergy; all factors that did not favour its survival. If the book is rare now, and preserved in rare or unique copies in libraries in all corners of the western world, we must still bear in mind that the thirty editions now recorded must mean that in the last thirty years of the fifteenth century the text became available in at least several thousands of copies.

We shall now take a closer look at the family tree. The inter-relationship of these editions is based on textual investigation which I cannot relate in any detail here.[20] The result shows that at about the same time, 1470-1471, four editions were printed. Three were undated, the edition printed by Christopher Valdarfer in Venice, and the two editions printed in Rome by Georg Lauer. They are closely related to one another, and, on rather complicated grounds that I shall leave aside now, I could establish their relative order. The Venetian edition, a very handsome book, must have been printed from a manuscript *exemplar*, and a copy of this printed book served as *exemplar* for the first Rome edition. There are a few very slight textual variants, enough to distinguish its descendants from those descending straight from the Valdarfer edition. One of its offspring, the second edition printed by Georg Lauer, here called Rome B, was meant to be a straightforward reprint of his first edition (Rome A). About a quarter of the way through the printing of Rome B, a minor error of imposition was made in the printing house, causing a page of text to be skipped. It was soon discovered, and cunningly amended by inserting the missing text a little later with noticeable but minor loss of coherence. They were jests after all – what did it matter? Nevertheless this change causes all the descendants of Rome B to be instantly recognizable, as if by an inherited birthmark. We can thus distinguish three branches in the printed editions, after they had all descended from Venice. One branch, the most handsome of the family, descended through the also very beautiful reprints in Nuremberg and a number of later descendants to the version in the collected works of 1538. Textually this branch remained very close to the first Venice edition.

The second branch, slightly corrupted by its descendance from the second Rome edition, was often reprinted in Rome, and developed a sequence of French descendents, a Paris edition reprinted twice in Lyon. It was also reprinted in Milan by the same Christopher Valdarfer who had printed at Venice the *editio princeps*, and who took as *exemplar* not his own beautiful book but the slightly flawed version. A manuscript, now in the Biblioteca Apostolica Vaticana but written in Germany, must have descended from this branch of the Rome family, since it also shows the error in the order of the jests that originated in the printing house. It is remarkable that all the descendants of Rome B, itself a very modest book, are unassuming in appearance, distinctly lower on the social scale than the direct descendants of Venice. The concentration of editions in Rome shows that the book was particularly popular near the place where the text had its origin, the apostolic see. The fact that the author reveals that these irreverent stories were told in the papal antechambers, and their natural tone of gossip and banter, will have appealed in particular to ecclesiastical readers until the time when the text was turned against them. The *Facetiae* may have been one of those books one brought back from a journey to Rome. There is much to indicate that printers in Rome did not work for established trade channels to send books all over the reading world, as Venetian printers and so many others in the great mercantile centres did; in Rome the printers depended on the carriage trade, as it were. They worked for the many visitors attracted to the spiritual centre of the Western world. A copy of the first Rome edition may well have travelled in a priest's saddlebags to Wrocław, in Poland, where in 1475 it served as printer's copy for Caspar Elyan. From this edition the text was reprinted somewhere in a Polish religious house – the exact site of this press is under discussion, but it was possibly situated in central Poland. The Lübeck edition is still a problem. It belongs to this branch, but must have been printed from an imperfect and disordered copy. In any case we can see that the descendants of the first Rome edition move in a distinctly middle or eastern European circle.

There is yet something else to observe in the dissemination of the text shown in this stemma, and that is that there are six editions quite independent from the main family. They belong to shorter and presumably earlier versions of the text. I may remind you of Poggio's own claim that his text was widely circulated over many countries. It is known that over the years his collection of jests grew and grew, until it numbered 273 jests. But before it had reached this number the text had already been circulating in manuscript form. It was the final version, with 273 jests, that was printed by Valdarfer in Venice and reprinted so many times. The dated edition, printed at approximately the same time by Andreas Belfortis at Ferrara in 1470, contained only 175 jests, and shows many textual variations. Anton Koberger in Nuremberg did slightly better, working about one year later from a manuscript with 218 jests; Johannes de Westfalia in Louvain used a manuscript in a completely different version, the 251 jests having titles which deviate from everybody else's, and were presented in a different order. Even in Rome, where from 1470 onwards so many copies of the printed version were going round, Ulrich Han (or the successors to his material) produced a shorter version with only 206 jests, in an undated edition which is thought to have been printed around 1480, and for which the printing house must have used a manuscript.

These four independent versions have in common that they were not reprinted, with the exception of that of Johannes de Westfalia. The reason that these presumably earlier versions of the text were generally not reprinted was probably because it did not escape printers – nor their clients – that these books did not represent the full set of *Facetiae* available in print elsewhere. In these four witnesses we can see a reflection of the wide dissemination of the text in manuscript, in a variety of versions, but we see also a selection process at work: only the most extensive form of the text proliferated in print, in a connected but by no means straight line of descendance.

The exception, Johannes de Westfalia's version, offers an interesting illustration of this point. He himself reprinted his book in unaltered form a few years after the first had appeared, probably around 1477. In this form the book was also reprinted in nearby Antwerp by Mathias van der Goes, in 1486. But in the following year Van der Goes, apparently not content after seeing other printed versions with the full set of jests, published another edition which contains all 273 jests and which must have had one of Creussner's edition as model. It appears to be an act of repudiation of the shorter version.[21]

Finally, it is impossible to do justice to another aspect of the dissemination of Poggio's text: the copies of the editions represented in the *stemma* spread over a much wider area than the places of printing can evoke. We have already seen that the germ of its proliferation in eastern Europe was an edition printed at Rome. At the other end of the western world of its time we can see that the two editions printed at Louvain are each preserved in a unique copy in an English collection, each bearing traces of a contemporary English owner.[22] Obviously the survival rate of printed copies is such that the real dissemination of the text in copies of printed editions has largely to be left to the imagination.

Manuscripts play a part in the transmission of Poggio's *Facetiae*, but one element, often found in fifteenth-century textual tradition, is missing here due to the nature of the text. Poggio's jests did not make a serious book: nobody was concerned with the *minutiae* of this text. Although we could see that the shorter versions were passed over in favour of the longer ones, there is no sign at all of any collation or other comparing of sources. Collation, the comparison and critical assessment of a text against another source, was a continuous process that tends to be underestimated by textual historians who come to the fifteenth century from other periods.

The fact that print caused so many more texts to become widely available had a marked effect: there was much more material to serve as a basis for critical assessment. Manuscripts gained a new significance as sources to find earlier authority, a basis for collation or simply a better alternative to previously published versions. In the work of early printing houses we can very soon find attempts at textual perfection, but not until the printing presses had provided the world for several decades with a wide variety of texts did this process come fully into its own. Towards the end of the century manuscripts came to be sought after for new reasons, as independent sources; we all know the extra force given to this trend early in the sixteenth century when scholars like Erasmus broke away from established textual tradition by returning to earlier manuscripts which provided fresh evidence for the text of the Bible and the church fathers. The wider availability of texts in print had fostered this critical spirit. It had taken more than fifty years to achieve this effect.

When we speak of textual scholarship of this order we are at the very top of the intellectual scale. Having recognized the principle, however, we can see it at work much earlier than Erasmus's time, but in a far less spectacular fashion.

Printers sent a text into the world in hundreds of copies. Naturally they were concerned that it should not be defective, that it should remain reasonably up to date, that faults would not be multiplied hundreds of time if this could be prevented. They and their customers compared editions and sources. At the same time they created the resources, or to put it in modern jargon, they created a mode of access to further knowledge, that brought critical assessment within the grasp of far and far larger numbers than ever before. The parallel with modern communication developments is again obvious.

By the end of the century there had been a revolution in the dissemination of books. A beginning had been there before the advent of printing, but of a very limited nature. For example, Christopher de Hamel's book on illuminated manuscripts contains a chapter on books of hours which he quite tellingly entitles: 'Books for Everybody'; these prayer books were small books owned by individuals and carried round by them for their private devotions. But no other kind of book was owned by individuals on such a scale, and even in the context of medieval books of hours 'Everybody' should be very heavily qualified. By and large manuscript books were owned by institutions, for communal use rather than by individuals, with the well known exceptions of great noble or royal libraries which had almost institutional status. The earliest printed books, the great Bibles, works of canonical law and patristic texts such as were produced at Mainz, were all printed with a well-defined market in mind, for monasteries and other ecclesiatical institutions. This changed very soon. Books began to be owned by people who had never owned books before; they now could afford them, and they began to use them. An individually owned book could be treated as one may treat a member of one's family, it could be cherished, or criticized, improved upon, consulted at all hours, abused and befriended again. Luckily these relationships have left many visible traces, notes of all kinds expressing fascination or boredom, the face of your teacher or of the girl of your dreams.

For the book as an object belonging to an individual I can think of no better example (almost a symbol) than a small book acquired a couple of years ago by the British Library. It was printed at Cologne by Arnold ther Hoernen about the year 1471-2,[23] and it is one of the earliest examples on record of printing in such a small format – 16mo – North of the Alps. Its text, a Soliloquy, was thought in the Middle Ages, and at the time it was printed, to have been written by St Augustine. It offers therefore a particularly telling contrast to the Augustine printed at Subiaco in 1467 discussed above. There is a copy of the Subiaco Augustine in the Vatican Library containing a stern note saying that this book belonged to the Regular Canons of the Lateran Congregation at Rome, for communal use, and let nobody dare to alienate it for his personal use from the communal use of the Canons.[24] The *Soliloquium* printed only five years later, in Cologne, could hardly be a greater contrast as a presentation of and a destination for a patristic text: its very small sextodecimo format allows it to nestle in your hands, an Enchiridion, or to be carried about in your sleeve, to be read whenever you had a moment to yourself, nothing interfering with your soliloquy (see fig. 3).

Since I began with an image expressing the spread of knowledge I shall end with one other image which expresses the theme in lighter vein: at the time of the manuscript codex, teaching was often represented by a teacher lecturing from a book, while the pupils apparently were lucky when they had one book between them. In contrast, a woodcut in a book printed in 1490 at Florence shows a class full of pupils with books in their hands, acting as if nothing was more ordinary.[25] They practically ignore their teacher, Landinus, and concentrate on their own, privately, individually owned books (see fig. 5). The message clearly is: when you buy this book you don't need to attend lectures.

It was for anonymous people like these that the printing presses worked and produced an ever growing number of copies of books, large and increasingly smaller. The great difference with manuscript production is that manuscripts were produced with either an individual or a very defined market in mind. Manuscripts written 'on spec' are rare, and in any case a late development of stationers in the fifteenth century. Printers

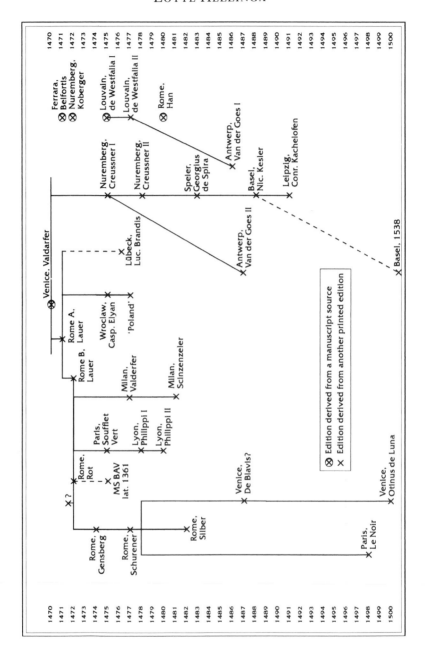

Fig. 4. Stemma of the dissemination of Poggio's *Facetiae* in printed editions before 1501.

CFormulario di lettere & di orationi uolgari con la
propofta & rifpofta cõpofto p Chriftofano landini

Fig. 5. Master with pupils, after the invention of printing: Christophorus Landinus, *Formulario di lettere*. [Florence, Bartolommeo di Libri, about 1490]. BMC VI 656. The British Library, IA.27450 (title woodcut).

soon learned to work for a far less well defined market, not for individuals or even a *type* of individual or institution. To this day we can observe the effect of the imaginative enterprise of the really great publishers such as Anton Koberger in Nuremberg, and Aldus Manutius and other less glamorous but equally prolific printers at Venice. To this day their work can be found in very many collections, not rare at all, but in numerous copies. Their survival rate is a testimony to their publishers' success in selling books through by then developed trade channels, selling them to buyers whom they themselves could not identify as individuals or even as institutions. For a publisher who really had discovered how to exploit the potential of the new medium of print the market should not be too defined: if the product was good they could trust it would be bought. Half a century of printing had taught them how to safeguard the quality of the product by making the fullest use of the resources accumulated over centuries in manuscript and then in print. We could call this the invention of publishing.

Barker and Adams remarked in their considerations about the communication circuit that the text is the *reason* for the cycle of the book; its *transmission* depends on its ability to set off new cycles. I think that in paying close attention to the process of transmission in the fifteenth century we may gain an insight into how transmission was controlled by the quality of the text itself, and the quality of presentation; both had to be adequate to the expectations of a wider environment. This applies not only to the fifteenth century, but the early development of the process may be illuminating when we consider later periods of book production.

NOTES

1 Werner Rolewinck, *Fasciculus Temporum*, Cologne, Arnold ther Hoernen, 1474. Hain-Copinger *6918; Goff R 254; BMC i, p. 204. This edition of Rolewinck's work (which appeared almost simultaneously with a different version, printed by Nicolaus Götz, also in Cologne) is the first to contain the observation on the invention of printing. A press-variant in at least six still extant copies of Ther Hoernen's edition is known which contains the important specification 'ortum sue artis habentes in maguncia'. The dissemination in later editions of the information contained in this variant was studied in Lotte Hellinga and Margaret Lane Ford, 'Deletion or Addition: A controversial variant in Werner Rolewinck's "Fasciculus Temporum" (Cologne, 1474)', in *Essays in Honor of William B. Todd*, ed. Dave Oliphant, University of Texas at Austin, 1991, pp. 61-79.

2 'Wernerus Rolevinck de laer ... vir in diuinis scripturis studiosissimus: et valde eruditus et ingenio subtilis: vita et conuersatione deuotus'. Johannes Trithemius, *De viris illustribus* (Mainz, Peter von Friedberg, after 14 August 1495), in 4°. Hain *15615, Goff T 433, BMC i, p. 47 (IA.389).

3 George D. Painter, 'Michael Wenssler's devices and their predecessors, with special reference to Fust and Schoeffer's', in *Gutenberg-Jahrbuch 1959*, pp. 211-19. A further development of tree symbolism in printers' devices can be found in the sixteenth century in the devices representing an olive tree with falling branches widely used by the Estiennes. The motto 'Non altum sapere, sed time' which accompanies this emblem in various forms of the device, is derived from the letters of St Paul (Romans 11:20) with the parable of the branches of the olive tree: '. . . if the root is holy, so are the branches . . .'. In his Hanes lecture *The Hanes collection of Estienne Publications: From Book Collection to scholarly Resource*, University of North Carolina, 1984, F. Schreiber, after identifying the letters of St Paul as source for the motto, revealed another aspect of the symbolism of the tree: the family name Estienne can be expressed through the symbol of olive branches which refer to the noun *stephanos* (wreath, specifically of olive twigs). This last interpretation would obviously not be relevant to the Fust-Schoeffer device and its descendants. The reference to the letters of St Paul may, however, be a layer of interpretation valid for all the devices with branches of trees; conversely, the olive tree of the Estiennes may represent on a general level the Tree of Knowledge (as thought by some modern bibliographers) as well as specifically and explicitly St Paul's olive tree.

4 Robert Darnton, 'What is the History of Books?' in *Books and Society in History*, Papers of the Association of College and Research Libraries Rare Books and Manuscripts Preconference, 24-28 June 1980, ed. Kenneth E. Carpenter, New York and London, 1983, pp. 3-26; a model for a communication circuit on p. 6. Cf. the modified circuit proposed by Adams and Barker in the present volume, *supra*, p. 14.

5 Henry Bradshaw's passage on the natural history method was originally published as Note D, 'Printing in Zwolle' attached to *A classified index of the Fifteenth Century Books in the De Meyer Collection sold at Ghent, November 1869* [Memorandum 21], Cambridge, 1870, reprinted in *Collected Papers of Henry Bradshaw*, ed. F. Jenkinson, Cambridge, 1889, p. 221. It has been much quoted (e.g. in the introduction to *Catalogue of Books Printed in the XVth Century now in the British Museum* (BMC) vol. I, p. xii), and much discussed. For recent discussions (which do not achieve a consensus of opinion) see G. Thomas Tanselle, 'Bibliography and Science', in *Studies in Bibliography*, 27, 1974, pp. 55-89; Paul Needham, *The Bradshaw Method: Henry Bradshaw's Contribution to Bibliography* (The seventh Hanes Lecture), University of North Carolina, 1988; Lotte Hellinga, 'Analytical Bibliography and the Study of Early Printed Books: with a case-study of the Mainz Catholicon', in *Gutenberg-Jahrbuch 1989*, pp. 47-96.

6 Examples of the use of typographical forms half-way between capital and lower-case are discussed in L. Hellinga, *Caxton in Focus*, London, 1982, pp. 55-62. These examples illustrate how such conventions were misunderstood by compositors and eventually rejected. Another stage in the developing balance between standard forms and duplicate forms can be demonstrated in the relation between scribes' hands and Greek types, discussed by N. Barker, *Aldus Manutius and the Development of Greek Script and Type in the 15th Century*, Sandy Hook, Conn., 1985, *passim*. Barker noted a substantial number of duplicate forms in several typecases of the 1490s, but in spite of these instances the types represent a

simplification of the many variations in form to be observed in the hands of the scribes.

7 A single example must suffice. In the (probably) public auction of the 69 books that had belonged to Canon Johannes de Platea, which took place in Mechlin in 1489, six items are specified as printed ('impressus'), 59 as manuscripts ('scriptus'), and only five items are not specified. In the first sixteen items the bindings are noted: seven books are bound on boards ('in asseribus'), one book is described as 'ligatus sine asseribus', and four merely as 'ligatus'. Of 24 books the material is noted as 'in pergameno', of 34 'in papiro'. A further analysis of this sale is in preparation. Partly published by E. Steenackers, 'La Bibliothèque de Jean de Platea, Chanoine de Saint-Rombaut à Malines, décédé en 1489', in *Mechlinia*, 6, 1928, pp. 177-83.

8 Christopher de Hamel, *A History of Illuminated Manuscripts*, Oxford, 1986.

9 Tomaso da Modena (c. 1325-1379). See Luigi Coletti (ed. Clara Rosso Coletti), *Tomaso da Modena*, Venice, 1963. The sequence of 40 frescoes of Dominicans was reproduced entirely by J. J. Berthier O.P., *Le chapitre de San Nicolò de Trevise: Peintures de Tommaso da Modena*, Rome, 1912.

10 An example of an early sheet with part of Jacob van Maerlant's *Wapene Martijn* written 'in plano' was illustrated and discussed in W. Hellinga, *Copy and Print in the Netherlands: An Atlas of Historical Bibliography*, Amsterdam, 1962, pp. 136, 137 and pl. 1 and 2. The date of this vellum sheet, on which the pages were wrongly combined and which must therefore have been discarded to be used as binders' waste, has variously been estimated as the first and the second half of the fifteenth century. Examples of such procedures which undoubtedly can be dated before the invention of printing were discussed by Graham Pollard, 'Notes on the size of the sheet', in *The Library*, fourth ser. 22, 1941, pp. 105-37. For a recent discussion see Jean Vezin, 'Manuscrits "imposés"', in: H.-J. Martin (ed.), *Mise en page et mise en texte du livre manuscrit*, Paris, 1990, pp. 423-25. The classical work on the *pecia* method is Jean Destrez, *La Pecia dans les manuscrits universitaires du XIIIe et du XIVe siècle*, Paris, 1935. Important modification to Destrez's presentation by Graham Pollard, 'The *Pecia* system in the Medieval Universities' in *Medieval Scribes, Manuscripts and Libraries, Essays presented to N. R. Ker*, ed. M. B. Parkes and A. G. Watson, London, 1978, pp. 145-61. For an excellent up-to-date summary see Christopher de Hamel, *Illuminated Manuscripts* (see note 8), pp. 126-9. See also R. H. and M. A. Rouse, *supra*, pp. 45-61.

11 Extensive sampling of incunabula printed before 1485, mainly copies in the British Library, showed that the earliest examples of printing on a two-pull press are found in Rome and Naples, followed by Venice. It took several years for this technical improvement to spread to other Italian cities, and it is not until the late 1470s that it is found north of the Alps. Publication of this sample is in preparation.

12 Literature has been summarized in note 79 of A. C. de la Mare and Lotte Hellinga, 'The first book printed in Oxford: The *Expositio Symboli* of Rufinus', in *Transactions of the Cambridge Bibliographical Society*, 7, 1978, pp. 184-244. See also Carol Meale, 'Wynkyn de Worde's setting copy for *Ipomydon*', in *Studies in Bibliography*, 35, 1982, p. 156 n1. An attempt to draw general conclusions from the various isolated case studies in Lotte Hellinga, 'The link between two early

printed books', in *Book Production and Letters in the Western European Renaissance: Essays in Honour of Conor Fahy*, ed. Anna Laura Lepschy, John Took and Dennis E. Rhodes, London, 1986, pp. 166-82.

13 Paul Needham, 'Division of Copy in the Gutenberg Bible: Three Glosses on the Ink Evidence', in *Papers of the Bibliographical Society of America*, 79, 1985, pp. 411-26.

14 As a result of Proton Milliprobe analysis Professor Schwab and his colleagues published readings in several sections of the Gutenberg Bible which suggest an alternate pattern of printing, or at least a pattern not in textual order within the quires. See Richard N. Schwab, Thomas A. Cahill, Bruce H. Kusko, Robert A. Eldred, Daniel L. Wick, 'The Proton Milliprobe ink analysis of the Harvard B42, Volume II', in *Papers of the Bibliographical Society of America*, 81, 1987, pp. 403-32.

15 GW 2874. A more extensive discussion of the Subiaco printers' copy in: Lotte Hellinga, 'Three notes on printers' copy: Strassburg, Oxford, Subiaco', in *Transactions of the Cambridge Bibliographical Society*, 9, 1987, pp. 194-204.

16 The original text of Benedictus' letter which I paraphrased in English is: 'Item si ordinate in divino officio subito mente non possunt concordari, paulatim componant unam formam breviarii, quae videlicet regula se conformet cum Rubrica Romana et ex post, si non omnia monasteria sint in puncto ad comparandum breviaria, tunc facile centum vel ducenta volumina possunt scribi in quacumque littera in torcularibus, sicut et nos scripsimus ducenta volumina sancti Augustini De Civitate Dei, in ista forma scripture, quam mittam. Et artem perfectam in instrumentis et personis habemus in monasterio sacri Specus. Eius in casu posito, quo se talis unio religionis dilataret usque ad nos, per quinque fratres, qui istam artem addiscerent, omnes libros, quotquot essent, per omnia monasteria sibi invicem coniuncta possent scribi et dilatari.' (Melk MS 91, quoted from Barbara Frank, 'Tipografia monastica sublacense: per una confederazione benedettina', in *Il Sacro Speco*, 74, 1971, pp. 69-72). I am most grateful to Dr Piero Scapecchi, Biblioteca Nazionale, Florence, who obtained for me a copy of *Il Sacro Speco*, an elusive periodical. The letter is of course also of interest for the information it yields about the edition-size of the Subiaco Augustine (200 copies) and the fact that some leaves were sent as type-specimen.

17 See literature quoted above in note 12.

18 E. J. Kenney, *The Classical Text: Aspects of Editing in the Age of the Printed Book*, Berkeley, 1974, classified the transmission process in print as 'unilinear, or monogenous', and expanded (p. 18): 'With remarkably few exceptions the descent of any given text through the printed editions is in a single line, and each editor is found to base his work on that of his (usually though not invariably) immediate predecessor. For each author the base text, the *lectio recepta* – the text *tout court* – is the printed text; this is now the uniquely stable point of reference.' The concept of the printed text as stable point of reference was given greater popularity by Elizabeth L. Eisenstein, *The Printing Press as an Agent of Change*, Cambridge, 1979.

19 What follows is derived from a study of editions of Poggio's *Facetiae* printed before c. 1482: Lotte Hellinga, 'The dissemination of a text in print: Early editions of Poggio Bracciolini's *Facetiae*', in G. Crapulli (ed.), *Trasmissione dei testi a stampa nel periodo moderno*, vol. II, Rome, 1987, [Lessico Intellettuale Europeo

XLIV], pp. 85-106. For the present paper I have extended researches to editions printed before 1501.

20 For details of textual variation I refer to the study quoted above in note 19. The later editions I examined could be classified according to the same textual criteria. In addition to the 23 editions listed in the article quoted above, all printed before *c.* 1482, I have examined the following five editions printed before 1501: Antwerp, Mathias van der Goes, 1486, in-4°, Campbell, *Annales* 1430. Antwerp, Mathias van der Goes, 3 August 1487, in-4°, Campbell, *Annales*, 1431. Basel, Nicolaus Kessler, 14 March 1488, in-4°. HC 13195. Paris, Michel le Noir, 1498, in-4°. Goff P871. Venice, Otinus de Luna, Papiensis, 1 December 1500, in-4°. Goff P872. The following edition (not examined by me) completes the list of editions of the *Facetiae* on record: Venice, Thomas de Blavis de Alexandria, 10 April 1487, in-4°. Goff P867. The edition Paris, Michel le Noir in-4°. Goff-P870 is according to CIBN p. 441 printed about 1514.

21 I am most grateful to my colleagues Mademoiselle Ursula Baurmeister (Bibliothèque Nationale, Paris), Mrs Elly Cockx-Indestege (Koninklijke Bibliotheek, Brussels) and Dr H. Härtel, Herzog-August Bibliothek, Wolfenbüttel, for their kind help in providing microfilms and photocopies of the two Antwerp editions.

22 The copy at Cambridge University Library of the book printed in 1475 (Oates 3763) bears the early inscription 'Ant. Cope' (?), and marks of ownership of later English collectors. The copy at Oxford, Bodleian Library, Proctor 9225, Sheppard 7120, is bound in a contemporary Oxford binding of the type usually designated as a 'Rood and Hunt' binding.

23 Augustinus, *Soliloquia* (text beginning: Agnoscam te ...).[Cologne, Arnold ther Hoernen, about 1475]. in-16°, British Library, IA.3136, unrecorded edition acquired in 1984. Miss M. L. Ford studied the type in connection with other Ther Hoernen printing and determined the dating. See Margaret L. Ford, 'An unrecorded small-format incunable', in *The Library*, 6th ser. XI, 1989, pp. 139-42.

24 The inscription is: 'Ad usum Canonicorum Regularium eiusdem patris Augustini Congregationis Lateranensis in Urbe Roma commorantium. Ubicumque habitaverunt: Ad nullum sic locum pertinet: sed ad personas tantum. Quare nullus sibi usurpare praesumat privato usufructu quod ad commune commodum est dedicatum' (Biblioteca Apostolica Vaticana, Stamp. Ross. 493).

25 Christophorus Landinus, *Formulario di epistole*. [Florence, Bartolommeo di Libri, about 1490]. in-4°. Reichling 587, BMC VI 656 (IA.27450).

AMERICAN PAPERMAKERS
AND THE PANIC OF 1819

John Bidwell

From affluence to recession, from boom to bust, the American economy expands and contracts with an ominous regularity that economists call a business cycle. Frequently a business cycle ends in catastrophe, a panic followed by a depression which might last for several gruelling years before prosperity returns. The economy of this newly created nation gathered strength and momentum during the nineteenth century despite major depressions beginning in 1819, 1837, 1857, 1873, 1882 and 1893 – in effect a series of periodic setbacks, some more severe than others. This chapter will examine how papermakers and other members of the book trade coped with America's first great financial disaster, the Panic of 1819.[1]

Hard times provide valuable evidence for the historian of the book. Printers and publishers belong to a trade that can easily tell the public about its problems, that can complain in print when petitioning for reforms or lobbying for relief. Bankruptcy proceedings contain useful information about the history of a firm, its customers and investors. An injured party may go to court and testify about business practices and financial arrangements that would otherwise be concealed from view. A severe depression exposes the weaker members of the trade as well as the most vulnerable, a hapless few who overextended their affairs at the wrong end of a business cycle along with the speculators and the recklessly ambitious, who often went out in a blaze of publicity.

James J. Barnes has argued that financial hardships were a force for innovation in the book trade, that publishing strategies often changed during difficult times. Anxious publishers contracted their obligations, lowered their prices, and tested the appeal of different genres and cheaper formats. The Depression of 1837 created a vogue for cheaply printed mammoth weeklies that could deliver a book's worth of text at a newspaper's price. The Panic of 1893 helped to curtail the traffic in

89

cheap paperbound reprints by eliminating the speculative publishers who had been overtrading in the lower end of the market. John Sutherland, on the other hand, has detected no major changes in the structure of the British trade during the Panic of 1826. He maintains that the Panic neither paralysed British publishing nor significantly thinned its ranks.[2]

Both Barnes and Sutherland judge the impact of financial crises entirely from the publisher's point of view. As much as their conclusions differ, their approach is basically the same. I propose to examine another sector of the book trade, the manufacture of paper, a highly capitalized industry acutely sensitive to changes in the economic climate. During the Panic of 1826, for example, the production of better quality paper dropped 17 per cent in a single year. The manufacture of wrapping paper and pasteboard also declined dramatically along with the trade's payments of excise duty, which fell about 19 per cent. If not changed dramatically, the book trade was certainly in a bad way to cut down on its consumption of its major raw material. The demand for printing stock collapsed at this time and, indeed, on most occasions when money troubles afflicted publishers and printers.[3]

Papermakers had to cope not just with poor business conditions but also with the misfortunes of their customers, who could neither order as much as before nor pay for what they had already received. Turmoil in the publishing end of the book business often seeped into the manufacturing end. Here we can see the book-trade network in action, the give-and-take between various social groups involved in the creation, manufacture and consumption of printed goods. We can learn more about the structure of this network by observing how it functioned in times of stress, by examining the social and economic relationships that linked its constituent parts, and by testing those links for tensions and fractures. By noticing how and where the normal course of business was disrupted, we can obtain a glimpse of the 'whole socio-economic conjuncture' entailed in book production, a conjuncture which Thomas Adams and Nicolas Barker have posited as the theme of this volume (see above, p. 14).

The Panic of 1819 provides one especially vivid example of these interdependent relationships within the book trade. Bibliographical data and documentary evidence make it possible to juxtapose the bankruptcy of Washington Irving, one of America's most successful authors, with the insolvency of Moses Thomas, one of America's most enterprising publishers. Their partnership came to an end when Thomas's business collapsed under the strain of an ill-timed, overly ambitious publishing venture that burdened him with debts he could not repay. One of his creditors was John Willcox, proprietor of one of the country's oldest and most distinguished paper mills. I will show that the cost of paper amounted to a major portion of the expenditures that drove Thomas out of business and compelled Irving to make his own publishing arrangements. Willcox drew up an eloquent account of his affairs, which I will use to elucidate the relationship between Irving and Thomas.

Papermakers embroiled in the Panic not only recorded their own difficulties but also their views on the state of the trade. The Panic occurred just on the verge of America's Industrial Revolution, when economic and cultural changes were favouring the introduction of papermaking machines and other mechanical improvements that would help to lower the cost of book production. New technology, new marketing methods and an expanding market demanded a heavy capital investment, which brought new blood and new ideas into the paper trade. Unprecedented growth, unparalleled opportunities and unforeseen vicissitudes made papermakers more conscious of their professional identity and of their changing position in the book-trade network. They came to realize that they were not alone in their predicament, that their problems were part of a national calamity. For the first time, I believe, they joined together in trade associations, not just with their competitors but with other manufacturers and the other book trades. From these early organizing efforts they gained an enhanced awareness of their craft, and a new appreciation of its important role in the realm of books and the world of finance.

The Panic devastated all classes of American society. Banks failed, merchants defaulted on their debts, factories closed their doors, factory workers lost their jobs, and farmers lost the lands they had bought with borrowed funds. Estimates of unemployment in Philadelphia ranged from 5,000 to 20,000. The courts of Pennsylvania heard 14,537 lawsuits against insolvent debtors during 1819 and sentenced 1,808 defaulters to prison in Philadelphia alone.[4]

In some ways America's monetary system was still too backward and its factory production still too meagre to fit the classic definition of a modern business cycle. Agriculture remained the main occupation of this rural country, sparsely inhabited except in a few cities where only a small number were employed in industrial concerns. Nevertheless, economists have detected some cyclical features in manufacturing after the War of 1812: a boom period while the hostilities reduced competition from abroad, a crisis when imports resumed, a depression while foreign goods glutted the American market, and then a recovery beginning in 1821. Meanwhile the financial mayhem was exacerbated by the strain of repaying the Louisiana debt, speculation in western land, and – an inevitable flaw in any rapidly developing economy – the spirit of speculation in general.[5]

A panic, strictly defined, reaches a peak of hysteria when the financial community scrambles frantically for hard cash after losing confidence in its paper money, deposits or investments. Bank notes, used in those days as negotiable currency payable on demand, were to blame for convulsions even more violent than the fluctuations in manufacturing. Most American banks could issue them, and some were not obliged to secure their value with specie reserves. When banks on the frontier ran short of cash, they paid their debts to the East Coast with their own bank notes, which were allowed to depreciate. A state could create more banks whenever it needed cheap money to finance internal improvements or commercial expansion. Kentucky chartered 46 during one legislative session. Generous to a fault, they lacked the capital to support their liberal lending policies, so they printed paper money, which naturally declined in value, so they printed even more. Kentucky bank notes had to be discounted at least 10 per cent and sometimes as much as 15 to 20 per cent if they were accepted at all. In many western and mid-Atlantic states, paper money drove gold and silver from circulation: coin became so scarce that the Baltimore Post Office was reduced to making change with a note of six and one quarter cents.[6]

Congress founded the Second Bank of the United States to discipline the banking system and to regulate the money supply. Unfortunately the Bank was poorly regulated itself and in some branches scandalously mismanaged. Instead of curbing the excesses of other banks, it accepted their notes, circulated notes of its own, granted loans, and otherwise expanded credit from January 1817, when it began operations, until the summer of 1818. By that time the situation had become impossible: specie was at a premium, and the Bank could no longer import enough to redeem its notes. Thereupon it reversed its policy, called in its loans, and began to refuse the devalued paper of other banks. Too brutally it forced them to contract their liabilities. Many that could not pay in specie or in paper backed by specie suspended operations or forfeited their charters. As banks began to fail, depositors withdrew their funds, investors dumped their stocks, and the economy collapsed.[7]

Tight money never bodes well for the book trade, nor for any trade that transacts most of its business on credit. Publishers and printers frequently transmitted funds with promissory notes instead of cash. After a stipulated interval a creditor could present a note at the local bank and receive its full value; before then he could have the note discounted for slightly less. The book-trade network depended on these credit instruments for settling debts at long distance and, sometimes, for gaining a grace period before repaying them. A debtor might be able to sell his goods fast enough to recoup his investment in supplies before his note came due. If, on the other hand, he misjudged the market and could not pay his obligations, and if the creditor refused to renew his note, it could be protested at the bank with embarrassing legal consequences. For safety's sake, a creditor might insist on having a note endorsed by somebody of proven worth and reliability, who effectively put his own funds up for collateral. Less cautiously, businessmen often accommodated their colleagues in the trade with endorsements to be used for raising capital rather than for paying debts.

In good times this system of accepting one another's notes, and of guaranteeing them, reinforced the book-trade network with moral and financial obligations not unlike family loyalties, only more difficult to detect. But this system could also be inconvenient when cash was scarce and dangerous when the failure of one party involved others in debts beyond their means. In 1820 the papermaker John Willcox complained that he had lost several thousand dollars from what he called 'the immence risk on *sales*'. By this he meant bad debts, almost certainly those of Moses Thomas, a prominent Philadelphia publisher whose downfall was to undertake an expensive edition of Johnson's *Dictionary* during the Panic of 1819. Not only Willcox but also a printer and an author had to cope with his insolvency, a perfect model of how trouble could spread from one part of the book-trade network to another. To understand how Johnson's *Dictionary* affected his business relationships and his publishing career, we must first see what other books he stocked in his bookshop at 52 Chesnut Street, Philadelphia – at the sign of Johnson's Head.[8]

From 1812 to 1819 Philadelphians avidly inquired at this address for the latest works of Byron, Scott and other fashionable English authors. Moses Thomas specialized in reprinting British bestsellers, a lucrative but fiercely competitive business in which only the swiftest survived. In the absence of international copyright, there were no restraints, no exclusive rights in this free-for-all. American publishers rushed British texts to market speedily before another edition could spoil their sales. By dint of 'quick work', Moses Thomas was able to sell Byron's *Mazeppa*

only 22 hours after receiving copy from London.[9] Americans sometimes
bargained with English publishers for galley proofs, unbound sheets, or an
advance copy, which, if expedited quickly, might give them a competitive
edge in the race to reach the market first. The Philadelphia publishers
Carey & Lea employed two agents for this purpose, a London bookseller
and an American who made his living from the traffic in British books.
Similarly, Moses Thomas relied on the American author Washington
Irving to spot likely reprint candidates as they arrived in New York and to
negotiate directly with the authors and publishers Irving met while
residing in England.[10]

From New York Irving forwarded Byron's *The Giaour* four months
after it was published by Murray. He promised to advertise Scott's *Lord
of the Isles* in New York newspapers before it went to press in
Philadelphia, the better to stake a claim and to scare away the competition. From Liverpool he sent *Lord Byron's Farewell to England*, which
smacked of scandal: 'You had better publish this pamphlet at once', he
warned, '& sell off the edition as fast as possible'. In London and
Edinburgh, he tapped English literature at its source, at the homes of
authors and at the publishing houses of Murray, Longman and Con-
stable. Since, he realized, these gentlemen could never hope to control
the transatlantic trade, they might accept whatever an American chose to
pay for their bestsellers: 'I have written to Thomas, advising him to remit
funds to me for the purpose; if he does so, I will be able to throw many
choice works into his hands'.[11]

Irving had already drawn a salary from Thomas as editor of *The
Analectic Magazine* during 1813 and 1814. After leaving for England in
1815, he continued to deal with Thomas in literary matters although his
main concern was the family's importing business. Like many American
merchants, the Irving brothers had overextended their affairs during the
boom period before the Panic and were then caught short when
American orders for British goods began to decline. 'No – no – if I must
scuffle with poverty let me do it out of sight', he wrote from his counting
house in Liverpool. Tempers flared when creditors met with Irving's
brother-in-law, who came to blows on the street and was horsewhipped
in his home. On 9 February 1818 a Birmingham paper announced
officially the bankruptcy of Irving, his brother and his brother-in-law. In
these desperate straits, Irving staked his last hopes on his literary career;
he took to his pen, prepared a new edition of Knickerbocker's *History of
New York*, and started on Geoffrey Crayon's *Sketch Book*. Both were
destined for Moses Thomas.[12]

Meanwhile Thomas had also run short of funds, after having embarked on a new venture far more costly than the bestsellers on his list. In early 1817 he had circulated proposals for the 'first American edition' of Johnson's *Dictionary*, to be published in parts at $20 to subscribers, $24 after publication. Although his edition was not cheap, neither were copies imported from London, which could be sold for as much as $30 in quarto and $50 in folio. The text was based on the eleventh edition of 1816, supplemented with symbols of pronunciation and a prefatory treatise derived from John Walker's *Critical Pronouncing Dictionary*. Subscribers could choose between two formats, either two volumes in medium quarto or four volumes in royal octavo, and pay in four easy instalments, upon receiving half volumes of the quarto or volumes of the octavo, either way priced at $5 each. The first part (letters *A-C*) was in press around November 1817; the second part (*D-K*) appeared in November 1818, the third (*L-R*) in July 1819, the fourth (*S-Z*) towards the end of the year. Ordinarily this arrangement should have mitigated the expense of printing a complex work in a large edition – an expense the newspapers estimated at $20,000. But the Panic caught Moses Thomas just after he had finished the letter *K*. Money was scarce, so were subscribers, and their enthusiasm waned for the letters *L* through *Z*.[13]

'A very large capital is engaged in the work', Thomas told the public, but otherwise it is hard to tell how deeply he was involved. If the puffs were correct in saying that he had undertaken a 'large impression', the size of the edition may have ranged from 1,500 to 2,000 copies at the very least. Quarto copies contained just over 290 sheets, the octavos just over 250. For an edition that large and books that size, the cost of the paper alone would have been enough to burden Thomas with debts far heavier than he had incurred from his dealings in twelvemo English reprints. Thomas promised in his advance publicity that the *Dictionary* would be printed on 'a handsome and substantial paper, manufactured expressly for the purpose'. And he kept his word by ordering premium goods from John Willcox, a third-generation papermaker, whose mill not far from Philadelphia specialized in making fine writing, printing and banknote grades.[14]

Willcox agreed to supply medium stock for the quarto copies at $5.25 a ream. If anywhere near the same quality, royal paper for the octavo copies would have cost as much as $7.00 a ream. However, a sheet of royal octavo accommodated a greater amount of text than a sheet of medium quarto, so the two formats did not differ greatly in cost. At these prices, Thomas's total expenditure for paper might have amounted to more than $7,500 for 2,000 copies, a thousand in quarto and a thousand in octavo.[15]

Thomas's financial obligations loomed even larger because he had other ambitious books in press. He had intended to publish *Picturesque Views of American Scenery* engraved by John Hill after paintings by Joshua Shaw, and had gone so far as to print a title-page, dated 1819, before turning the project over to another publishing firm, Mathew Carey & Son. They too abandoned the sale of Hill's expensive hand-coloured aquatints, after issuing only twenty of the 36 originally planned. Furthermore, he had invested heavily in Knickerbocker's *History of New York*, a large work printed in 1,500 copies, one volume by James Maxwell, the other by William Fry. Thomas did not economize by hiring William Fry, whose typography and presswork were highly esteemed in Philadelphia. But he did order two types of paper to lower the costs of this edition and also to widen its appeal, a publishing stratagem not unlike the one he devised for Johnson's *Dictionary*. He offered copies either on fine paper at the price of $3.50 or on ordinary paper at $3.00.[16]

Irving counted on Thomas to send more than just a token payment for Knickerbocker's *History*. 'I hope this new Edition will bring me in a little money soon', he wrote in September 1818, 'or my purse will soon run dry'. Indeed, Thomas may have speeded up production by employing a different printer for each volume. The title-page was deposited for copyright on 5 March 1819. But Johnson's *Dictionary* was not the only Thomas imprint to sell poorly during the Panic. By November 1819 he had sold only 400 copies of Knickerbocker and still owed $1,000 on the 1,100 remaining. Since he could not pay for them, he assigned the books on hand to his creditors with the understanding that the author could buy them back. Irving could not expect any payment for what had already been sold nor any income from the rest of the edition unless he managed to 'redeem' it with funds out of his own pocket. His literary agent in New York took over the remaining copies and was advertising them to the trade by August 1820.[17]

Irving first heard of Thomas's predicament in March 1819, while Knickerbocker was in press. He had already finished the first number of *The Sketch Book*, and put the manuscript in the mail, but it was not too late to reconsider. 'Were I a rich man I would give him my writings for nothing', he confided, 'as I am a very poor one, I must take care of myself'. So, reluctantly, he decided not to publish *The Sketch Book* as he had originally planned but rerouted it to New York, where his friends could oversee production and sales. An instant success, it sold so well that preparations were made to double the edition to 4,000 copies. This publication marked the end of an ignoble literary apprenticeship and the beginning of an independent career: instead of plundering British texts to supplement his income, he earned his living from his own writings, as one of America's first professional men of letters.[18]

Although disappointed by the Knickerbocker fiasco, Irving still esteemed his former employer – 'a worthy honest fellow', in his opinion, 'but apt to entangle himself'. Generously, he steered some of his business by Johnson's Head where Thomas was struggling with enormous debts and a tremendous inventory. While Irving could no longer entrust an entire edition to Thomas, he could still give him some copies to distribute in Philadelphia, which is why bibliographers must contend with Thomas's name on wrappers of *The Sketch Book* and spine labels of *Bracebridge Hall*.[19]

Thomas's printer also esteemed his former employer, and they too parted on friendly terms. James Maxwell worked off so many Thomas imprints that he could have been a silent partner or paid on retainer. Certainly he was a major creditor, having printed all of Johnson's *Dictionary* and half of Knickerbocker's *History*. Whatever his relationship with Thomas, it grew closer in this time of adversity. In 1820 and 1821 they shared openly in the publication of Robert Waln's satires, and from 1820 through 1823, Maxwell published odd volumes of Walter Scott over his own name, having either inherited the business or its methods. Maxwell took over a retitled *Analectic Magazine* as well as the sheets of the fatal *Dictionary*, which also appears over his own name. Since Thomas had to assign such assets as the *History* for the benefit of his creditors, it seems more than likely that he surrendered other, more saleable properties such as the *Dictionary*. Thomas may have passed on his bad luck as well as his bad debts to Maxwell, who made an assignment of his assets in 1823.[20]

The printer took over some of the publisher's stock in compensation for his losses; the author took his business elsewhere; but the paper-maker seems to have had no recourse but to lament the sorry state of his affairs and of his trade. John Willcox could not afford to be a gracious and indulgent creditor like Irving or Maxwell. If he had supplied all of the *Dictionary* medium, he would have had to stake nearly half of his annual production on the promises of one man, whose credit record was far from spotless even then. Willcox seems to have accepted this risky proposition since the paper was 'manufactured expressly for the purpose', and since Thomas, like other Philadelphia publishers, would have contracted with one mill at a time to assure uniformity of weight, size and colour as well as a regular supply. Exactly how Thomas shirked his obligations I do not know, but I do know that Willcox suffered losses from bad debts amounting to several thousand dollars at a time when Thomas was his major customer. It seems likely, therefore, that Willcox was one of the angry creditors that hounded Thomas out of business.[21]

Amicable or not, dealings between some members of the book-trade network affected the affairs of others at several removes. The desperation of a papermaker could threaten the profits of an author. Distress in the book trade influenced the literary career of Washington Irving as well as relations between him and his audience. Irving alleviated the expense of *The Sketch Book* by issuing it in parts costing 75¢ apiece, just as Moses Thomas sold the *Dictionary* in instalments each priced at $5. By publishing it in parts, the author could hope to please a newly cost-conscious, penny-pinching public; he could save on his initial investment in book production; and he could ensure a quick return on his investment as well as a steady income as long as the series retained its popular appeal. This publishing strategy enabled him to tap a large middle-class market in cities and also to reach into the hinterland, where these slim, lightweight, unbound part-issues could be shipped at minimal cost. Major distributors like Moses Thomas were allowed a 25 per cent discount, while country booksellers could purchase smaller lots at 60¢ each.[22]

Likewise, these tactics could be said to have influenced the loose, essayistic style that Irving adopted to package this series of part-issues, just as the depression period may have inspired the nostalgic tone, the escapist hankering after the past, the old country and the picturesque that suffuse these essays. Irving had previously contributed to a publication in parts but only on the most casual basis; this was a new departure. From his own experience, he could testify that the Panic of 1819 had changed the methods, market and membership of the American book trade.

The Census of 1820 confirms that the Panic affected the dealings of the book trade in at least one important sector, papermaking. So many papermakers participated in the Census that it contains a reliable cross-section of opinion on the state of the trade and on the measures needed to revive it. The Census not only counted heads, it examined the health and welfare of American industry, an unprecedented fact-finding effort mandated by Congress in direct response to the business crisis of the year before. Papermakers along with other factory owners were invited to fill out a supplementary census questionnaire with information about raw materials, machinery, labour, wages, capital investment, and, most importantly, 'General Remarks concerning the Establishment'.[23]

Many welcomed this opportunity to present their grievances to the nation's lawmakers; a few, fearing that these figures might be used for tax purposes, exercised their right to remain silent. They may have compromised the accuracy of the Census, but not so much as certain assistant marshals, who failed to circulate their questionnaires or neglected to see that they were correctly completed. For whatever reason, the Census omitted at least 40 paper mills. Statistics on the mills it did include are often unreliable because the respondents lacked training or interest in accounting. The marshals rarely questioned the figures they forwarded to Washington, nor did the Department of State, which subtotalled the returns by county and by trade and published the results. The Department's *Digest of Accounts of Manufacturing Establishments* (Washington, 1823) turned out to be so inaccurate and incomplete that one congressman proposed to build a bonfire, take the entire edition, pile the books up, and burn them.[24]

If not always reliable, the raw returns deserve better treatment than the *Digest*. Nearly 170 survive for paper mills of all shapes and sizes, a vast conglomeration of opinions, facts and figures, some of which can be correlated statistically or substantiated with external evidence. Papermakers did not have to be expert economists to describe the day-to-day activities of their trade, the prevailing wages, the cost of raw materials, and the price of their products on the open market. Their testimony reveals how paper mills were capitalized, which suffered most from the downturn in business, why some failed, and how others managed to survive.

Large and ambitious mills built by newcomers to the trade were, predictably, the earliest victims of the Panic. A four-vat mill in Baltimore succumbed in June 1817 after having been in operation for less than ten years. The Census states that this extensive establishment and an adjacent woollen factory cost about $100,000 – an extravagant sum, yet confirmed in a contemporary periodical. The director of this concern founded the mill when he was in his mid-twenties, apparently unacquainted with the paper trade but amply supported by wealthy relatives who had manufacturing and mercantile interests in the Baltimore area. After the mill closed down, he continued his career in high finance as cashier of a Washington bank, which folded two years later.[25]

In the same enterprising spirit, the poet David Humphreys built a factory complex of seven workshops, three boarding houses, and a warehouse on an industrial estate of sixteen acres in Humphreysville, Connecticut. He ran a paper mill, a saw mill, a grist mill, textile mills and a machine shop, largely staffed by children recruited from the streets of New York, the city orphanage and the surrounding countryside. His manufacturing ventures never prospered even though he obtained a charter of incorporation, apparently authorizing a capitalization of half a million dollars. Only $85,000-$100,000 had been invested by 1819, by which time the property was for sale.[26]

Perhaps the most flagrant example of speculation in the paper trade took place in Lexington, Kentucky, where two Boston merchants named James and Thomas Prentiss obtained a charter of incorporation for a woollen and paper mill called the Lexington Manufacturing Company. The Prentiss brothers built an impressive five-storey factory, the largest of its kind in that part of the country, containing textile and papermaking machinery tended by 200 hands and powered by a steam engine of 40 horsepower. They persuaded local merchants to buy 60 per cent of the stock in this grandiose venture, at one point thought to have been capitalized at $150,000. The Prentisses used the money they raised with their manufacturing operations to plot even more daring speculations in the financial sector of the Kentucky economy. They seized control of a bank in Lexington, and then raided other banks in the vicinity with the assistance of Col. Richard M. Johnson, a war hero and prominent local politician. (Johnson was later elected vice president of the United States even after he was implicated in this scandalous affair.)[27]

Richard Johnson loaned James Prentiss a vast sum of money in an exceedingly complex and dubious exchange. Prentiss in turn conveyed a large parcel of stock in the Bank of the United States to Johnson for the benefit of his brother James Johnson, who had underwritten some of the Prentisses' debts. This stock in turn served as collateral for a considerable loan. Possibly one party or the other had indulged in the dangerous but common practice of buying bank stock with a promissory note and using the stock itself to secure the note. The Johnsons not only fronted loans to James Prentiss but also their good name to help him obtain a mortgage on land and the Lexington Manufacturing Company, a similarly suspect transaction which obliged him to pay twice the legal rate of interest to another unscrupulous investor, a manufacturer in Rhode Island. The Johnsons and Prentisses used their fictitious capital to bolster their credit and to found a bank in Georgetown.[28]

The Prentisses' financial empire began to crumble when the state bank refused to accept the notes of the Lexington bank and advised other banks to beware of its suspect currency. When its charter expired in 1818, the depositors lined up to close their accounts and redeem the notes they held, but after only a quarter were paid, the rest were turned away, the bank closed, and the Prentisses disappeared. The creditors of the bank discovered that some of their funds had been used to service the usurious mortgage on the paper mill. After this debacle, the Johnsons purchased the mill at public auction despite the protests of the mortgagee, who sued, and fought the case all the way up to the Supreme Court.[29]

The Johnsons removed the papermaking machinery and tried to rent the mill for textile manufacture but without success. Other factories failed as soon as nervous investors heard about the schemes of the Johnson and Prentiss brothers, including another steam-driven paper mill which had been incorporated in 1816 with local capital. Lexington's overheated frontier economy ruptured even before the Panic swept the nation, partly because papermaking had become a fashionable investment, an object of speculation.[30]

The banking crisis may have spared some of the smaller one- and two-vat mills, which consumed less capital and incurred fewer risks than the factories built by syndicates and speculators. The American trade had not yet developed to the point where it could support manufactories as ambitious as the Lexington Manufacturing Company. The Census of Manufactures records only fourteen mills with more than two vats and only four with steam engines, a formidable investment at that time. These larger mills mobilized capital averaging around $43,500. Forty-three mills tallied in the Census contained two vats, a preferred configuration for making higher quality paper with a moderate capital outlay. In a typical return, owners of a two-vat mill in Taunton, Massachusetts, estimated that they had invested $10,000 in fixed capital – in the land, water privilege, mill building and machinery they owned – and $10,000 in active capital to finance their day-to-day business operations.[31]

One-vat mills were even less expensive and even more common in America. The Census records 81 of this size, generally employing fewer than seven men and capitalized between $4,000 and $8,000, though it should be noted that the respondents calculated their capitalization in many different ways. Some included the cost of the mill building, others didn't. Some owned their land, others rented it. Furthermore, some had

installed only a minimum of machinery in modest quarters to manufacture coarse grades like newsprint, wrapping or pasteboard, an investment
often less than $1,000.

At the other end of the scale, figures of over $10,000 represent either
the cost of setting up a mill for fine writing paper (in which case they are
fairly accurate) or else the wishful thinking of the proprietor. A one-vat
mill valued optimistically at $20,000 in 1820 was sold by the sheriff for
$7,330 in 1824. (The owner may not have exaggerated quite so much if
he had inherited a mill of two vats and then shut one down, as some
evidence suggests.) To take a more straightforward example, writing
paper generated half the annual income of Jacob Ulrich, who figured his
fixed capital at $10,666.66 and his active capital at $2,766.[32]

Modest, family-owned, one- and two-vat paper mills also foundered
during the Panic even though less capital was at stake. Slow sales,
dwindling profits and tight credit could endanger these mills too,
especially those that had been recently improved or expanded with
borrowed funds. At least fifteen one- and two-vat establishments went
out of business or changed hands under duress between 1820 and 1822.
Some fifteen others drop out of sight immediately after the Census, as if
they had fallen beneath the notice of other sources. Newspapers and
reminiscences often passed over their obscure and solitary tribulations to
consider more pervasive failures of community interest. However, the
Census indicates that many of these mills were operating on the verge of
insolvency, suffering as much from competitive pressures from outside
the country as from the financial squeeze within.

These competitive pressures came mainly from imported merchandise
dumped on the American market at cut-throat prices. In self-defence,
American manufacturers urged the government to enact protective tariffs
and exhorted their countrymen to boycott foreign goods. Friends of
domestic industry spurned European luxuries, not just articles of fashion
but even English writing paper. The journalist Hezekiah Niles, a
vociferous protectionist, scolded government officials who sent him
letters watermarked with a royal crown.[33]

Although annoyed by English imports, American papermakers suffered most from under-priced printing and writing grades shipped from
France, Spain and Italy. Of the 35 who deplored foreign papers in their
replies to the 1820 Census, seven traced their troubles to the Mediterranean; not one complained about British competition. John Willcox
repeatedly expressed his concern about European imports, while twice
mentioning his losses from bad debts:

The present proprietor is now carrying on the business that his Grand Father did in part of the same walls above one hundred years ago, and it looks more than likely that if a great alteration does not take place in the business, that *it* must sink with the *walls*. The great quantity of paper that has been Imported from France & Italy the last *Three* years, (all has [been] of an inferior quality) has much decreased the demand for the american paper, so much so, that not more than one half the paper manufactured, at the present time, in the United States can find a *market*.

My business this last two years, with all my exertions has not neated [i.e., netted] more than 7 per cent on the actual capital, deducting the *rent* of the *work*, without taking into consideration the immence risks on *Sales* – and actual losses, which has amounted to Several thousand dollars.

The business from 1815 to 1819 afforded a reasonable proffit, but since that time French and Italian paper have been frequently sold in the market, for very little more, than what the metirials would cost with us to make paper of a similar quality.

It will be perceived that the expenses and the interest on the active capital at the present prices leaves a balance in favour of the proprietor of $541.80 giving all his own trouble and attention, the rent of the Mill and the immence risk on *sales*.[34]

Likewise, a papermaker in Orange County, New York, attributed the plight of the American trade to 'the general stagnation of business' and to European merchants who overestimated the demand in the American market. He believed that some stationers had ordered paper from abroad to please 'Fourenners & natives amongst us, who give a preference to foureign articles'. After filling those orders, European merchants had sent more on speculation, hoping to have discovered a new market for their goods. When their shipments failed to sell, they had to settle for whatever they could get, he reasoned, even if they had to take a loss. In his opinion the best way to deal with the glut of imported paper would be to stop purchases from overseas altogether.[35]

Consignments from abroad poured into the market through several channels. Some Europeans sold their goods outright to an American agent; others entrusted their wares to a consignment house to be sold on commission; and many exploited a new outlet for imported manufactures, the auction sale. In Philadelphia, New York and other ports on the Atlantic seaboard, speculators unloaded vast quantities of foreign paper at auction; they set rock-bottom prices and still made a modicum of profit by realizing quick returns on large volume with no overhead. Industrialists complained of these auction sales so persistently that Congress considered a bill to tax them as an unfair monopoly and as a vicious influence on public morals akin to gambling.[36]

Unable to compete against this deluge of foreign paper, American manufacturers stockpiled their products on the off chance that the glut would end and prices would improve. A New Jersey papermaker could sell only one quarter of his mill's output, even after shutting down a vat and a beating engine. Half of what a Maryland mill had made in the previous year remained unsold, and paper two years old was still gathering dust in a Massachusetts warehouse. Some pessimists not only left the marketplace but also closed down their paper mills, hoping to trim their expenses along with their inventory. Clark & Sharpless of Columbia County, Pennsylvania, abandoned their establishment in August 1819, not to return again until sometime in late 1821 or early 1822.[37] It would seem that they left when the crisis was at its worst and returned not long after prices bottomed out, not just in the papermaking industry but in other trades as well. Economists report that wholesale prices in Philadelphia plummeted by 14.3 per cent from January to September 1819 and then declined at a slower pace until April 1821, when the local economy reached its lowest point since 1794.[38]

In the paper trade only the cost of labour seems to have remained stable.[39] The cost of raw materials plunged sharply, from 7¢ a pound for middling-quality rags in 1816[40] to 5¢ a pound in 1820. Here was one question on the Census forms that papermakers knew how to answer with confidence and precision. Forty-three agreed on the current price of rags, calculated either at 5¢ a pound or $100 a ton, and the others supplied answers so close to this figure that the price per ton reported in 137 returns averages out to $99.25. They also agreed on the amount of rags they consumed every year, estimated at twenty tons per vat in 30 returns. On the basis of these figures, a proprietor of a one-vat mill who manufactured ordinary printing paper would have seen his annual expenditure on rags decline from $2,800 in 1816 to $2,000 in 1820.

The price of raw materials fell so low partly because the price of the finished product had also dropped alarmingly. Papermakers had no reason to buy supplies as long as they couldn't sell their wares. One complained to the Census that 'Good writing paper' had declined in value from $4.50 a ream in 1818 to $4.00 in 1819 to $3.50 in 1820, or 22 per cent altogether; another figured that prices had slumped by 30 per cent since 1817; and two agreed on a middling pessimistic figure of 25 per cent.[41]

Philadelphia booksellers arrived at a similar percentage in December 1820, when they estimated that their cost of paper and binding had decreased from 20 to 30 per cent.[42] As far as paper is concerned, the Census returns confirm their calculations, as do the accounts of paper purchased by Mathew Carey & Son. Fine medium printing, a staple of book publishers during this period, cost the Careys as much as $5.50 in

1818 and as little as $4.00 in 1820. Three of the Census returns quoted a standard price of $3.50 for the medium size, two others somewhat less, probably because they were manufacturing low-grade stock.[43]

A few pennies less per ream made a big difference to papermakers whose annual output generally ranged from 1,500 to 2,000 reams per vat. One of the papermakers who priced medium printing at $3.50 lamented that he could no longer work his mill 'to any advantage', although in better years he could expect an annual profit between $1,500 and $2,000. George Lewis of Delaware County, Pennsylvania, once enjoyed a return between $1,200 and $1,500 a year but now subsisted on such a slender income that he couldn't afford to work one of his two vats, nor even pay the policy on his fire insurance. Altogether 95 papermakers complained about hard times in their Census returns, about 78 per cent of those who commented on the state of the trade. Business seems to have been bad

Table 1. *Papermakers' comments on profitability and sales in the 1820 Census of Manufactures*

state	pessimistic responses	optimistic responses
Connecticut	8	5
Delaware	3	
Kentucky	5	2
Maine	2	
Maryland	7	
Massachusetts	13	2
New Hampshire	1	1
New Jersey	8	1
New York	13	6
North Carolina	1	
Ohio	2	4
Pennsylvania	20	2
Rhode Island	1	
Tennessee		1
Vermont	11	2
Virginia		1
Total:	95	27

Source: Responses to question 14, 'General Remarks concerning the Establishment, as to its actual and past condition, the demand for, and sale of, its Manufactures', 1820 Census of Manufactures.

everywhere except Ohio and other remote localities, where paper was in short supply.[44]

The price squeeze and related financial hardships politicized American papermakers. For the first time they protested adverse trading conditions as a group and acted in concert with other book trades suffering from similar complaints. They sought orderly and effective ways to discuss their problems and seek redress from the nation. If still too few and too isolated to form a national trade association, mill owners organized pockets of resistance in Massachusetts, Baltimore and Philadelphia.

Invariably their lists of grievances began with unfairly priced imported paper. The Massachusetts contingent petitioned Congress for a protective tariff of $2 a ream, a request twice brought before the House and twice referred to a committee. Baltimore papermakers mustered the support of local newspaper editors, booksellers and publishers, who begged unanimously for a protective tariff, not just to prevent market fluctuations but also to foster a valuable domestic industry employing 5,000 persons.[45]

Philadelphians also commiserated with local papermakers. In August 1819 Philadelphia manufacturers appointed fifteen of their colleagues to compile statistical reports on their respective trades, comparing their current state of affairs with their situation in the years of 1814 and 1816. Although listed last but one, the papermaker John G. Langstroth joined in the deliberations of such prominent Philadelphia bookmen as the printer William Fry, the publisher Mathew Carey and the typefounder James Ronaldson. The results of Langstroth's survey so impressed his fellow manufacturers that they singled out his trade as a model industry in distress. In 1816 the mills of the Philadelphia vicinity consumed 2,600 tons of rags and employed 950 men, women and children to manufacture products worth $760,000, a 'clear gain to the community' since the rags they consumed could serve no other useful purpose. Patriotic citizens should encourage this laudable enterprise, the Philadelphians argued, since it harms no one, employs many, and makes a valuable commodity out of refuse – but instead, Americans have squandered their wealth on imported paper, a shortsighted economic policy that has stripped 775 workers in this region of their jobs and has cost their employers as much as half of their capital investment. Langstroth's report indicated that production had declined by 82 per cent since 1816 because so many hands had been laid off, and so many mills shut down.[46]

A few months later the Society of Paper Makers of the States of Pennsylvania and Delaware repeated Langstroth's figures in a memorial to Congress. The memorial reviewed the history of the craft, recited the usual protectionist arguments, and pleaded for a duty of 25¢ a pound on writing, printing and copperplate papers, and 15¢ a pound on the rest. It urged Congress to adopt a specific duty (calculated by weight and quality) instead of its current *ad valorem* duty (determined by invoiced value). A specific duty would protect the lower end of the market from underpriced imports and prevent speculators from sneaking undervalued goods through customs. England, for example, had imposed a specific duty of nineteen pence per pound, with a drawback of three pence to encourage exports. So formidable was this tariff barrier that purveyors of cheap Mediterranean paper had retreated from the English market and dumped their merchandise in America instead. Let us emulate England, close the floodgates, stop the auction sales, and defend our domestic resources, the memorial concluded.[47]

This impressive account of foreign trade bolstered the papermakers' arguments far more convincingly than Langstroth's survey. The memorialists exaggerated their plight, whether by copying, misprinting or twisting Langstroth's figures I cannot tell. Only 17 vats in the Philadelphia area were still in operation, the memorial claimed, whereas the Census records at least 26. If Langstroth committed that error, then he compounded it by multiplying 10 persons per vat to arrive at the number employed. These rules of thumb skewed other statistics as well but did not sway very many votes in Congress. These petitions died in committee, and the tariff bills of 1820 and 1821 also failed to muster adequate support.[48]

To my mind, the importance of Langstroth's survey lies more in its origins and purpose than in its accuracy or consequences. I have tried to link the economic concerns of papermakers with other members of the book trade, such as the publisher Moses Thomas, the printer James Maxwell and the author Washington Irving. I have dwelled on a single instance of distress to demonstrate how trouble could spread from one sector of the trade to another, from publishing to papermaking, for example. And to show where those troubles began, I have discussed general trends in the economy and in the business conditions papermakers encountered during the Panic of 1819.

The boom, crisis and depression disrupted the papermaking trade at all levels, both at the top, where large mills were toppled by financial pressures, and at the bottom, where small mills suffered from low prices and the onslaught of imported paper. Speculators were driven out of business, and veteran papermakers plied their trade less confidently than before. The survivors looked out at the world downstream and realized that even their rural occupation could be jeopardized by market factors beyond their control. Other members of the book trade appreciated their concerns and rallied to their support, recognizing that they formed an integral part of the book-trade network.

Papermakers surveyed their losses, marshalled their forces, and defended themselves on the political front. They emerged from the crisis of 1819 as hardened professionals, fewer in number but more closely allied. They withstood other trade upheavals, business cycles and trying times by mastering not just water and fibre, but men and machines, and the vagaries of finance.

NOTES

1 Samuel Rezneck, *Business Depressions and Financial Panics: Essays in American Business and Economic History*, New York, 1968, p. 4; Charles P. Kindleberger, *Manias, Panics, and Crashes: A History of Financial Crises*, New York, 1978, pp. 255-8.

2 James J. Barnes, 'Depression and Innovation in the British and American Book Trade, 1819-1939', in *Books and Society in History*, ed. Kenneth E. Carpenter, New York and London, 1983, pp. 231-48, reprinted in *Economics of the British Booktrade, 1605-1939*, ed. Robin Myers and Michael Harris, Publishing History Occasional Series, 1, Cambridge & Alexandria, Va., 1985, pp. 209-31; James J. Barnes, 'The Depression of 1837-43 and Its Implications for the American Book Trade', in *Authors, Publishers and Politicians: The Quest for an Anglo-American Copyright Agreement, 1815-1854*, Columbus, 1974, pp. 1-29; John Sutherland, 'The British Book Trade and the Crash of 1826', *The Library*, 6th ser., 9, 1987, pp. 148-61.

3 A. Dykes Spicer, *The Paper Trade: A Descriptive and Historical Survey of the Paper Trade from the Commencement of the Nineteenth Century*, London, 1907, p. 242.

4 William A. Sullivan, *The Industrial Worker in Pennsylvania, 1800-1840*, Harrisburg, 1955, p. 51; Samuel Rezneck, 'The Depression of 1819-1822, A Social History', *The American Historical Review*, 39, 1933, 28-47, reprinted in his *Business Depressions and Financial Panics*, pp. 53-72.

5 Murray N. Rothbard, *The Panic of 1819: Reactions and Policies*, New York and London, 1962, pp. 2-18; Otto C. Lightner, *The History of Business Depressions: A Vivid Portrayal of Periods of Economic Adversity from the Beginning of Commerce to the Present Time*, New York, 1922, pp. 109-14.

6 Kindleberger, *Manias, Panics, and Crashes*, pp. 5 & 113-15; Rothbard, *Panic of 1819*, p. 98; *Niles' Weekly Register*, 12 June 1819, pp. 260-1; *Things as They Are; or, America in 1819. By an Emigrant, Just Returned to England*, Manchester, 1819, pp. 13-15.

7 Rothbard, *Panic of 1819*, pp. 7-12; Rezneck, 'The Depression of 1819-1822', p. 29.

108

8 Return of John Willcox, Delaware County, Pennsylvania, *Records of the 1820 Census of Manufactures*, National Archives microcopy no. 279, Washington, 1964-5, reel 14, item 706.

9 Washington, D.C., *Daily National Intelligencer*, 25 August 1819, p. 3.

10 David A. Randall, 'Waverley in America', *The Colophon*, n.s., 1, Summer, 1935, pp. 39-55; David Kaser, 'Waverley in America', *Papers of the Bibliographical Society of America*, 51, 1957, pp. 163-67.

11 Irving appears to be responsible for the majority of Thomas's English reprints during 1816-1818, including James Hogg's *Mador of the Moor*; Scott's *Rob Roy*; and the fourth canto of Byron's *Childe Harold's Pilgrimage*. See Washington Irving, *Letters, Volume 1, 1802-1823*, ed. Ralph M. Aderman et al., The Complete Works of Washington Irving, 23, Boston, 1978, pp. 359, 391, 441-2, 448-9, 489, and passim.

12 Irving, *Letters, 1802-1823*, pp. xxxii, 382 & 484-6.

13 Two prospectuses are at the Houghton Library, Harvard University, titled *First American Edition of Dr. Johnson's Dictionary*, Philadelphia, 1817(?), and *In Press, the First American Edition of Dr. Johnson's Dictionary*, Philadelphia, 1817. Michael Winship very kindly provided photocopies of these documents. Publicity also appeared in the *Daily National Intelligencer*, 10 Nov. 1818, p. 3; 12 Nov. 1818, p. 2; 19 Jan. 1819, p. 2; 1 July 1819, p. 4; and 14 July 1819, p. 3 as well as in *The Baltimore Directory, Corrected up to June, 1819*, Baltimore, 1819.

14 *Daily National Intelligencer*, 12 Nov. 1818, p. 2; *In Press, the First American Edition of Dr. Johnson's Dictionary*, Philadelphia, 1817.

15 Joseph Willcox, *Ivy Mills, 1729-1866. Willcox and Allied Families*, Baltimore, 1911, p. 45. A thousand quarto copies would have consumed 677 reams, a thousand octavos about 590 reams. I have based these figures on the Philadelphia ream of 432 printable sheets, a smaller ream than used elsewhere but still standard in that city through the 1830s; see *Early American Papermaking: Two Treatises on Manufacturing Techniques Reprinted from James Cutbush's* American Artist's Manual (*1814*), New Castle, Del., 1990, pp. 23-8.

16 Richard J. Koke, *A Checklist of the American Engravings of John Hill (1770-1850), Master of Aquatint*, New York, 1961, pp. 16-19. Publication details of Knickerbocker's *History* appear among other advertisements on 'wrapper B' on part 1 of *Salmagundi, Second Series*, described and reproduced in the *Bibliography of American Literature*, comp. Jacob Blanck et al., New Haven and London, 1955-91, entry 15695, hereafter cited as *BAL*. Ordinary-paper copies are at the British Library and the New York Public Library; a fine-paper copy is at the Huntington Library.

17 Irving, *Letters, 1802-1823*, p. 534; *Letters of Henry Brevoort to Washington Irving*, ed. George S. Hellman, New York, 1918, pp. 116-17; *BAL* 10226; Edwin T. Bowden, *Washington Irving: Bibliography*, The Complete Works of Washington Irving, 30, Boston, 1989, p. 145.

18 Irving, *Letters, 1802-1823*, pp. 539 & 542; *Letters of Henry Brevoort to Washington Irving*, p. 119.

19 Irving, *Letters, 1802-1823*, p. 542; *BAL* 10106 & 10109; Bowden, *Washington Irving: Bibliography*, pp. 132, 143, 145 & 185.

20 Gordon M. Marshall, 'The Golden Age of Illustrated Biographies: Three Case

Studies', *American Portrait Prints: Proceedings of the Tenth Annual American Print Conference*, ed. Wendy Wick Reaves, Charlottesville, 1984, p. 51.

21 At the standard rate of five and a half reams per day, six days a week, it would have taken a one-vat mill more than five months working at top capacity with no time off for repairs or maintenance to manufacture 680 reams for a thousand quarto copies. Annual production of the Ivy Mills was estimated at 1,500 reams in Benjamin Pearson, comp., *Report of the Committee of Delaware County, on the Subject of Manufactories, Unimproved Mill Seats, &c. in Said County. 1826*, Chester, 1826, p. 20. Thomas had already made an assignment of his assets in Jan. 1815, when he was 'dragged down' by the insolvency of the Philadelphia publishers Bradford & Inskeep (Irving, *Letters, 1802-1823*, pp. 385-7); he appears to have recovered his credit standing by July of that year.

22 William Charvat, *The Profession of Authorship in America, 1800-1870: The Papers of William Charvat*, ed. Matthew J. Bruccoli, Columbus, 1968, pp. 32-34. Charvat, however, mistakenly interpreted the publishing tactics adopted by Irving and his agents as standard practice in 1820 rather than as a last-minute change in plans, prompted by Thomas's failure and the decline of the economy. I believe that if Charvat had been less exclusively concerned with author-publisher relations, and if he had studied Thomas's dealings with other members of the book trade, he would have gained a better understanding of the economic factors, profit motives and the marketing approach that influenced Irving's plans for *The Sketch Book*.

23 *Records of the 1820 Census of Manufactures*, reel 1, pp. iii-vi; Carroll D. Wright, *The History and Growth of the United States Census*, 56th Cong., 1st sess., S. Doc. 194, 25-7.

24 *Debates and Proceedings*, 17th Cong., 2nd sess., 887-90.

25 Horatio Gates Jones, *The Levering Family; or, A Genealogical Account of Wigard Levering and Gerhard Levering ... and Their Descendants*, Philadelphia, 1858, pp. 57-60; *Daily National Intelligencer*, 29 July 1818, p. 1; 2 June 1819, p. 3; return of the Franklin Paper Mill, Baltimore County, Maryland, *Records of the 1820 Census of Manufactures*, reel 16, item 50. This return estimated the capital invested in Levering's paper mill at twice the amount of other four-vat mills. In 1810, however, its capitalization amounted to $70,000 in the opinion of John D. Craig, author of an article on 'Domestic Manufactures' in *The Agricultural Museum*, 2, 1811, pp. 161-5. I am very grateful to William B. Keller and Donald L. Farren for information about Baltimore papermaking and the Levering family.

26 Return of Ann F. Humphreys, New Haven County, Connecticut, *Records of the 1820 Census of Manufactures*, reel 4, item 66; *Daily National Intelligencer*, 17 June 1819; p. 3; John C. Pease and John M. Niles, *A Gazetteer of the States of Connecticut and Rhode-Island*, Hartford, 1819, p. 117; Frank L. Humphreys, *Life and Times of David Humphreys, Soldier – Statesman – Poet*, New York and London, 1917, pp. 364-5, 384-7 & 417-21.

27 Dale Royalty, 'James Prentiss and the Failure of the Kentucky Insurance Company, 1813-1818', *The Register of the Kentucky Historical Society*, 73, 1975, pp. 1-16; return of the Lexington Manufacturing Company, Fayette County, Kentucky, *Records of the 1820 Census of Manufactures*, reel 20, item 43; Ebenezer Hiram Stedman, *Bluegrass Craftsman, Being the Reminiscences of Ebenezer Hiram*

Stedman, Papermaker, 1808-1885, ed. Frances L. S. Dugan and Jacqueline P. Bull, Lexington, 1959, pp. xv & 16.

28 Royalty, 'James Prentiss', pp. 3-16; *Kentucky Gazette*, 26 March 1819, p. 3; *The Papers of Henry Clay*, ed. James F. Hopkins and Mary W. M. Hargreaves, Lexington, 1959- , 3, p. 120.

29 Royalty, 'James Prentiss', pp. 12-16; *Kentucky Gazette*, 6 March 1818, p. 3; De Wolf v. J. Johnson, R. M. Johnson, W. T. Barry, and J. Prentiss, 23 United States Reports (10 Wheaton) 367-95 (1825).

30 Stedman, *Bluegrass Craftsman*, pp. xv-xvi, 101 & 219; returns of the Fayette Paper Manufacturing Company and the Lexington Manufacturing Company, Fayette County, Kentucky, *Records of the 1820 Census of Manufactures*, reel 20, items 42 & 43.

31 Return of John West and Richard Park, Bristol County, Massachusetts, *Records of the 1820 Census of Manufactures*, reel 2, item 141.

32 Return of Jacob Ulrich & Co., Berks County, Pennsylvania, *Records of the 1820 Census of Manufactures*, reel 15, item 876; return of John Mattson, Delaware County, Pennsylvania, reel 14, item 705. For the sale of Mattson's mill, see Anthony F. C. Wallace, *Rockdale: The Growth of an American Village in the Early Industrial Revolution*, New York & London, 1980, p. 80.

33 *Niles' Weekly Register*, 7 August 1819, p. 389; 1 Jan. 1820, pp. 292-3; 8 Jan. 1820, p. 305.

34 Return of John Willcox, *Records of the 1820 Census of Manufactures*, reel 14, item 706.

35 Return of Hector Craig, Orange County, New York, *Records of the 1820 Census of Manufactures*, reel 10, item 1523.

36 Among those who spoke in favour of the bill was the congressman Charles Kinsey, who had operated a paper mill in Paterson, New Jersey, before the War of 1812 and appears to have taken the business up again sometime after this bill was debated in 1820. See *Debates and Proceedings*, 16th Cong., 1st sess., 2176, and the *Biographical Directory of the American Congress, 1774-1971*, 92nd Cong., 1st sess., S. Doc. 92-8, 1239.

37 Return of Jesse Cox & Sons, Burlington County, New Jersey, *Records of the 1820 Census of Manufactures*, reel 17, item 134 (Cox & Sons also remarked that they had been running two vats at time and a half in better days); return of Zimmerman & Smith, Frederick County, Maryland, reel 16, item 168; return of Eliphalet Thorp, Worcester County, Massachusetts, reel 2, item 78; return of Clark & Sharpless, Columbia County, Pennsylvania, reel 15, item 1109. In their return, dated 1 Jan. 1821, Clark & Sharpless reported that the mill had been left 'standing for upwards of 17 months'. At the latest, they must have been back in business in Feb. 1822, when they ordered paper moulds from the firm of N. & D. Sellers (who recorded that order in ledgers now at the American Philosophical Society, Philadelphia).

38 Anne Bezanson, Robert D. Gray & Miriam Hussey, *Wholesale Prices in Philadelphia, 1784-1861*, Philadelphia, 1936-7, 1, p. 7.

39 Jacob Ulrich (Berks County, Pennsylvania) told the Census that he had cut his men's weekly wages from 'occasionally' $5.00 in 1816 to 'occasionally' $4.50 in 1820. However, George Helmbold, Jr. (Philadelphia County, Pennsylvania) still

paid his journeymen at $5.00 a week, and John G. Langstroth claimed that this standard salary had not varied since 1814; see 'American Manufactures', *Niles' Weekly Register*, 23 Oct. 1819, p. 117. Skilled workers in Massachusetts continued to be paid at approximately a dollar a day (Rothbard, *Panic of 1819*, p. 15).

40 Jacob Ulrich calculated his cost of rags at 7¢ a pound in 1816, 4¢ a pound in 1820. Aaron Levering of Baltimore was said to have been buying rags at 7¢ a pound before his mill went down in 1817.

41 The decline of prices was estimated variously at 22 per cent by Charles Cadwallader, Huntingdon County, Pennsylvania, *Records of the 1820 Census of Manufactures*, reel 12, item 279; 30 per cent by Charles Lungren, Delaware County, Pennsylvania, reel 14, item 703; 25 per cent by J. Patterson & Co., Allegheny County, Pennsylvania, reel 12, item 5; and 25 per cent by Markle & Drum, Westmoreland County, Pennsylvania, reel 13, item 513.

42 *Address to the Booksellers of the United States*, Philadelphia, 1820, p. 1. The Huntington Library has a copy in its collection of American book-trade ephemera (Eph. MI-4).

43 Account books of Mathew Carey & Son, vols. 32-34, American Antiquarian Society, Worcester, Mass.

44 Return of James S. Tuttle or Tuthill, Suffolk County, New York, *Records of the 1820 Census of Manufactures*, reel 10, item 1377; return of George Lewis, Delaware County, Pennsylvania, reel 14, item 691.

45 *Debates and Proceedings*, 15th Cong., 1st sess., 565 & 737; *Niles' Weekly Register*, 15 Jan. 1820, p. 331.

46 *Niles' Weekly Register*, 4 Sept. 1819, pp. 7-8; 23 Oct. 1819, pp. 116-20.

47 'Protection to Paper Manufacturers, Communicated to the Senate, January 18, 1820', *American State Papers*, III: *Finance*, 3, pp. 460-2; see also *Niles' Weekly Register*, 22 Jan. 1820, p. 341. Mathew Carey presented a copy of *The Memorial of the Society of Paper Makers, of the States of Pennsylvania and Delaware* (Philadelphia, 1820) to the American Antiquarian Society in 1821.

48 Rezneck, 'The Depression of 1819-1822', p. 42.

BOOKBINDING AND THE
HISTORY OF BOOKS

Mirjam M. Foot

One can study the history of bookbinding in a variety of ways. In the nineteenth century and the first three quarters of the present century, the history of bookbinding was virtually synonymous with the history of binding decoration. With the exception of Mademoiselle de Regemorter who studied the construction of Coptic and Anglo-Saxon bindings in the 1940s, 1950s and 1960s[1] most scholars who devoted themselves to the history of binding were primarily interested in the styles and designs that embellish the covers and in the tools used to effect these designs. In England, the late Graham Pollard became interested in binding structure during the 1950s and published interesting articles on the lacing-in patterns of Anglo-Saxon and early medieval bindings, on medieval binding structures, and on changes in the technique of bookbinding between 1550 and 1830.[2] Other binding historians, such as Jean Vézin in France, Guy Petherbridge and Gulnar Bosch in the USA, Janos Szirmai in the Netherlands, and Roger Powell, Bernard Middleton, Chris Clarkson, and Nicholas Pickwood in Great Britain, have followed this trend and have produced very good work on the history of binding techniques. A descriptive study of contemporary binding technique is, of course, nothing new, and one has but to glance at the chronological table in Pollard and Potter's excellent *Early Bookbinding Manuals* (Oxford, 1984) to see that references to bookbinding as a craft have been traced as far back as the six century AD. A tenth-century Oriental craftsman, Abū Ja'far al-Naḥḥās, was the first to describe in any detail how to bind books,[3] and this kind of 'trade' literature has continued over the centuries until the present day.

A different way of looking at the history of binding concentrates on the binder and his role in society. Not much work has been done in this field, as most historians of the book trade seem to have concerned themselves mainly with scribes, or printers and publishers, rather than with binders.

Paul Christianson has done some work on binders in medieval England[4] and Ellic Howe's delightful book on *The London Bookbinders, 1780-1806* (London, 1950)[5] looks at the economical and social position of these craftsmen at the end of the 18th and the beginning of the 19th centuries. In the introduction to his *List of London Bookbinders, 1648-1815* (London, 1950) he again touches on these themes. The publisher, John Dunton, in his *Life and Errors* (London, 1705) wrote biographical sketches of 17 bookbinders at work during his lifetime and from these one can catch a glimpse of their social standing. They appear a pious assembly, 'true sons of the Church', 'keeping close to the private and public duties of Divine Worship'; politically sound (e.g. R. Baldwin who 'was a true lover of King William, always voted on the right side'); 'tender Husband[s]', 'kind Father[s]', 'dutiful Son[s]', judicious, honest and industrious, in short, pillars of society. This is not the impression created in John Jaffray's manuscript volume relating to the binding trade in the period from 1786 to 1820,[6] where they come across as a quarrelsome lot, fond of strong drink and not averse to a brawl. Dibdin, whose colourful descriptions of books and their producers are an unfailing source of amusement, hints, for example, at the social status of Charles Lewis, the leading London binder of the early nineteenth century, who went about with 'tassels to his half-boots',[7] a flamboyancy of style which some of his patrons evidently thought unbecoming for a tradesman. From other sources concerning the book trade, both archival and printed, one can get a picture of the bookbinder as one of the humbler members of the trade, not very highly regarded, although evidently a number of binders prospered and added publishing and bookselling to their binding business, thus becoming employers and businessmen, rather than craftsmen.

Yet another approach to the history of bookbinding is that which shows how the binding as a physical object, its form and its construction, as well as its decoration, can teach us something about the history of the book in general, its development, its use and its readership. Potentially this is a gigantic subject, only three aspects of which I will try and develop here. The first is *how the purpose of the book, its use and its readership can dictate its form and construction and vice versa*, and for this we turn to antiquity and look at the development from scroll to codex.

In the West, the most important development in the history of books before the age of printing was the change from scroll to codex. The codex can be defined as a collection of sheets of any material, folded and fastened together at the back or spine and usually protected by covers. There has been very little doubt that the physical origin of the codex is to be found in the writing tablet. When the change from scroll to codex took place, why, and in what circles the codex was first used has been the subject of a debate that has not yet reached its final conclusion.[8]

Scrolls or rolls were long strips of leather or papyrus, the papyrus strips being made of individual sheets glued together. They were inscribed in columns, usually on one side only, and rolled up for storage. When stored the rolls might simply be tied with tapes, or they might have leather wrappers or cylindrical boxes. They might have a wooden or bone roller attached to one end to facilitate rolling and unrolling.

Writing tablets were commonly formed of two or more pieces of wood, held together either by a clasp or by strings passed through pierced holes. The centre of the tablet was usually hollowed out to receive wax (though writing with ink or chalk directly on wood is not unknown). There is epigraphic evidence that the ancient Greeks used writing tablets of this kind and they are mentioned in Homer, Sophocles and Euripides. In later Greece they were used for any writing of an impermanent nature, such as letters, bills, school exercises, memoranda, or author's first drafts. Pliny the younger describes how his uncle compiled his *Natural History*: a slave would take down on wax tablets the author's thoughts, but the final version would be written on rolls, filled on both sides.

Already in the fifth century BC tablets of several leaves were in use, but the nature of the material would set a limit to their number and no specimen surviving from antiquity has more than ten leaves. The Latin word for more than one tablet or for multi-leaved tablets was codex, whether the material was wood (as was usually the case) or ivory. Seneca, Cato, and Cicero all used the term, and the latter frequently describes tablets used for business or legal purposes as such. But the word codex did not, until much later, mean a book.

The poet Martial, writing in or near AD 85, described literary publications in codex form (without using the term), but they were still curiosities and, for at least two hundred years more, at least pagan literature continued to be written on rolls. The earliest use of the word codex for a book dates from the third century AD and it was first used by a Christian writer. This is significant, as it is the Christian literature that was first found in codex form. The earliest surviving fragments of the Christian Bible, dating from the second century, are in codex form. It is not until the fourth century, roughly at the time when the Roman Empire became officially Christian, that we find the codex form normally used for non-Christian literature.

The wooden tablets were gradually replaced by pieces of parchment or papyrus. The earliest evidence for a parchment diptych, two leaves of equal size held together by a leather thong, is a deed of registration, written in the last century BC or the first century AD. Both Horace and Persius refer to writing on parchment leaves (*membranae*) and later authors refer to their use for letters, accounts and legal documents. When Quintillian *c.* AD 90 writes about *membranae* as the best way for students to take notes, we have reached a stage in the history of the codex where it is more than a tablet but less than a book.

There are arguments in favour of the practicality of the codex form vis-à-vis the roll, and Martial points out the convenience to the traveller and the way the codex saves space in a library. It was also cheaper and more compact, as in a codex both sides of the parchment were used, while usually only one side of the roll was covered in writing. For reference use or for finding a specific passage, it has advantages over the roll for the reader, as everyone knows who has ever used a microfilm.[9] All the same, the transition from papyrus or leather roll to parchment codex as the normal form for a book was not a single step. The question whether the parchment codex ante-dates the papyrus codex is still wide open. The format and material are not essentially linked. The slow growth in the use of parchment may be explained by the fact that special skills were required to produce a good-quality article. Equally, the yield per animal slaughtered would not have been very great.

All this does not explain why it is that the earliest surviving biblical and other Christian manuscripts are in codex form. In 1954 C. H. Roberts put forward the hypothesis that St Peter's auditors in Rome would have been using parchment notebooks and that St Mark as the first evangelist might have used such notebooks, which were then transmitted to Alexandria, where papyrus was the normal writing material.[10] In 1983 Roberts and Skeat rejected this as implausible, because neither St Mark's Gospel nor the Church of Alexandria were so influential in early centuries as to be likely to impose a new pattern of book production on other cities. They suggested instead that the earliest Christian communities, such as those in Antioch and Jerusalem, borrowed the Jewish custom of writing rabbinic sayings on tablets of papyrus. According to Jewish law, oral law, i.e. rabbinic sayings, could not be formally published (formal publication meant having been written on rolls). Instead, they were recorded in 'unpublished' ephemeral form on tablets, and the early Christians were writing the sayings of Jesus down in the same way. A contributing factor may have been the wish of the early Christians to emphasize the break with the pagan cultural tradition; pagan literature being written on rolls, like the formal Jewish law, while the new Christian literature was to be written on tablets or notebooks. Whatever the reason, the surviving evidence bears out the fact that for Christian literature the codex was the preferred format. For pagan literature the codex was practically unknown in the first century, little used in the second century, while the use increased during the third century and in the beginning of the fourth century, and gradually became the normal form during the fourth century. It is striking that the tendency to use the codex more and more runs parallel with the Christianization of the Roman Empire.

The second aspect which I would like to develop is *how the spread of learning and the increase in readership, and hence the increase in book production, can be demonstrated in the changes in styles and techniques of bookbinding.*

Let us go to France in the twelfth century, where the development of the Cathedral schools stimulated the book trade and gave rise to new developments in decorated leather bindings. Prior to this, very few European decorated leather bindings are known. Apart from the seventh-century Anglo-Saxon binding of the Stonyhurst Gospel, and three eighth- or ninth-century bindings now at Fulda,[11] there are no other known European decorated leather bindings until the twelfth century. These earliest Romanesque bindings were made in France and they mostly cover glossed books of the Bible. Christopher de Hamel[12] has shown that they were made in monasteries in and around Paris, where the manuscripts themselves were produced. These bindings differ from the run-of-the-mill undecorated medieval bindings, not only in the fact that they are embellished with stamps, but also in that they are made of tanned brown leather, instead of the white tawed leather of which most plainer bindings are made. Like the plainer bindings they also had clasps. These clasps were made of leather thongs, attached to the outer edge of the upper board, with pierced metal finials that fitted over pins, protruding from nearly half-way across the lower cover. This method of keeping a book shut tells us something about the storage of such books. They could not have fitted side by side in a book chest, as the protruding pin on the lower cover would have damaged the book next to it. These books were therefore meant to be either held in the hand or displayed on a lectern or desk with the lower cover uppermost. Likewise, the use of ornamental stamps indicates that these books were not purely for reading but that they were in themselves ornamental objects. Why were they made at all? G. D. Hobson believed that these books were prepared by the stationers for sale and that their decorated bindings might be intended to attract potential customers.[13] De Hamel questioned this explanation and put forward as an alternative version that they may have been cheaper copies of the jewelled or metal bindings made for the use in churches. De Hamel suggests that these glossed books of the Bible were essentially privately owned manuscripts. They were produced in schools where masters gave lectures on the Sacred Text. These schools were monasteries and religious houses with traditional association with students and scholarship. Here the masters made the gloss available for copying, they also provided the blank vellum, the exemplars, and – when the book was finished – a cheap and decorative binding.

In addition, the Cistercian belief that an excess of ornamentation was wrong and distracted from the sacred text (clashing with the ancient tradition that it was almost a religious duty to embellish the sacred page), and that monochrome impressed ornamentation was perhaps in order, may have had its influence, especially if we consider that the earliest examples of French Romanesque bindings were presented to the monastery of Clairvaux by Prince Henry, son of Louis VI, a personal friend of St Bernard. Why then did the production of these stamped bindings virtually stop in Paris in the early thirteenth century, not to be revived until the end of the Middle Ages? Around 1200 we see the appearance in Paris of the professional stationer, the entrepreneur who controlled the exemplar, but who did not himself make the parchment, nor write the text nor paint the initials, nor make the binding. He simply arranged for these matters to be done by different craftsmen and scribes, and sold the result. The settlement in Paris of these lay craftsmen meant that the close link between the owner of the exemplar, the scribe and the binder no longer existed. It is interesting that this change in production and publishing pattern resulted in a change of finished product. We now find law books and complete Bibles, but the individual books of the Bible with their glosses in stamped bindings, part of the standard library of the Parisian student during the last quarter of the twelfth century, disappear in the early thirteenth century.

The technique of decorating leather bindings with engraved tools appears to have re-emerged in Paris in the 1370s, but a revival on any scale of stamped bindings on the continent of Europe goes hand in hand with the monastic revival of the first half of the fifteenth century. The reform movement among the Italian Benedictine abbeys spread rapidly all over Europe. The two major religious reform movements in Germany were those of the Benedictine monasteries, centralised in the Bursfeld

Congregation, and of the Canons Regular of St Augustine. In the Netherlands, it was the Windesheim Congregation and the Brotherhood of the Common Life whose influence on the history of learning and on book production was considerable. The monastic reform with its return to the strict observance of the rules of the religious orders and its emphasis on study, on reading and on writing, stimulated the formation of monastic libraries and necessitated the binding of books. The Brotherhood of the Common Life especially, made a profession of binding books. These bindings were decorated with blind lines and blind tools and many examples from the fifteenth century, especially from Germany and the Netherlands, but also from Italy and Spain, have survived. Fewer French and English bindings of this period are still in existence. In France the destruction of monastic libraries at the time of the Revolution was thorough, but earlier, during the seventeenth and eighteenth centuries, many old books had been lovingly rebound. In England the destruction, first at the suppression of the monasteries under Henry VIII and then by the Puritans of Cromwell's time, made sure that very few monastic bindings survived.

The increase in book production after the invention of printing caused an increase in the production of blind-tooled bindings. Soon a cheaper and quicker way of binding decoration was developed at the end of the fifteenth century with the introduction first of rolls and then of panels.

These changes in the styles of binding were not limited to decoration only. A number of changes took place in the construction of books, mostly as a result of the need to speed up production and to cut the cost of binding.

Late medieval manuscript books are no different in form and construction from printed books. The main difference in book production after the invention of printing was the possibility of producing comparatively easily and comparatively quickly duplicate copies of the same text. This led to an increase in the number of books available, which in turn led to an increased demand for the binder's skill. As is well known, up to the beginning of the nineteenth century books were as a rule sold unbound in sheets. No publisher, printer or bookseller would go to the expense of having large numbers of books bound without being sure that he could sell them. There are, of course, exceptions to this and certain types of books, such as schoolbooks, popular editions of the classics and certain religious or devotional books sold sufficiently well for a publisher to have a considerable quantity ready bound in stock.

But with the greater availability of books, the demands made on the binding trade, even by the private owners, increased and with them increased the need for the binders to speed up their production and to cut their costs. This can be demonstrated in the change to cheaper materials and to less time-consuming practices from the beginning of the 16th century onwards, accelerating after the industrial revolution in the second half of the eighteenth century, and culminating in the gradual mechanisation of binding processes in the 1820s and 1830s.[14] To give a few examples: in the Middle Ages most binding boards were made of wood and, from the tenth century onwards, most volumes were sewn on split or double leather or vellum thongs with a fairly complicated sewing pattern, and formidable methods of lacing the thongs into the boards. By the middle of the sixteenth century boards were, as a rule, made of pasted sheets of waste, or low-quality paper or – a little later – of paper shavings; by that time the practice of sewing on single thongs or cords (made of rope or hemp) was well established; and lacing-in patterns had become noticeably simpler. During the sixteenth century recessed cords came into use, thereby reducing the actual sewing time (as the thread would simply be passed over the cord, instead of circling round it), and we find that not all cords are laced in. Often only the first, middle, and last cord are laced in, the rest are simply cut off. The sewing process itself was further speeded up by sewing two or more sections at a time, a common practice for trade bindings in the seventeenth century and later. Most manuscripts and early printed books had proper headbands, first consisting of turned-over spine leather, sewn through, then sewn over separate cores, sometimes elaborately plaited, always laced in and with the sewing thread tied down in the centre of each section. Already in the sixteenth century we find false headbands being used: a simple strip of alum-tanned leather, folded over a core and sewn, or strips of vellum over-sewn along the width of the spine (but not tied down) and either stuck on the backs of the sections with the ends laced in, or stuck on the boards. For cheap work, pulpboard was used as well as pasteboard in the seventeenth and eighteenth centuries, to be replaced by strawboard in the nineteenth century.

The search for cheaper covering materials goes back a long way. Already in the fourteenth century we find limp vellum used for account books, and limp vellum bindings for schoolbooks and classical texts were popular, especially in the Low countries and Germany, but also in Spain and Italy, in the sixteenth and seventeenth centuries. Attempts at using sheepskin rather than the more expensive calf came in for censure from the Stationers' Company in London in the seventeenth century. Paper covers for thin pamphlets were used all over Europe, and in the eighteenth century we find canvas used instead of leather to cover schoolbooks, to be followed by the various kinds of book cloth in the nineteenth century. Cutting production cost and time sometimes resulted in sewing as many as six sections at a time, in less lacing in, and in the development (at the very end of the eighteenth century) of sewing on tapes that were then inserted into split boards. We find more and more false headbands, simply made of rolled paper, oversewn with silk, and stuck on the outside of the top and tail of the spine, or, simpler still, made of strips of coloured linen or calico, rolled round a piece of string and stuck down.

The introduction of casing in the mid- to late 1820s meant that the cases could be made simultaneously with the book being sewn, rounded and backed, thereby again speeding up production, as well as laying open the way to mechanisation.

There are many more examples, but it should by now be clear that an increase of readership and an increase of book production compelled the binders to look for cheaper materials and speedier processes, thereby altering, and in most instances weakening, the traditional structure of the hand-bound book.

The third aspect to be considered is *how the existence of trade bindings, their structure, and consequently their price, reflect the demands of the reading public.* I mentioned above that publishers or booksellers would have copies of certain types of saleable books ready bound in stock. What kinds of books they were I have already indicated, but we can be more precise. There is evidence from the seventeenth and eighteenth centuries that the bookbinders of London and Westminster, and also those of the city of Dublin, agreed among themselves on set prices for binding specified kinds of books in certain ways. These prices were published and presented to the booksellers, or in the seventeenth century in London to the Master, Wardens and Assistants of the Stationers' Company. Nine such published documents still survive, five dating from the seventeenth century and four from the eighteenth century.[15] They take the form of broadsheets, printed in two or three columns. The categories into which the entries are divided, either reflect various standard styles of binding or – more commonly – sizes and types of books. The first price list dates from 1619. The various binding styles include 'crosse-bound' or dos-à-dos bindings, two small books bound together, back to back, sharing one cover, a fairly common feature at the end of the sixteenth century and still current in the 1620s and 1630s. Usually one finds the New Testament at one end and the Anglican prayer book and the psalms in metre at the other. There are a number of decorative styles, such as 'Gilt ouer', which for the smaller formats may well refer to decoration in gold with the impression of a single large block; 'gilt, edges and corners', i.e. decorated with corner tools or corner blocks and with gilt edges; 'fillets' and 'ouills', both common during this period. There are also entries for 'Bookes sheepes leather' which are cheaper than the others which are bound in calf, and for 'Bookes in hard bords', presumably books that have been sewn and laced-in in boards, but not covered, ready for the professional embroiderers to fit their embroidered covers on.

The 1646 price list is arranged by type of book, an arrangement that remains more or less standard for the rest of the century. The last half-column is devoted to 'Sheeps Leather' binding. Under each heading, indicating kind and size of the books (e.g. 'Bibles in follio', 'Bookes in quarto Lattine', 'Bookes in Octavo English', etc.), the various binding styles are indicated. We find again 'Gilt over', 'Corners', 'Edges', 'Fillets' and 'Ovills', but a distinction is made between 'Gilt over' and 'Small tooles ordinary'. The latter way of decorating is more expensive and refers to the application of small hand tools. There is also 'Chequer', slightly more expensive than 'Gilt over', but cheaper than 'Small tooles', which refers to an all-over pattern made with one or two repeating tools. Cheaper still are 'Rolles'.

The sizes of the books are indicated by format (folio, quarto, octavo, etc.) but also by paper and type sizes (e.g. 'Crown' and 'pot' for paper sizes and 8° 'Minnion', as distinct from 8°, referring to a type size between non-pareil and brevier).

Under each size there are examples of what must have been popular books. Apart from Bibles and prayer books, which merit categories of their own, we find under 'Bookes in Lattine' such frequently read authors as Aristotle, Plutarch, Erasmus, Grotius and Vossius. Books in English include various herbals, such as those by Gerrard and Parkinson, Foxe's *Book of Martyrs*, Lancelot Andrewes' *Sermons* (1641), Josephus's *History*, and – in smaller formats – Rider's Dictionary, Diodati's *Annotations on the Bible* (4°, 1643) and Henry Scudder, *The Christians Daily Walke* (12ᵐᵒ, 1642), The 1669 list is again divided into Bibles and service books in various sizes, and books in Latin and in English. We find the same binding styles as before. Among the non-liturgical books we find editions of classical authors, such as Aristotle, Plutarch, Virgil, Horace and Homer, both in Latin and in English translations; dictionaries (Polyglott Lexicon, Cotgrave's Dictionary); history books (Davila, *The Historie of the Civill Warres of France*, London, 1647, 1648, Th. Fuller, *The Historie of the Holy Warre*); devotional works (R. Baxter's *The Saints Everlasting Rest*, 1669, Jeremy Taylor, *The Rule and Exercises of Holy Living* and *Holy Dying*, Allestree's works); and schoolbooks (e.g. *Corderius's School-Colloquies*, grammars and primers).

The same pattern is repeated in the 1695 list. The titles of the books are usually given in an abbreviated form (e.g. 'Hales's Contemplations' [Sir Matthew Hale, *Contemplations Moral and Divine*, London, 1695], 'Lake of the Sacrament' [Edward Lake, *Officium Eucharisticum*, London, 1690], 'Burnet's Abridgment' [Gilbert Burnet, *The Abridgment of the History of the Reformation of the Church of England*, London, 1683]). They were obviously very-well-known, popular books, for which there was a steady market, and which, consequently, could be held in stock ready bound. The fact that these well-known titles were used as examples is borne out by the frequent addition in the lists of the words 'or the like'.

The earliest eighteenth-century list to survive, a 1743 Dublin price list, reverts to the pattern of the 1619 list, in that it has been arranged according to style or method of binding. Under each heading the prices are quoted for the various sizes. We find 'Gilt Back only' (with gold-tooling on the spine), 'Books Filleted on the Back only with a Tool added thereto' (calling to mind the frequently found flat spines decorated with a double fillet, evenly spaced to suggest bands, with a small tool in each compartment). There are also categories of 'Books bound in Vellum plain' and 'Forril' (vellum made from unsplit sheepskin), which could be had in yellow or green. The heading 'Russia Bands' refers to a form of stationery binding with two or three Russia-leather bands across the spine, extending about half way down the sides.[16] As well as 'Plain Sheep', we find 'Grains', charged for by the hundred. This refers to the grain split or outer split of a sheepskin, the cheapest available leather. Under this heading are entries for 'Testaments Saw'd' and 'Grammars ditto', which indicate an early form of perfect binding. The backs of the sections were sawn in, the cords pressed into the grooves and the whole glued up without any sewing: a very cheap and very unstable way of holding a book together, bearing out what I have said earlier about the trade binders' efforts at finding cheaper and quicker methods to bind the ever-increasing numbers of books for sale.

In the 1744 list bindings are charged for entirely according to size and one could order them in sheep or calf, plain or with edges (probably marbled, sprinkled or even gilt edges) and 'Letterd' (on the spine). In the last London list of the century, published in 1760, the bindings are also priced according to size and many titles of available books are mentioned. The same pattern of classical texts, reference works (altases, dictionaries), schoolbooks and devotional works can be seen, but we now also find travel books (Harrison's *Voyages*, *The Universal Traveller*, Sloane's *Voyage to the Islands . . . and Jamaica*), books on architecture (Gibbs's *Architecture*, Ware's *Architecture*), and what one may call 'leisure reading' (e.g. two translations of Don Quixote [Smollet and Jarvise], Pope's works, Milton's *Paradise Lost and Paradise Regain'd*, *Rasselas*, and *Tristram Shandy*, both just published,[17] and even the *Miss's Magazine* and the *Young Lady's Magazine* [in sheep for 5*d.* per volume]). It is interesting to see such a clear indication of the broadening of the reading public in the second half of the eighteenth century.

One could move on from the humble trade bindings discussed above to the expression of luxury, of power even, that can be seen in the splendid bindings made to glorify the Word of God, or in the presentation bindings for the high and mighty. Binding patronage reflects the importance attached to books as embodiments of knowledge, but also as objects of art. However, even the run-of-the-mill trade binding, its form, its structure, and its decoration, can tell us a certain amount about the development of the book, its use and its readers.

In the scroll and the earliest manifestation of the codex, we saw how form and structure were closely linked to use and to readership. The two occurrences of blind-tooled decoration on tanned leather bindings followed increases in book production as a result of a spread of learning. Increases in book production also caused changes in binding techniques born out of the need to bind more books more quickly and more cheaply, while from the kind of books that were bound for the booksellers' stock and that were given these cheaper treatments, one can infer a changing and growing readership.

In the eighteenth and nineteenth centuries bookbinding was classified among the 'useful arts'. It is more than that, it is a mirror which reflects the history of the book and, if one looks closely, the history of society at large.

NOTES

1 E.g. B. de Regemorter, 'La Reliure des manuscrits de S. Cuthbert et de S. Boniface', *Scriptorium*, III, 1949, pp. 45-51; de Regemorter, 'La Reliure des manuscrits gnostiques découverts à Nag Hamadi', *Scriptorium*, XIV, 1960, pp.

225-34; de Regemorter, 'Ethiopian Bookbindings', *The Library*, 5th series, XVII, 1962, pp. 85-8.

2 G. Pollard, 'Some Anglo-Saxon Bookbindings', *The Book Collector*, XXIV, 1975, pp. 130-59; Pollard, 'The Construction of English Twelfth-Century Bindings', *The Library*, 5th series, XVII, 1962, pp. 1-22; Pollard, 'Changes in the Style of Bookbinding, 1550-1830', *The Library*, 5th series, XI, 1956, pp. 71-94.

3 G. Bosch, J. Carswell and G. Petherbridge, *Islamic Bindings and Bookmaking*, Chicago, 1981, pp. 2-3.

4 C. P. Christianson, 'Early London Bookbinders and Parchmeners', *The Book Collector*, XXXII, 1985, pp. 41-54; Christianson, 'Evidence for the Study of London's Late Medieval Manuscript Book Trade', in *Book Production and Publishing in Britain, 1375-1475*, ed. J. Griffiths and D. Pearsall, Cambridge, 1989; Christianson, *A Directory of London Stationers and Book Artisans, 1300-1500*, New York, 1990.

5 Reprinted, London, 1988. See also E. Howe and J. Child, *The Society of London Bookbinders, 1780-1951*, London, 1952.

6 Referred to by E. Howe in his *London Bookbinders, 1780-1806*, London, 1950; a typescript of the fourth of a series of manuscript volumes relating to 'The Art and Trade of Bookbinding', compiled by John Jaffray, dated 1864 (London, *c.* 1945) is at the British Library (667.r.19).

7 T. F. Dibdin, *The Bibliographical Decameron*, London, 1817, vol. II, p. 522.

8 C. H. Roberts and T. C. Skeat, *The Birth of the Codex*, Oxford, 1983 (2nd edn. 1987), and below further.

9 See also M. Gullick, 'Old Books for New', *Fine Print*, XII, 4, October 1986, pp. 205-8, who argues that the roll as a book form was perfectly adequate for those who used it. I agree that the reasons for the change from roll to codex were probably religious and political, rather than purely practical.

10 C. H. Roberts, 'The Codex', *Proceedings of the British Academy*, XL, 1954, pp. 169-204.

11 T. J. Brown (ed.), *The Stonyhurst Gospel of Saint John*, Oxford, 1969, pp. 13-23, 45-55; de Regemorter, 'Manuscrits de S. Cuthbert et de S. Boniface', *Scriptorium*, III, 1949, pp. 45-51; D. M. Wilson, 'An Anglo-Saxon Bookbinding at Fulda', *Antiquaries Journal*, XLI, 1961, pp. 199-217.

12 C. de Hamel, *Glossed Books of the Bible and the Origins of the Paris Booktrade*, Woodbridge, Suffolk, 1984.

13 G. D. Hobson, *English Binding before 1500*, Cambridge, 1929; Hobson, 'Further Notes on Romanesque Bindings', *The Library*, 4th series, XV, 1934-5, pp. 161-211; Hobson, 'Some early Bindings and Binders' Tools', *The Library*, 4th series, XIX, 1938-9, pp. 214-33.

14 For change in and development of binding structures in England, see B. C. Middleton, *A History of English Craft Bookbinding Technique*, 2nd edn, London, 1978.

15 M. M. Foot, 'Some Bookbinders' Price Lists of the seventeenth and eighteenth Centuries', in *De Libris compactis miscellanea*, ed. G. Colin, Brussels, 1984, pp. 273-319. A fourth eighteenth-century price list, 'A Regulation of Prices Agreed to by *The Company of Bookbinders* of the City of Dublin ... 1791', was discovered by Miss M. Pollard (in private ownership).

16 See [H. Parry], *The Art of Bookbinding*, London, 1818, pp. 44-6 and frontispiece.
17 S. Johnson, [*Rasselas*] *The Prince of Abissinia*, 1st edn, London, 1759. L. Sterne, *Tristram Shandy*, vols. 1 and 2, 1st edn, York, 1760 [1759]; the other seven volumes were published between 1761 and 1767.

THE 'TRADE OF AUTHORSHIP' IN EIGHTEENTH-CENTURY BRITAIN

W. B. CARNOCHAN

I

SOME TIME AGO an advertisement appeared for a book called *The Blood of Kings: Dynasty and Ritual in Maya Art* (figure 1). At first glance, perhaps nothing in it appears out of the ordinary. Ask someone to look at it, quickly, and then to say what is unusual about it, and your 'subject' will usually notice the image of the Maya figurine first, for it seems to dominate the verbal text, not only by its placement within the frame but also by its commanding presence and gesture. The title, *The Blood of Kings*, darkens as it crosses the body of this figure, drawing attention to the mysterious object in his left hand. What is unusual, at first sight, about the imagery of the advertisement is the prevalence of the visual over the verbal, of the primitive original over the derivative commentary.

What is more unusual is that no author's name appears, although four names do appear: those of a reviewer, a famous anthropologist, a photographer and a publisher. Allen Wardwell's gnomic metaphors of light and darkness, set in white against a dark ground, have epigrammatic force. The name of Claude Lévi-Strauss, ultimate figure of 'authority', appears in a position that hints at a type of authorship: star billing places the actor above the vehicle, the author above the title. In small print, between a copyright mark and a date, is the name of the photographer, Justin Kerr. Finally there is George Braziller, whose identity hovers between the personal and the corporate, and who is in position to compete with Lévi-Strauss for authorship were it not for the statistical data that intervene between the title and his name.

The total effect is one of ghostly presences, on the one hand, and multiple authorship, on the other – a multiple authorship that obscures the names and existence of the actual authors of what is in fact an exhibition catalogue, albeit an unusual one.[1] This helps to explain the situation, exhibition catalogues not being the product of authorship in the

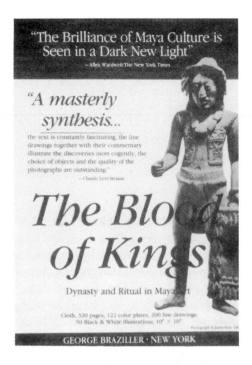

"The Brilliance of Maya Culture is Seen in a Dark New Light"
— Allen Wardwell The New York Times

"A masterly synthesis...

the text is constantly fascinating, the line drawings together with their commentary illustrate the discoveries most cogently, the choice of objects and the quality of the photographs are outstanding."
— Claude Lévi-Strauss

The Blood of Kings

Dynasty and Ritual in Maya Art

Cloth, 320 pages, 122 color plates, 200 line drawings, 50 Black & White illustrations, 10" × 10".

GEORGE BRAZILLER · NEW YORK

same sense as novels or poems. The Maya kings, long gone, are present and dominant in an image that co-exists with the authority of copyright, hence with a kind of proprietary authorship. The book itself, inevitably absent, is represented as a collection of data: 'Cloth, 320 pages, 122 colour plates, 200 line drawings, 50 black & white illustrations, 10" × 10".' By a convention that would be obscure to an alien observer we call into being the physical object that the data represent. Somewhere else, there is a book.

The sense of ghostly presences corresponds to the absence of any explicit attribution of authorship and the associated sense of multiple authors. *The Blood of Kings: Dynasty and Ritual in Maya Art* seems to rise out of a collective, even a ritual experience. Allen Wardwell, Lévi-Strauss, Justin Kerr, George Braziller, all contribute to the making of the absent book, while some 'real' author or authors seem to exert a spectral influence. It is by him or her or them that 'the brilliance of Maya Culture is seen in a dark new light'. The dark new light of their passive seeing is also that of divinity hidden behind its own aura yet capable of seeing to the heart of things, emblematic of mastery and of a synthesis to which the data of the text are subordinate if not incidental.

II

In a conversational sally that has found its way into editions of the *Pensées*, Pascal anticipates Roland Barthes and Michel Foucault by three centuries: 'Authors who say "My book", "My commentary", "My history", etc. resemble those bourgeois with a house of their own who are always saying "chez moi"' – 'qui ont pignon sur rue, et toujours un "chez-moi" à la bouche' – 'when they should say "Our book", "Our commentary", "Our history", etc. since there is in them usually more of other people's wares than their own.'[2] This is plain truth, of course, and it underlies the current concern with the interdependence of literary (and other) texts. It also underlies Joyce's attempt in *Finnegans Wake* to create a new language and, as well, the paradox of *Finnegans Wake* that, because it is made from the ruins of an old language, it reads like a vast, collective effort of the tribe. *Finnegans Wake* seems to anticipate the conditions of the new world that Foucault presents as an anticipatory vision in 'What is an Author?': 'I think that, as our society changes, at the very moment when it is in the process of changing, the author-function will disappear.' In this new world, all discourses will 'develop in the anonymity of a murmur'. Questions about authorial intention, about the relationship between author and narrator, about authenticity and originality, will fall away like the state in a Marxist Utopia, to be replaced by different questions, such as: 'What are the modes of existence of this discourse?' and 'Where has it been used, how can it circulate, and who can appropriate it for himself?' Behind these questions, says Foucault, 'we would hear hardly anything but the stirring of an indifference: "What difference does it make who is speaking?"'[3]

Foucault's idiom is not everyone's. But his vision of the future stands comparison, at first sight a surprising one, with another forward-looking manifesto: 'A new Model for the Study of the Book', by Thomas R. Adams and Nicolas Barker, included in this volume. Foucault predicts that others will ask of a 'discourse', where it has been used and how it can circulate; Adams and Barker remark that the distribution of a book or text from one person to another is 'a densely woven network about which we still know comparatively little'. Where Foucault asks who can appropriate a discourse for himself, which is to ask, among other things, who can buy a book and for what reasons. Adams and Barker speak of 'the power conveyed by the book itself, an incalculable, inarticulate, but none the less potent factor in the mixture of motives that makes people want books'. Foucault could not have said it better. The history of the book, in the new life that Adams and Barker imagine for it, resembles the forms of life imagined by Foucault in a world that has lost, as one of its distinctive signs, the 'author-function'. To be sure, Adams and Barker regard authorial intention as part of the history of the book, but it is far from being central.[4] In the history of the book, authorship is one function among others. Our difficulty in admitting that fact may be one reason why we have been so slow to develop a history of the book that is not subordinate to other fields and other interests. The coming of a new history of the book, as envisaged by Adams and Barker, might coincide with a declining power of authorship.

III

The ascendant power of authorship over the last few centuries mirrors the self-possessive habits of modernity. We hardly understand the psychology of anonymous publication except as a stratagem of self-protection, and in such cases our custom is that of pseudonymous rather than anonymous performance. We can hardly bear to bring a book into the world without authorial attribution, even if it involves pseudonymous concealment. This inability has made it hard to understand fully the motives for anonymous publication that underlie, for example, *A Tale of a Tub*, or even to understand exactly the response of Swift's contemporaries to anonymous publication. On first appearance, the *Tale* generated eager speculation about the author's identity; but what did Swift believe he was doing – authorially speaking – when he published the *Tale*, one among his many anonymous publications and dazzling in the very fact of its anonymity, as in so much else? Was it only a matter of self-protection?

No doubt anonymity protected Swift in obvious ways: he had his career to think about, and even if he had entirely and disingenuously believed that this satire on the abuses of religion and learning was in no way subversive, it would have been prudent for any young clergyman with large aspirations to be cautious. But self-protection is just part of the story. Beyond it lies a satire both on authorial possessiveness and on the reader's need to identify the author. And beyond that specific intention lies a larger claim, itself subject to satirical treatment, to participation in an original act of creation – the same claim as seems to lie behind, or within, the apparent anonymity of *The Blood of Kings*. From the start of the *Tale*, a sense of unseen forces created by the learned mysteries of the title page provides a commentary on the habits of the Grub Street writer trying relentlessly to lay claim to 'his' book, 'his' commentary, 'his' history, 'his' tale. Swift stands in the same relationship to the 'author' of the *Tale* as does Pascal to those authors whose bourgeois pride and presumption lead them to false claims of ownership.

In early editions of the *Tale*, a jocular list of 'Treatises writ by the same Author' appears facing the title page. This list, with such entries as '*A Character of the present Set of* Wits *in this Island*' and '*A Panegyrical Essay upon the Number* THREE', establishes the *Tale* as a piece not just of modern writing but of modern *authorship*, a ragbag of digressions and vulgarisms, all accompanied by large claims of originality. These claims are then mocked in the text by the author's everlasting harping on his own authorship. The word 'author' is a leitmotif. In the Dedication to Somers, the tale-teller immediately turns the floodlight on himself, announcing that, although 'the Author has written a large Dedication' to Prince Posterity, the Prince is unlikely to be his patron and therefore he will turn to Somers instead. Near the end of the *Tale* we learn that the disappointment of being a bad conversationalist gave the tale-teller the idea of 'setting up for an *Author*' in the first place. In between, in the 'Digression on Madness' (among many other instances), the tale-teller identifies himself, with mad pride, as being the author of momentous truths, hence a kind of divine original: 'even, I my self, the Author of these momentous Truths, am a Person, whose Imaginations are hard-mouth'd, and exceedingly disposed to run away with his *Reason*'.[5] Possessed with the idea of possessing, the author of the *Tale* displays the dark side of the cult of originality.

Yet Swift took pride in his own originality and was deeply offended by claims that the *Tale of a Tub* was not all his. In the 'Apology' of 1710, he counters William Wotton's charges of plagiarism. These charges, says Swift, acting as his own apologist, touch '*the Author in a very tender Point, who insists upon it, that through the whole Book he has not borrowed one single Hint from any Writer in the World; and he thought, of all Criticisms, that would never have been one. He conceived it was never disputed to be an Original, whatever Faults it might have.*'[6] The gross hyperbole that the author has not borrowed a single hint from anyone else calls attention to itself and is self-implicating; here, as so often with Swift, he recognizes what he shares with victims of his satire, which derives much of its strength from such self-recognitions. This does not alter the fact that his sense of his own originality is extremely strong. In an 'Advertisement' to the second volume of Faulkner's 1735 edition of Swift's *Works*, the publisher records '*what we have heard from several Persons of great Judgment; that the Author never was known either in Verse or Prose to borrow any Thought, Simile, Epithet, or particular Manner of Style; but whatever he writ, whether good, bad, or indifferent, is an Original in itself.*[7] Swift unquestionably approved the judgement – and unquestionably realized its implications.

The title-page of the *Tale* (figure 2) comments on the pretensions of modern, authorial ownership. The sense of cosmic forces bringing the text into being is both parodic of the author's huge claims to originality and exemplary of the collective nature of all authorship: the *Tale* has been mysteriously and anonymously written for the benefit of mankind, it has long been desired by the world, the *Battle of the Books* has been added to it, all in a series of unassignable transactions in some collective enterprise. In this context, the babble of Gnostic heretics transcribed by Irenaeus has something of the true Joycean flavour. While these babblings may have been mere sound in their original, here they hint at meanings and hence the need for deciphering: the history of collective utterance has a meaning, however ludicrously obscure.

The excerpt from Lucretius on the title-page makes the satiric point most directly, that originality is relative. Emblems of this sort provide protective authority by establishing the author's place in a line of intellectual transmission. The Lucretian verses, from the invocation to

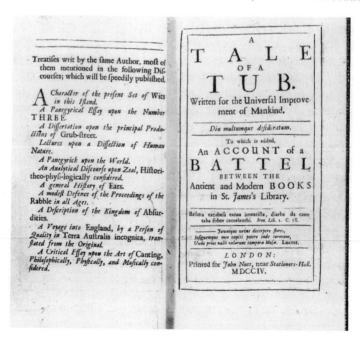

the fourth book of *De Rerum Natura*, celebrate the poet's originality. In translation: 'I delight in plucking new flowers, seeking a noble garland for my head in fields whose flowers the Muses never placed on human brows before.' Whatever may be true of *De Rerum Natura*, the *Tale*'s claim to originality in the presence of this motto becomes self-cancelling: even if everything else in the *Tale* were miraculously original, the claim itself is not. Whatever Swift's conscious intentions when he added his 'Apology' to the 1710 edition, its assertion of his own originality is not only hyperbolic but unavoidably ironic, Lucretius having pre-empted the claim.

IV

While preparing this paper, I tried the patience of the Clark Library's staff – or I would have done so, if they had not been so resolutely helpful. I called up what seemed like volume after volume to look at title-pages, prefaces, advertisements and afterwords: the places and moments in books where authors or publishers leave visible traces of themselves. A study that did the job in truly thorough fashion, however, would try the patience of the hardiest librarian, for what in fact I looked at were only a few familiar texts: Faulkner's 1735 edition of Swift, *Pamela*, *Clarissa*, *Sir Charles Grandison*, *Joseph Andrews*, *Tom Jones*, Sarah Fielding's *David Simple*, and one or two more. What one would need to look at, to understand the multiplicity of situations that define eighteenth-century authorship, is not much less than everything: novels, poetry, tracts, histories, pamphlets, indeed all that was published during an age when conditions of authorship were enormously fluid. Eighteenth-century title-pages, prefaces and the like have the allure of obscurely encoded systems.

Here I will look at authorial traces displayed in a few texts and then, in a closing section, reflect on the 'trade of authorship'[8] as practised in a time when the modern author, as we know him or her, came into being. In the eighteenth century, Pascal's advice to authors was definitively rejected and the way cleared to say 'my book' with hardly a reflection on the assumptions behind such assertions of proprietary right. This story can be told in other terms – for example, those afforded by the history of copyright, which begins, formally speaking, with a statute of 1709 and makes part of the larger histories of intellectual property, of print technology and of professionalism.[9] These are allied stories, the one variously anticipating or reinforcing the other. The curious evidence of title-pages, prefaces and advertisements, provides a more intimate laboratory, however, than that of corresponding laws or large social movements.

The texts I have chosen are: Faulkner's 1735 edition of Swift; Richardson's three novels; *Joseph Andrews* and *The Adventures of David Simple*; Johnson's *Dictionary*; and Hume's posthumous 'My Own Life'. This list conspicuously leaves out poetry and, with the exception of *David Simple*, works by women. In the case of poetry, other than satiric poetry, the situation is less intricate, largely because poetry was a more respectable business than fiction and anonymous publication therefore less the norm. In the case of fictions by women, the situation is if anything more complicated and can be summed up in the familiar aphorism, 'anonymous was a woman'. What I am looking at, then, is the emergence of an authorial, male class. In the listing that follows, the arrangement is roughly chronological; the movement, roughly in the direction of growing authorial possessiveness.

1. In *The Works of J.S., D.D., D.S.P.D.*, printed 'by and for' George Faulkner in 1735, Swift's usual strategy of anonymity collides with the demands of a collected edition designed to record and to memorialize a career, a form that assigns particular value to the author whose life binds the individual texts together. Decisive acts of authorship, collected editions gather and identify what is the author's own and save what might otherwise have been lost. When a living author publishes a collected edition, it amounts to saying 'this is mine' or 'this is what I want to call mine'. But Faulkner's edition, attributed to J.S., D.D., D.S.P.D., maintains a fiction of pseudo-anonymity. In its editorial apparatus Swift sometimes appears as '*the supposed Author*' or as '*this Author, whoever he be*'; or we are told, of 'On Poetry A Rapsody' – a particularly inflammatory piece – that '*the Author* [is] *not known*.'[10] Swift's career was a fantasia on the theme of anonymity; the collected works bring the fantasy to completion by specifically inviting the reader to constitute the author from all manner of signs and equivocations. The equivocations merely reinforce the attribution of authorship to J.S., D.D., D.S.P.D., because J.S. was so well known to be the prince of equivocation. The real though closeted author of the *Tale* has edged out into the light of day.

2. Part I of *Pamela* came into the world with Richardson's name nowhere in view. The title-pages of the two volumes announced that they were printed for Richardson's friend, Charles Rivington, and sold by

another of Richardson's friends, John Osborn. Copyright was in the names of Richardson, Rivington, and Osborn. In a preface by the 'editor', Richardson distinguished between editors and authors: *'an* Editor *may reasonably be supposed to judge with an Impartiality which is rarely to be met with in an* Author *towards his own works.'*[11] The fiction of editorship, though a convenient avenue to self-praise, means more to Richardson than that, just as anonymity means more to Swift than a way of self-protection. As printer, publisher and editorial reviser of others' works, Richardson came to the writing of *Pamela* with a history of literary activity behind him that had shown him how elusive were the gradations between editorial and authorial functions. If the concept of authorship was then far less hardened than it would become, so was the concept of editorship more capacious and less cautious than it has become (as Richard Bentley's high-handed emendations of Milton make clear). Richardson's editorship of *Pamela*, far from being merely a disguise, asserts the power of an anonymous will as strong as that of any author's. In the second edition of *Pamela*, Richardson admitted into the prefatory material an ecstatic letter from Aaron Hill which, though addressed to the editor of *Pamela*, nonetheless praises the 'wonderful **AUTHOR**', in bold capitals, 'of *Pamela*'.[12] And in the second part of the novel, Richardson emerged partly from the shadows: the volumes were described as printed for him and sold by Rivington (and Richardson held sole copyright). Still he never explicitly gave up his role as editor. *Clarissa* was described as printed for Richardson and published by the editor of *Pamela*; *Sir Charles Grandison*, as printed for Richardson and published by the editor of *Pamela* and *Clarissa*. It is not far-fetched to say that if the history of the novel had taken different turns than it did, we might by now think of it as natural to claim the editorship, rather than the authorship, of literary fictions.

3. One reason the history of the novel took the turns it did, rather than the turns it did not, was Fielding's example. In 1741 he published *Shamela*, using the pseudonym of Conny Keyber. *Joseph Andrews* followed the next year, without Fielding's name on the title page but described as 'written in the manner of Cervantes, author of Don Quixote' – thus signalling primacy of authorship. Who would not have known that Cervantes was the author of *Don Quixote*? In 1743 came the three-volume *Miscellanies* 'by Henry Fielding', who thereby identified himself forthrightly as the author of the fiercely satirical *Jonathan Wild*, included in the third volume. *Tom Jones* (1749) and *Amelia* (1751) were both 'by Henry

Fielding, Esquire'. Just as Fielding valued the authorial *persona* in his fiction, so he valued the role of authorship in his life.

When his sister Sarah published *The Adventures of David Simple* (1744), described on the title-page as written 'by a lady', some thought Fielding to be the author. Offended by this, he furnished a preface to the second edition, in which he not only denied authorship but made the whole matter into a case of conscience. He would not have troubled to reply, he says, 'had not the Imputation directly accused me of Falshood, in breaking a Promise, which I have solemnly made in Print, of never publishing, even a Pamphlet, without setting my Name to it: A Promise I have always hitherto faithfully kept; and for the Sake of Men's Characters, I wish all other Writers were by Law obliged to use the same Method....' Then he renounces his promise: '"till they are, I shall no longer impose any such Restraint on myself'.[13] This is all quite odd, since Sarah Fielding had after all published anonymously and it was this anonymity that led to the mistaken attributions. Is it that Fielding's rules need not apply to women? Perhaps, yet he may also be dissembling: he claims to be offended because he believes, for reasons of moral responsibility, in setting his name to what he writes, yet is he not also upset to have been taken for the author of his sister's fiction, this novel 'by a lady' and, no doubt, a work of less power than he himself was capable of? Is this not a case of possessive (and male) authorial pride concealing itself as high-mindedness?

4. The title-page of Johnson's *Dictionary* (1755) reads as follows:

A
Dictionary
of the
English Language
in which
The Words are Deduced from their Originals
and
Illustrated in their Different Significations
by
Examples from the best Writers
to which are prefixed
A History of the Language,
and
An English Grammar
By Samuel Johnson, A.M.

Seeing this for the first time, a modern reader might suppose that the attribution of authorship refers only to the history of the English language and to the grammar. We no longer think of dictionaries as authorial products. But Johnson and his age did. Among the 'unhappy mortals' who 'toil at the lower employments of life', Johnson says, 'is the writer of dictionaries. ... Every other authour may aspire to praise; the lexicographer can only hope to escape reproach, and even this negative recommendation has been yet granted to very few.'[14] It is not only because early dictionaries depended so much on individual efforts that lexicographers had the status of authors but also because the distinction had not yet been made between writing a dictionary and compiling it. The distinction might have been made; Johnson's third definition of 'author' is 'The first writer of any thing; distinct from the *translator* or *compiler*'. But Johnson's understanding of what a dictionary is emphasizes the actual writing of definitions. The famous, witty ones, like 'lexicographer: a writer of dictionaries; a harmless drudge', announce Johnson's sense of what is distinctive in his enterprise. Even so, the claim to authorship carries a sense of some presumption to modern eyes. In our sense of things, to be the 'author' of a dictionary would be to create language itself, and with the advantage of linguistic history behind us we sense in Johnson a tug between assertions of humility and of power; between the belief that making dictionaries is one of the lower employments of life and the imposing aura of authorship. Pascal could have said, 'Certain authors ... say "My book", "My commentary", "My history", "My dictionary", etc.' It is an irony that Johnson's dictionary initiated the custom of providing examples from other authors and thus emphasized the collective nature of linguistic meanings. When we call the dictionary Johnson's, we attribute to him more than we may realize.

5. When David Hume was ill in spring, 1776, and only a few months from death, he wrote a short autobiographical account that he called 'My Own Life'; in a codicil to his will he expressed the wish that it appear in a posthumous edition of his works. In the event, his publisher William Strahan brought out 'My Own Life' in a separate edition, together with a letter from Adam Smith to Strahan that described Hume's last illness and death (1777). Facing the half-title was a listing, under works *'Published by the Same Author'*, of three editions of Hume's *History* and three editions of *Essays and Treatises on Several Subjects*, all 'published by T. Cadell in the Strand'. The half-title announces *The Life of David Hume, Esq*, and a price, 1*s*. 6*d*. There follows a portrait of Hume and then

a title-page announcing *The Life of David Hume, Esq.: Written by Himself.* These reiterated signs of posthumous authorship, represented in both biographical and autobiographical modes, proclaim the author-function with a curious insistence.

The concern that dominates 'My Own Life', as it dominated Hume's thoughts during his last illness, was his posthumous reputation. Near the end he remarks that 'I see many symptoms of my literary reputation's breaking out with additional lustre' and calls the 'love of literary fame' his ruling passion.[15] Had he been able to know that 'My Own Life' would be published independently of his works, he would have had reason to be pleased, for separate publication confirmed the triumph of his reputation. However intimately responsible for generating a work, the modern author lives apart from it. The author's life, in so far as the ascendancy of authorship has become an article of modern faith, pre-empts or is independent of the work and assumes a value larger than that of what has been written: a situation that the 'new criticism' strove to alter, though with modest and temporary success. The author achieves a reputation by virtue of *being* an author. When Strahan decided to publish 'My Own Life' separately, he took a step that we can recognize as parallel in implication to Rousseau's *Confessions* or Boswell's *Life of Johnson.* Separate publication of Hume's 'Life' – especially with its emphatic title of 'My Own Life' – implies the apotheosis of his own authorship. It therefore seems unsurprising to find Hume, in the text of 'My Own Life', reiterating claims of possession: 'I composed my *Treatise of Human Nature*'; 'my Enquiry concerning the Principles of Morals'; 'my Political Discourses, the only work of mine that was successful on the first publication'; 'my Natural History of Religion': 'my History'; 'my writings'.[16] Hume speaks the quintessential language of proprietary authorship.

V

Chapter 11 of *Biographia Literaria* is headed '*An affectionate exhortation to those who in early life feel themselves disposed to become authors*'. This tongue-in-cheekiness matches the mood of some of what follows in an essay that begins with a semi-solemn exhortation, 'NEVER PURSUE LITERATURE AS A TRADE' – that is, don't write to make a living – and ends with a jokey aside that concedes a large part of what it began by challenging: "woefully will that man find himself mistaken who imagines that the profession of literature, or (to speak more plainly) the *trade* of authorship, besets its members with fewer or less insidious temptations, than the church, the law, or the different branches of commerce.'[17] Coleridge's scrambling of the distinction between trades and professions both asserts and denies a nostalgia for a professionalism uncontaminated by economic motives. The long stability of the distinction between trades and professions had coincided with a stability of class relationships, and when Coleridge advises aspiring authors not to pursue literature as a trade, he manages to imply that to be an author is to be truly disinterested and not one of the grub-street mob. Yet he realizes how badly this image misses the reality.

Coleridge's ironic perception of the situation of authorship still colours our self-understanding and sense of vocation. When we say, as scholars who happen to be authors, that so-and-so's study of such-and-such is only journalism – the term 'journalism' having been imported from the French in the early nineteenth century to help professionalize so far as possible the trade of authorship – we are still insisting, with a sense of advantage, on the distinction between trades and professions. Yet we insist (not unreasonably) on the rewardability of our authorial labours, occasionally to the point of creating or threatening to create academic trade unions. These conditions of the academy can be generalized. In moments of self-reflection, any modern author could assent to the ironic self-understanding of Coleridge's formulation, 'the profession of literature, or (to speak more plainly) the *trade* of authorship'.

At the same time, two hundred years have blunted the edge of realization: our recognitions are further from the surface of consciousness than they were when the emerging character of authorship was of immediate concern. Johnson's famous apothegm, that no one but a blockhead ever wrote except for money, is the gruff assertion of one who began his literary life in trade; he is denying the distinction between professionals whose economic interests are supposed to be secondary and tradesmen who write to make a living. If history had taken Johnson's apothegm more seriously, we would have seen more readily the ambivalence of Coleridge's injunction, never pursue literature as a trade.

The conditions of modern authorship, as established in the eighteenth century, can only be exemplified here, not summarized. To that end, I will close with the case of William Whitehead, Poet Laureate for almost thirty years and a writer whose reflections on writing and on the laureateship, in their conventionality, shed light on the history of authorship and on the institution of the laureateship, itself a considerable footnote in that history.

I choose Whitehead in part because Coleridge's pious advice to 'youthful literati' is lifted from one of Whitehead's poems. 'Exerting the prerogative of his laureatship', says Coleridge, Whitehead 'addressed to youthful poets a poetic CHARGE, which is perhaps the best, and certainly the most interesting, of his works.'[18] Coleridge refers to *A Charge to the Poets* (1762), in which he found these lines:

> If nature prompts you, or if friends persuade,
> Why, write; but ne'er pursue it as a trade.
> And seldom publish: manuscripts disarm
> The censor's frown, and boast an added charm,
> Enhance their worth by seeming to retire,
> For what but few can prate of, all admire.
> Who trade in verse, alas! as rarely find
> The public grateful, as the Muses kind.[19]

Whitehead has in mind the risk of being criticized that writers who publish cannot help but run. But his advice evokes those old and better days when writers became famous not by publishing but by circulating manuscripts from hand to hand: 'what but few can prate of, all admire'. The rejection of literature as a trade mirrors a desire to recreate a literary elite, graceful and mutually supportive, and not, like the modern rabble, vulgar and inept. Whitehead describes the mob of modern critics: 'One epithet supplies their constant chime, / *Damn'd* bad, *damn'd* good, *damn'd* low, and *damn'd* sublime.'[20] It is every writer's complaint, but the moral of the poem underscores the modern kinship between the mob of critics and the mob of authors.

And who was this Whitehead, the laureate poet who closed his *Charge to the Poets* with the stoic and consolatory proposition 'that verse and virtue are their own reward?'[21] In brief, he was the son of a baker who somehow managed to send him to Winchester College, where the boy spent his adolescence in the company of students far above him in social rank. His friendships, it was said, 'were usually contracted either with noblemen, or gentlemen of large fortune'.[22] After Winchester, he applied to New College, Oxford, where Winchester students typically enrolled; but he was not admitted and instead became a sizar at Clare Hall, Cambridge, with a tiny scholarship of four shillings a week, reserved for orphan sons of Cambridge tradesmen (Whitehead's father having died soon after he entered Winchester). At university, as at school, Whitehead courted his betters. He became tutor to the son of the Earl of Jersey and, having established some reputation as a poet and playwright, spent two years leading a grand tour of the continent, returning to England shortly after Cibber's death left the laureateship vacant in 1757.

The laureateship was not offered to Whitehead first but to Gray, who refused it and, in a letter to William Mason, made some famous remarks that capture forever the oddity of the office, in both its pretensions and its reality:

Tho' I very well know the bland emollient saponaceous qualities both of Sack & Silver, yet if any great Man would say to me, 'I make you *Rat-catcher* to his Majesty with a salary of £300 a-year & two Butts of the best Malaga; and tho' it has been usual to catch a mouse or two (for form's sake) in public once a year, yet to You, S^r, we shall not stand upon these things.' I can not say, I should jump at it. nay, if they would drop the very name of the Office, and call me *Sinecure* to the K^g's majesty, I should still feel a little awkward, & think every body, I saw, smelt a Rat about me. ....[23]

In short, Gray could afford, temperamentally and financially, to act out the fantasy of the disinterested professional and turn the offer down. Whitehead could not.

But even though the position could not have come more conveniently into his hands, Whitehead eventually chafed under its requirements. At his death he left an unpublished poem called 'A Pathetic Apology for all Laureats, Past, Present and to Come'. Though it is a poor thing, it provides a commentary on his earlier innocent exhortation not to pursue literature as a trade. The laureate's role, which in fact Whitehead performed with almost touching diligence,[24] requires the poet to versify on royal command:

> *His* Muse, *obliged* by sack and pension,
> Without a subject, or invention –
> Must certain words in order set,
> As innocent as a Gazette;
> Must some half-meaning half disguise,
> And utter neither truth nor lies.[25]

These sentiments, so self-conscious in their awareness of the costs that accompany the laureate's stipend, can stand as a final, oblique comment on the trade of authorship since the eighteenth century. Poets and writers like to imagine themselves as pure creatures. In this fantasy, the laurel proves that verse and virtue are truly their own reward. Money does not matter. Fame is incidental. But of course the real situation is different, as Coleridge, Johnson, Whitehead and we ourselves all know. The possessive habits of modern authorship, so insistently asserting ownership, are reciprocal with the unavoidable, equally modern habit of writing from a deep, ambiguous sense of need.

NOTES

1 Linda Schele and Mary Ellen Miller, *The Blood of Kings: Dynasty and Ritual in Maya Art*, Fort Worth, 1986. In a foreword, Emily J. Sano states that the director of the Kimbell Museum advised the authors that 'I would like to see the publication developed as a book rather than an exhibition catalogue' and that it should contain 'eight long chapters' (p. xi) – as it does. More than ever, *The Blood of Kings* appears the product of multiple authorship; it also bears the imprint, in different printings, of different publishers – the Kimbell Museum and George Braziller. Still, one wonders whether the omission of Schele's and Miller's names from the advertisement was intended or not.

2 'M. Pascal disait de "ces auteurs qui, parlant de leurs ouvrages, disent: 'Mon livre, mon commentaire, mon histoire, etc.'", qu' "ils sentent leurs bourgeois qui ont pignon sur rue, et toujours un chez-moi à la bouche, Ils feraient mieux, ajoutait cet excellent homme, de dire: 'notre livre, notre commentaire, notre histoire, etc.,' vu que d'ordinaire il y a plus en cela du bien d'autrui que du leur."' *Les Pensées de Pascal*, ed. Francis Kaplan, Paris, 1982, p. 589.

3 'What is an Author', in *Textual Strategies: Perspectives in Post-Structuralist Criticism*, ed. Josué V. Harari, Ithaca, N.Y., 1979, p. 160. Cf. Roland Barthes, 'The Death of the Author', in *Image, Music, Text*, trans. Stephen Heath, New York, 1977, pp. 142-8. Barthes does not cite Pascal but, appropriately, seems to do so: 'The text is a tissue of quotations drawn from the innumerable centres of culture' (p. 146).

4 'A new Model for the Study of the Book', *supra*.

5 London, 1704, pp. A3ʳ; 220; 182.

6 London, 1710, [p. xiii].

7 *The Works of J.S., D.D., D.S.P.D.*, Dublin, 1735, II, A1ʳ-A1ᵛ.

8 See below, n18.

9 The literature on these topics is large and growing larger, and works such as Elizabeth Eisenstein, *The Printing Press as an Agent of Change*, Cambridge, 1979, have become well known. At the same time, a synoptic history detailing the consequences for literary culture of what C. B. MacPherson called 'possessive individualism' (*The Political Theory of Possessive Individualism*, Oxford, 1962) remains to be written. For a recent informed study of copyright and authorship, see Mark Rose, 'The Author as Proprietor: *Donaldson v. Becket* and the Genealogy of Modern Authorship', *Representations*, no. 23, Summer 1988, pp. 57-85.

10 *The Works of J.S., D.D., D.S.P.D.*, II, A1ʳ; A1ᵛ; 433.

11 London, 1741, I, p. vi.

12 London, 1741, I, p. xvii.

13 Fielding had made the promise that he here renounces in his preface to the *Miscellanies*: 'I will never hereafter publish any Book or Pamphlet whatever, to which I will not put my Name' (*Miscellanies by Henry Fielding Esq.*, London, 1743, I, p. xxvii). On this promise and its renunciation, see R. C. Jarvis, 'The Death of Walpole: Henry Fielding and a Forgotten *Cause Célèbre*', *MLR*, 41, 1946, pp. 113-30, especially 120-1. Jarvis argues that the renunciation of the promise was owing to the difficult – even 'desperate' – financial situation Fielding found himself in at the time.

14 London, 1755, I, A2^r.

15 London, 1777, pp. 31-2, 33.

16 *Ibid.*, pp. 6-7, 13-14, 16, 21, 22, 24.

17 *Biographia Literaria*, ed. James Engell and W. Jackson Bate, Princeton, 1983, I, pp. 223, 230. This is volume VII of *The Collected Works of Samuel Taylor Coleridge*, ed. Kathleen Coburn and Bart Winer, Princeton, 1969-

18 *Ibid.*, p. 223.

19 *The Poems of William Whitehead*, in *The Works of the English Poets*, ed. Alexander Chalmers, London, 1810, XVII, p. 232.

20 *Ibid.*, p. 233.

21 *Ibid.*, p. 234.

22 'The Life of Whitehead', *ibid.*, p. 190. Whitehead's editor and biographer, William Mason, is quoted.

23 Gray to Mason, 19 December 1757. *Correspondence of Thomas Gray*, ed. Paget Toynbee and Leonard Whibley, Oxford, 1935, II, pp. 543-4.

24 Between 1758 and 1785, Whithead wrote (if we assume the compilation in *The Poems of William Whitehead* to be complete) twenty-five birthday odes to the king and twenty-three odes for the new year. Birthday odes are missing only for 1760 and 1764; New Year's odes are missing only for 1764, 1766, 1769, and 1775.

25 'A Pathetic Apology for All Laureats, Past, Present and to Come', *The Poems of William Whitehead*, p. 277.

MOUNT AND PAGE

Publishers of Eighteenth-Century Maritime Books

Thomas R. Adams[1]

The great technological 'revolutions' between the fifteenth and eighteenth centuries were artillery, printing and ocean navigation. Braudel[2]

HERE WE ARE CONCERNED with an eighteenth-century English publishing firm that specialized in an area where Braudel's three 'revolutions' overlap: that is to say, maritime books. While neither the history of the book nor maritime history is in the mainstream of the study of history, both have extensive literatures and both are receiving increased attention from scholars. With a few exceptions, Anglo-Americans have not concerned themselves with the bibliographical aspect of early maritime books. Of those who have done so the most prominent are R. C. Anderson,[3] Lawrence C. Wroth,[4] E. R. G. Taylor[5] and D. W. Waters.[6] Another area in which printing and the sea come together is in the production of charts. While carto-bibliography deals with sheets printed from an engraved plate, bibliography deals with sheets printed from movable type. The maritime manual and the chart function together in navigating ships; each differs in the way in which it was created, manufactured and distributed and thus presents different problems when it comes to understanding how the two forms functioned both in the book trade and in maritime affairs. In the present case we are primarily concerned with publications that came from movable type; and with charts only when they appear as part of a book. More particularly we shall be concerned with the history of the London firm of Mount and Page as derived from the books they published between 1684 and 1800, 116 years, during most of which they dominated or at least played a prominent role in maritime publishing. These were the years that saw Britain, applying the maritime knowledge and skills acquired during the previous century and a half, become the dominant sea power of the world.

I. THE NATURE OF THE PROBLEM

One of the most difficult aspects of writing the history of the book trade is a lack of archival source material such as business records and correspondence. Although there are notable exceptions, generally we have to depend for our primary information on the books that bear a bookseller's imprint. This certainly is true in the case of Mount and Page. There are of course ancillary sources such as the records of the Stationers' Company[7] and contemporary memoirs like John Nichols's *Literary Anecdotes of the Eighteenth Century*, 1812-16, and *The Life and Errors of John Dunton*, 1705. They are of some help in providing biographical information about the two families concerned, but they are not very informative about their business affairs. Both families had dropped out of the firm by 1800, although the business that they founded is still (1993) listed in the London telephone directory as the printing firm of Smith and Ebbs.

Until recently, identifying the books issued by an English publisher in the eighteenth century was difficult. Now, however, *The Eighteenth Century Short Title Catalogue* is far enough along so that the ability to search it by names in the imprint, through the RLIN network, can give one a good start. This, coupled with the lists of Mount and Page books and charts advertised for sale which were printed almost every year on fly leaves, or elsewhere, in some of their publications, and in *The National Union Catalog of Pre-1956 Imprints*, can provide a fairly comprehensive list. With these data as a starting point, over thirty libraries in the United States and England were searched. The result was *The Non-Cartographical Maritime Works Published by Mount and Page, A Preliminary Hand List*.[8] Since its publication additional locations and editions and new titles have been added and the scope has been enlarged to include all the books published by the firm. It is this source that forms the basis for this paper. One characteristic of these books was immediately apparent: many are extremely scarce. Thirty-two per cent of those on the *Hand List* are recorded in only one copy. Almost every library searched produced new editions. It is also quite clear that there are many more which await discovery or which have not survived. This appears to be a characteristic of English maritime books. D. W. Waters's study of the 1528 to 1640 period shows much the same pattern.[9]

The pioneer study of Mount and Page by Captain W. R. Chaplin of Trinity House was published over forty years ago. He outlined the history of the firm from its beginnings to the present century, but provided little indication of where his information came from.[10] It is clear that Chaplin found the Stationers' Company records important, as well as Nichols and Dunton. Chaplin also had access to certain wills and deeds. He refers to records still held by Smith and Ebbs, but they seem not to date back to the eighteenth century. Chaplin notes a fire at the premises in Postern Row in 1880, the firm's removal in 1886 to Northumberland Alley a few blocks away, and its further removal in 1927 to larger quarters in the same street. The most recent address is in the same neighbourhood in Wormwood Street. Chaplin did his best to identify and use the books published by the firm, but in 1948 the first of the 263 volumes of the third edition of the British Museum's *General Catalogue of Printed Books* was eleven years away. Without it any attempt to investigate in detail eighteenth-century English books was extremely difficult. One source that was available to me which he apparently did not use are the Mount family papers in the Berkshire County Record Office in Reading. These, however, are almost entirely nineteenth-century and deal with the family after they left the business. They have been useful, however, in sorting out genealogical questions.

II. THE MEMBERS OF THE FIRM

The firm of Mount and Page had its origins in that of William Luggar, who began business about 1600 in Holborn. By 1633 he had moved to Postern Gate on Tower Hill, near Trinity House. Trinity House was the corporation of English mariners, founded in 1514, which regulated merchant shipping and the working conditions of master and sailors, and was responsible for the erection and maintenance of navigational aids, buoys and lighthouses. Luggar had evidently chosen his new site strategically. He began specializing in mathematical and navigational books. In 1640 his name appeared on the title-page of the third edition of Blaeu's *The Sea Mirror Containing; a Briefe Instruction in the Art of Navigation*. It was an English translation from the Dutch printed in Amsterdam: the imprint, hitherto 'Amsterdam, W. Johnson Blaeu', now became 'Amsterdam, sold by W. Luggar' in London. Two years later, in 1642, he published Henry Bond's *The Boates swaine's Art*, one of the most popular seaman's manuals, a title Mount and Page were to reprint almost 150 years later in 1786. The progress by which he and his successors acquired the copyright in most of the successful navigational books had begun; it was to lead to the establishment of a virtual monopoly that lasted for over a century.

In 1645 Luggar took his last apprentice, William Fisher, whom he freed in 1652. Four years later the two published John Brown's *The Description and Use of the Carpenter's Rule* which Mount and Page were to reprint as late as 1704. Luggar died in 1658 and Fisher succeeded to the business in Postern Row. Of the six apprentices he took during his years in business only one became established in the book trade. This was Richard Mount, bound in 1670, the son of Ralph Mount, Yeoman, of Chislet, Kent. Chislet, located halfway between Canterbury and Margate, was only three miles from the North Sea approaches to the Thames. It is reasonable to suppose that the young man grew up exposed to the increasing importance of the sea in the affairs of England.

Richard Mount's apprenticeship was irregular but not unusual. Normally he would have been freed in eight years, that is, in 1678. The records of the Stationers' Company show that he was freed, by patrimony, in June 1683, a year and a half after William Fisher's death. By that time he had, in 1682, married Sarah, one of Fisher's four daughters, and had published at least fifteen books either jointly with Fisher or on his own account. One can surmise that his father arranged for articles that involved a high binding price, in effect an investment in the firm, an arrangement traditionally sealed by marriage. By 1684 a de facto partnership must have existed when Mount's name appeared jointly with those of Fisher and others on three books, two of which were Henry Phillippe's *Mathematical Manual* and Samuel Sturmy's *The Mariner's Magazine*.[11] Fisher's will was proved on the 11th of January 1691/2, ten days after he signed it. Perhaps he had overlooked the formality of freeing Richard Mount so the latter's status had to be regularized with the Stationers' Company once he and his wife gained control of the business.

Whatever the formalities may have been, Richard Mount lost no time in capitalizing on his inheritance. In the year Fisher died he added to his list four well-established navigational works, including Richard Norwood's *Seaman's Practice* which between 1637 and 1689 had appeared in sixteen editions. In 1693, a year of signal importance to the firm, he published or republished four books, two of which were to become staples, *Great Britain's Coasting Pilot* by Greenville Collins and Nathaniel Colson's annual *The Mariner's New Kalendar*. The next year saw three more reprints: another Norwood, Andrew Wakely's *The Mariner's Compass Rectified* (an annual seaman's almanac) and John Seller's popular *Practical Navigation*. In 1694 Mount also advertised James Atkinson's *Epitome of the Art of Navigation*. Colson, Wakely and Atkinson were to

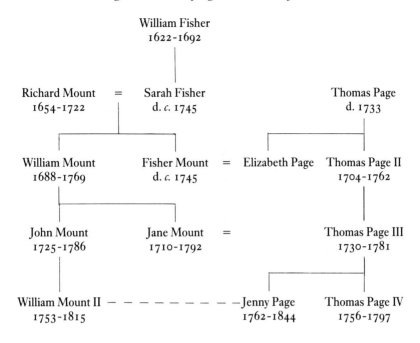

Fig. 1 A genealogy of the members of the Mount and the Page families associated with the firm

become standard navigational manuals and almanacs until the 1790s. (To avoid repeating titles, they will often be referred to by author. A list of the publications in question is to be found in appendix A.)

The earliest known printed advertisement by Richard Mount alone appeared in the 1694 edition of Seller.[12] It begins 'Mathematical and Sea-Books, Printed for, and sold by Richard Mount, Book-seller, at the Antient Shop by the Postern on Tower Hill'. After listing twenty-four titles it goes on, 'There are also sold all sorts of Mathematical and Sea-Books in English, or Books of any other Subject, as Divinity, History, Poetry, &c. Waggoners, Sea Charts of all Parts of the World; all sorts of paper and Paper-Books, rul'd or unrul'd, at the cheapest rate; also Bibles, or any other Books new bound and clasp'd and Writing-Ink, Pens, Wax, Wafers, Pencils, &c.' At this stage Mount was clearly a general bookseller in addition to being a stationer and to his interest in maritime books and charts. By 1705 the heading of Mount's advertisements is 'Books of Navigation' and reference to non-maritime books disappears. Among the twenty-four titles noted in 1694 were a number of items that Mount had inherited from William Fisher and never reprinted, although he kept them in stock, one apparently into the 1740s.

In 1701 Richard Mount took as a partner Thomas Page, a relative by marriage.[13] The imprint now was changed from 'R. Mount' to 'R. Mount & T. Page' and appeared on *The English Pilot, the First Book, Part I*. (For the forms of the name of the firm see appendix B.) The firm was ultimately to take over all five books in the series which John Seller, the first Englishman to publish maritime atlases, had started by 1671.[14] These, with Greenville Collins's *Coasting Pilot*, equalled Colson, Wakely and Atkinson in longevity. Three years before this, in 1698, Mount took his first apprentice, his son William, and in 1704 he was joined by a second son, Fisher. Apparently there was also another son John about whom little is known.[15] Five years later William became a partner in 'R. & W. Mount & T. Page', the name by which the firm did business for the next thirteen years. During this time family connections were further strengthened after Thomas Page II was bound to his father and his sister Elizabeth Page married Fisher Mount, the first of three intermarriages. (For a genealogy of the two families as they relate to the firm see fig. 1).

When Richard Mount died in 1722, after being kicked in the leg on London Bridge by a carthorse at the age of sixty-six, he was well established in both the book and maritime trades. He was the Upper Warden of the Stationer's Company in 1715 and Master in 1718 and 1719. A contemporary said of him: 'Mr Mount is not only a moderate, but has a natural antipathy to excess: he hates hoarding either money or goods and being a charitable man, he values nothing but the use of it, and has a tender love for truth.'[16] His maritime connections included appointment as the Printer for Trinity House, as well as printing for the Navy Office, the Transport Board, the Office of the Receiver for Greenwich Hospital for Seamen, and the Office of the Commissioners on Tower Hill (the Sixpenny Office) which collected the dues for the maintenance of the Hospital. He also did work for St Thomas's Hospital and the South Sea Company. On his death the prominent Presbyterian preacher John Newman delivered a sermon which the family had printed privately.[17] Appended to it is Richard Mount's 'Advice to his Children'. He recommended no particular sect as long as his children remained Protestants; he counselled moderation and good works and urged that they avoid lawsuits and 'be very cautious of being decoyed by the specious Pretense of *Projectors*, or of trusting others too far in the Management of any Part of your Estate; and gave a care of adventuring on hazardous Undertakings'. As we shall see, his advice was not ignored.

Thomas Page became senior partner, Fisher Mount joined the firm, and the imprint 'T. Page & W. & F. Mount' appeared on at least seven different books between 1723 and 1728 when Fisher Mount decided to leave the business. It then became 'T. Page & W. Mount' until Page's death in 1733. Although his son Thomas Page II had been freed in 1725 and in 1728 married William Mount's daughter Jane, it was not until after his father's death that he became an announced partner in 'W. Mount & T. Page'. During his years as senior partner Thomas Page did little to change the way the business was conducted.

William Mount's thirty years as senior partner (1733-1763) constituted the longest span of service of any member of the family. Like his predecessor, he heeded Richard Mount's warning about risky ventures. Few new titles were added to the dependable and profitable list. The one major exception was Thomas Haselden's *The Seaman's Daily Assistant, being a Short, Easy and plain Method of Keeping a Journal at Sea*, first advertised in 1745. The earliest recorded edition, however, is that of 1757.[18] The work joined Colson, Wakely, Atkinson, Greenville Collins and *The English Pilots* as one of the firm's mainstays. William Mount carried on in his father's pattern and took an active part in both the book and maritime trades. In 1731 and 1732 he was Upper Warden and in 1733, 1734 and 1735 the Master of the Stationers' Company. He continued the connection with Trinity House and other agencies with which the firm did business. He also strengthened the family's connections with the firm. His second son John was apprenticed in 1739. (His first son Richard was apprenticed in 1729 but disappears from the record; presumably he died.) After receiving his freedom in 1746 John became a partner in 'W. & J. Mount & T. Page'. In that same year Thomas Page III, son of Thomas II and Jane Mount, was apprenticed and in 1752 became a partner in 'W. & J. Mount & T. Page and Son' or sometimes 'T. Page & Son'.

The firm did not, of course, depend solely on the two families for its apprentices. Between 1703 and 1762 ten other young men signed articles. Eight of these went on to become Masters. Among them was James Davidson, bound to Thomas Page II in 1731, who became a bookbinder. In 1762 his son James Davidson II was bound to John Mount and also stayed with the firm, ultimately becoming a partner in 1790. Three other apprentices, Ralph Arnold, Robert Black and George Jarvis, along with Davidson, established themselves in Tower Hill and were bookbinders for more than twenty-five years. There is no direct evidence, but it is reasonable to suppose that their former masters

THOMAS R. ADAMS

provided them with a certain amount of business. Surviving copies of many of Mount and Page books are in bindings that clearly came from a common source. Among the distinguishing marks is a blind-stamped scalloped roll along the hinge which appears on the bindings of successive editions of Colson year after year.

Thomas Page II died in 1762 and for a brief time the firm reverted to 'W. & J. Mount & T. Page', but the next year William Mount decided to retire and his son John became the senior partner of 'J. Mount & T. Page'. The firm, now in the third generation, was losing its leading position. Rivals began to appear, particularly John Nourse in books and Sayer and Bennett in charts. Although John Mount increased the number of new titles, they tended to be published jointly with other booksellers or for some agency such as the Commissioners of Longitude.

John Mount showed little interest in civic affairs. He did not become an officer in the Stationers' Company but he heeded another piece of his grandfather's advice. 'As often as opportunity presents spend some Time *alone* and sometimes in the *Country*', Richard Mount had written, in the familiar vein of successful merchants who used their wealth to join the landed gentry. In 1760 John Mount purchased Wasing, an estate ten miles south-west of Reading, where he built a manor house which was to be the family home throughout the nineteenth and twentieth centuries. His status was confirmed in 1770 when he became Sheriff of Berkshire. About this same time Thomas Page III bought an estate in Sussex.

By the mid-1770s the fourth generation began to enter the firm but without passing through an apprenticeship. In 1775 John's son William Mount II, at the age of twenty-two, became a partner in 'J. Mount & T. Page & W. Mount'. Three years later Thomas Page IV, at the same age, joined, and the name was extended to 'J. Mount & T. Page & W. Mount & T. Page', or, sometimes, 'T. Page jr'.

The final phase began in 1781. In April Thomas Page III died and a few months later John Mount retired. Also in that year William Mount II married Jenny, the daughter of Thomas Page III. The two partners decided to become simply 'Mount and Page'. In the past this form had been used to shorten the name for imprints that included other booksellers. The new arrangement did little to revitalize the firm. With one exception all they did was to republish existing books. The exception was John Adams's *The Mathematician's Companion* in 1781, which might well have been the result of an initiative of John Mount who had made the arrangements before he retired. At the end of the decade Thomas Page IV lost interest and left the firm. William Mount II then took James

152

Davidson II as his partner and the firm became 'Mount & Davidson'. The decline continued as old titles were republished in a desultory fashion until the imprint disappeared after the 1800 edition of Haselden's *The Seaman's Daily Assistant.* Mount left the firm and Davidson associated himself with Smith and Venner, but he died the next year, 1801, before anything appeared with his name in the imprint. 'Smith and Venner' republished a couple of old titles in 1803, the Haselden and *The English Pilot Part III, Describing the Sea-Coasts ... in the Whole Mediterranean Sea*, which Mount and Page had first published just 100 years earlier. Thus ended the maritime publishing of a business which had its origins 167 years before.

III. THE NATURE OF THE PUBLICATIONS AND THEIR DISTRIBUTION

In terms of longevity Mount and Page rank with such eighteenth-century firms as the Tonsons, Rivingtons, Woodfalls and Longmans. Yet the firm's output was comparatively modest. Their imprint appears on about 140 titles in some 600 surviving editions. An extreme contrast is to be found in the brief career of the political publisher John Almon. During the eighteen years when he was most active, 1763 to 1781, he produced 448 titles in 753 editions.[19] With a few exceptions, to be mentioned later, Mount and Page concentrated on books in maritime and related fields and depended for their profit from books on a continuing demand for a few titles. Over seventy per cent of their publications went through three or more printings, with an average of fifty-two years between the first and last printings. The most frequently reprinted titles were the annual Colsons and Wakelys, *The English Pilot ... West India Navigation, The English Pilot ... Southern Navigation*, Atkinson, Haselden (another annual), Collins's *Great Britain's Coasting Pilot* and the annual *The Nautical Almanac.* These eight titles accounted for forty per cent of the books published between 1684 and 1800. The key to this constant pattern of reprints lies in the fact that, excluding the three pilot guides, all these books had astronomical tables that changed annually, requiring a new edition regularly. Although tables for more than one year were included because a normal oceanic voyage took more than one calendar year and often longer, *The Nautical Almanac* contained tables for a single year. However, beginning in 1769 they covered two or more subsequent years. Thus a need for frequent revision, to make them usable, was built into such books. Of comparable importance were the titles which lacked this characteristic. Primarily they were textbooks or manuals of instruction. The eleven most important went through between five and thirteen editions over twenty-six and sixty-seven years with an average time-span of five years between editions. The earliest to become popular were Norwood's *The Seaman's Practice*, John Seller's *Practical Navigation* and Henry Gellibrand's *Epitome of Navigation*. After the 1730s these were replaced by two works. Of those Henry Wilson's *Navigation New Modell'd* was first published in 1723 but did not catch on until the third edition of 1750, after which it went through eleven editions by 1777. The other was Archibald Patoun's *A Compleat Treatise of Practical Navigation* published between 1747 and 1770. One other work reprinted less frequently, because of a more restricted market, but which had a long life, that of eighty-three years, was William Sunderland's *The Ship Builder's Assistant*, which appeared between 1711 and 1794 in six editions. Another indication of the longevity of the firm's list was the number of titles still being advertised for sale long after the latest known printing.[20] Half the titles continued on the lists for between fifteen and sixty-five years. It is possible that some of these books were in fact out of print, but the case of John Seller's *Practical Navigation* suggests otherwise. This well-regarded text was last printed in 1739 but was still being advertised in 1781 forty-two years later. In 1755 William Bradford of Philadelphia issued a list of books 'Just Imported' on which Seller's book appears. It would be interesting to find out how many other booksellers kept such works in stock and whether they were so held for long periods of time or were in fact reprinted from standing type unaltered.

Mount and Page did not, however, doggedly reprint time and time without alteration. The calendar change in 1752 obviously required reworking of the astronomical tables. In addition, eighteen of the more popular works were revised at one time or another: Atkinson's, by William Mountaine in 1740 and John Adams, in 1785; the same two men revised Wakely in 1741 and 1781; Colson's by Mountaine in 1753; Barrow's edition of Euclid by Haselden in 1732, Haselden's own work by John Adams in 1783, Gellibrand's by Atkinson in 1701 and Wilson's by Mountaine in 1764. A closer comparison of editions may show even more alterations than those indicated by statements that appeared on the title-pages.

Maritime books were not the only things sold at Postern Row. Charts and maps have already been mentioned. In addition to separate charts they also published sea atlases made up entirely of engraved charts. Their best known one was *Atlas Maritimus or The New Sea Atlas*, begun about 1672 by John Seller. Richard Mount acquired the copyright in 1708 and the firm continued to publish it until at least 1750. The charts in these atlases could be and probably were sold separately. Because of the nature of engraving, the charts included could vary from copy to copy. They are not as useful as the printed books in documenting the history of the firm because engraved plates could go on being used year after year without being altered, so making the imprint information misleading. This could also occur with books kept in standing type. Normally, however, a printer did not want to tie up his type in this way and distributed it after the printing was done. This could not happen to a printing surface that was a solid piece of copper – which however could be corrected by being beaten out from the back and re-engraved.

The answer to the question of whether the firm actually printed any of its own books is not clear. Almost all their imprints read 'Printed for'. On the other hand, they printed for a number of organizations. Apparently, 'They maintained a complete establishment capable of producing everything from letterpress to engraved plates.'[21] In light of the wording of their imprints one would suppose that the more substantial books were sent out to other printers. Their charts, on the other hand, were probably printed on their own premises. This seems to be confirmed by Benjamin Franklin, who in 1768 took Captain Timothy Folger's sketch of the Gulf Stream 'to be engraved by order of the general post office, on the old chart of the Atlantic at Mount and Page's'.[22]

Almost half the titles published by Mount and Page dealt with some aspect of navigation. The next largest group, closely allied to navigation, were mathematical books, about evenly divided between works of instruction and tables of one kind or another. The remaining quarter were devoted to seamanship, gunnery and tactics, health at sea, ship-building, astronomical observations, and trade and commerce.

Without any business records from Mount and Page it is impossible to ascertain exactly how many copies of their books were printed. The normal press run in the eighteenth century was 2,000 copies but we also know that schoolbooks were printed in as many as 20,000.[23] On the other hand, we do know something about the size of England's maritime community. Shipping records kept at ports by Customs and others have made it possible to arrive at some estimate of how many ships were operating at various times and how many men were involved in manning them. D. W. Waters has provided me with the following estimates of the potential size of the market for navigational books, based on the latest estimated populations of England, Wales, Scotland and British America and his own estimates of the probable minimum numbers of seamen in each country practising the art of navigation and therefore requiring books and charts – all, with the rarest of exceptions, published in London only: 7,750 in 1702, 10,500 in 1740, 16,800 in 1774, 17,500 in 1780 and 18,500 in 1788, by which time there were 9,375 ships totalling over one million tons registered in England and Wales alone.[24] Mount and Page, with their connections to Trinity House and other nautical bodies already mentioned, and from the proximity of their premises to the Customs House a few hundred yards up river, should have been able to assess their market potential and its needs better than was usual for publishers of the time.

An avenue of investigation that casts more light on how the books were made is provided by a detailed comparison of copies. Over 150 have been described in detail. A number of cases show clear evidence of the use of standing type, not surprising in the case of some of the more frequently reprinted works, such as the Colsons, in which the text remained unchanged for edition after edition. Yet there is at least one Colson where an edition, that for 1711, exists in two entirely different settings of type. Was this the result of an unexpected demand or other vagaries in the printing process? An interesting oddity is the 1751 edition of the same work. On the only recorded copy the imprint date has been changed in a contemporary hand to 1752. There are also two recorded copies of the actual 1752 edition. One place where the use of standing type might be expected is in tables that do not change from edition to edition, such as logarithmic tables. They were set in very small type and the composition was exacting and tedious. Yet there are clear examples where all or parts of these tables were reset from one edition to another. From the user's point of view the desirability of leaving these tables undisturbed must have been great because of the potential introduction of errors in resetting, errors that could have serious consequences.

That the firm's eighteenth-century success depended on established titles is further confirmed by the origin of the seventeen titles that went through ten or more editions. Eleven originated before 1700, and only six were from the eighteenth century. Their authors were teachers of mathematics and navigation at places such as Gresham College, Christ's Hospital, or nearby naval establishments at Chatham Dock, Plymouth and Greenwich. Some had their own schools clustered around Trinity House near the Tower and conveniently near Mount and Page's premises or down river at Wapping Old Stairs. Generally these men made no fundamental contribution to the science of navigation. Instead they taught how to apply what was already known.

On a few occasions Mount and Page ventured beyond the maritime and related fields. This was not a significant part of the business but it deserves mention. They did so about sixteen times between 1694 and 1799, half of which were during Richard Mount's tenure. In almost every case the book was published jointly with other booksellers. The most popular were Robert Ainsworth's Latin dictionary and reprints of Richard Allestree's *The Whole Duty of Man* which they sold for J. Eyre of Oxford. Two works which were extensions of their primary interest were printed only once. In 1694 the reprinting of Richard Norwood's *Fortification or Architecture Military*, first published in 1639, suggests Braudel's first 'revolution', a field that the firm did not otherwise develop except in so far as it involved naval affairs. The other allied field that was not followed up was architecture. In 1700 Mount published an edition of Vincenzo Scamozzi's *The Mirror of Architecture*, a title inherited from Fisher. It was taken over by J. Sprint, who went on publishing it well into the eighteenth century. Two other unusual books are worth noting. In 1729 Thomas Page joined J. Osborne and T. Longman in republishing William Roper's *The Life and Death of Sir Thomas More* which had first appeared in 1626, and in 1731 he joined J. March and W. Parker to publish, for the first time, John Wycliffe's translation of the New Testament. The reason why the firm became involved in those projects may lie in the Mount family's Kentish origins. The editor of both books was John Lewis (1675-1747), an antiquarian and Vicar of Minster in the Isle of Sheppey who held livings in east Kent at Margate, Canterbury, Dover and Hythe, all of which pretty much encircled Richard Mount's native town of Chislet. It is certain, however, that the firm never extended its activities into literary or political areas where so much of the book trade was active.

An aspect of the diversification of Mount and Page's stock in trade about which we know comparatively little is the Irish dimension. Dublin editions of English books are often called piracies, but to a large extent they were simply cheap reprints done in collusion with the author or London bookseller. Mount and Page books were reprinted frequently in Dublin by George Grierson and his successors. This began as early as 1714 and continued to at least 1776. At present there is a record of thirty-six such editions of the following twelve works: Atkinson, Bond's *The Boate swaines's Art*, Colson, Wakely, *The English Pilot ... Southern*

Navigation, The English Pilot ... West India Navigation, Patoun, Wilson, *The English Pilot ... Northern Navigation*, Haselden, Mountaine's *Seaman's Vade-Mecum* and Seller. Many of these Dublin books carried lists of maritime books offered for sale there by the Griersons that were almost identical to those in Mount and Page's London lists. The list in the 1714 Seller reads 'Books of Navigation, Printed for Richard Mount'. It was printed on the verso of the title page and thus was a part of the book printed in Dublin rather than a separate leaf which Mount might have sent over for insertion. This suggests that there was an arrangement of some kind between the two firms. The Griersons were the King's Printers in Dublin. They may well have also been Mount and Page's agents with an arrangement to reprint works when the demand was such that they could not be supplied from London. The only other editions known to have appeared outside London are a 1777 reprint of Haselden in Philadelphia, presumably to meet a shortage caused by the war, and a 1788 revision of the same work that appeared in Glasgow.

Mount and Page's publications were not sold in Postern Row alone, but at present we do not know to what extent other booksellers in London carried them except, of course, for those published jointly with others. Booksellers in seaport towns must have carried them, but how and under what circumstances must await a study of their advertisements in newspapers and elsewhere. We do know, however, that they were regularly shipped to the colonies. The earliest American auction catalogue issued by Samuel Gerrish of Boston in 1717 includes a copy of Norwood, while his next one, for 1719, lists almost a dozen Mount and Page titles. These continued to appear in American advertisements down to the 1790s when John Norman, Lawrence Furlong, Edmund Blunt, Nathaniel Bowditch and others began to make independent American contributions to the art of navigation.[25] American seamen, however, continued to depend upon works based on British prototypes. Their *Nautical Almanac* was the only one available until the *American Nautical Almanac* appeared in 1855. The first completely original American contribution to the science of navigation were the works of Matthew Fontaine Maury, begun in the late 1840s with his *Winds and Current Charts* series.[26]

IV. THE AUDIENCE

Determining its effect is one of the most difficult aspects of the history of the book. Compared with other publishers Mount and Page had a more precise idea of who their customers were and what they were going to do with the books than did many of their fellow booksellers. They were involved with ships and the sea. By the eighteenth century mariners were so important in the life of the nation that, as has been noted, records were being kept of their activities. Most of the publications were addressed to those involved in the most crucial part of taking a ship to sea, navigation. Such books were used both to navigate and to train seamen in that art.

Ancient myth notwithstanding, England was comparatively late in becoming a sea power. At the time of the Armada in 1588, when seamen of Spain and Portugal were sailing the oceans of the world and the Dutch had laid the groundwork for their empire in the East Indies, most English merchant ships were still sailing local waters, the west coast of Europe and the closed seas of the Baltic and Mediterranean, where piloting rather than celestial navigation was the skill needed. Iberian sailors had had more than a century of experience using the sun, moon and stars when sailing out of sight of land and Spain had developed a substantial published literature on celestial navigation. It was the translation of some of these books, the first appearing in 1561, that introduced Englishmen to the 'Haven Finding Art'.[27] During Elizabethan and early Stuart times Englishmen caught up and created an extensive literature of their own on the subject.[28] Not until the second half of the seventeenth century, with the development of trans-Atlantic trade on a regular basis with British America, confined from 1651 by the Navigation Acts to English ships, did a need for seamen systematically trained in navigation emerge. The necessary pre-condition for this training was the existence of a large number of mathematical practitioners: between 1650 and 1700 their number doubled.[29] In theory, navigation requires the same preparation regardless of the kind of ship involved. In practice two different procedures developed, one for the Royal Navy and another for the merchant service.

The emergence of the Royal Navy following the Restoration is well known. So also are the reforms begun under Samuel Pepys during his years on the Navy Board (1660-76, 1686-8). Among his projects was the addition, in 1672, of a mathematical side to the school at Christ's Hospital for children 'to be educated in Mathematics for the particular Use and Service of Navigacon'.[30] At the end of their course the boys were examined by Trinity House, which had the responsibility for certifying Masters in the merchant service. In 1677 Pepys also saw to the establishment of examinations for promotion to Lieutenant in the Royal Navy.[31] In that same year, with the assistance of Sir Anthony Deane, the first step toward the standardization of the design of naval vessels was taken.[32] In 1702 the position of Schoolmaster to serve aboard ships was created.[33] The increasing demand for instruction was met in a number of ways. Teachers set up their own schools not only in London and other seaports but elsewhere throughout England. Sir Joseph Williamson endowed a mathematical school in 1701 in Rochester, near Chatham Dock, and Joseph Neale endowed another that opened in Fleet Street in 1715.[34] Instruction at or near naval establishments has already been mentioned. In 1730 this was carried further with the founding of a naval academy in Portsmouth which, however, did not amount to much until the nineteenth century.[35]

From what we know it is possible to assemble some picture of how navigation was taught to midshipmen and master's mates, the two ratings regarded as future sea officers in the Royal Navy. On board ship such instruction was the responsibility of the Schoolmaster, when one was inclded in the complement. Schoolmasters were posted to 3rd, 4th and 5th rate ships only, perhaps because these ships spent more time at sea than did the larger 1st and 2nd raters and the smaller 6th raters, sloops and the like.[36] The schoolmaster was rated as an inferior warrant officer on a par with the surgeon's mate, below the surgeon but above petty officers such as the boatswain's mate. Contemporary published descriptions of individual schoolmasters are not very flattering.[37] We ought, however, to be sceptical of generalizing from these writers. Between 1712 and 1824 at least 349 men served as schoolmasters, some for extended periods of time. Thomas Brown, who served in seventeen ships between 1717 and 1754, must have done his job well or so many captains would not have signed him on.[38] Regular sea officers must also have participated in the instruction, and they certainly did on ships without a schoolmaster.

All the evidence points to the books published by Mount and Page as the principal texts used, particularly in the first half of the eighteenth century. Among those written by naval schoolmasters were John Barrow's *Navigatio Britannica: or A Complete System of Navigation* and Joshua Kelly's *The Modern Navigator's Compleat Tutor*. We can only conjecture just how they were used. The schoolmaster certainly had his own copy, but what about his students? Midshipmen could have bought their own texts before coming aboard, but how did they know which one was going to be used? Is it not likely that the schoolmasters brought along a number of copies to sell to their pupils? As D. W. Waters has noted: 'Officers, both of naval and merchant ships, were obliged to provide themselves at their own expense with the necessary navigational instruments and books and, if they were responsible for the navigation of the vessel, the charts for the intended voyage.'[39] In any case, we can presume that the young men were required to work out the ship's position regularly. Indeed, there is a watercolour by Thomas Hearn of the quarter-deck of the *Deal Castle* in 1775 showing midshipmen assembled to practice taking noon sights.[40]

We know a great deal less about how merchant officers were taught. The service varied all the way from the coastal coal trade where few navigational skills, other than pilotage, were needed, to East Indiamen where the demands were not unlike those of the Royal Navy. The mathematical schools also played a part, although one cannot learn navigation without going to sea. In 1714 John Cremer was sent to 'one Mr. Atkinson, a mathematical schoolmaster on Roerifwall', before he was sent to sea on a Newcastle voyage.[41] This was James Atkinson, senior author of the long-lived *Epitome* published by Mount and Page. In 1626 Captain John Smith in his *Accident or Path-way to Experience Necessary for all Young Sea-men*, after listing the books his readers should be familiar with, says 'get one of these books, but practice is best'. The usual course, in the early part of the century certainly, was to be apprenticed to a ship's master, but the articles had to specify the teaching of navigation as part of the apprenticeship.[42] Here again circumstances point to Mount and Page as the most frequent source of textbooks. The book the master chose would usually, almost certainly, be the one he was using and probably had originally learned from himself. Again it was very likely that, on occasion, the apprentice bought his copy from the master. As we shall see, we have at least one example that implies this.

When we turn to how these books were used in the actual navigating of ships we have very little to go on except that we know that by modern standards the result was often highly inaccurate.[43] Making a landfall after a long period at sea, subject to the effects of unknown ocean currents and no dependable way of determining longitude, was a chancey thing. To what extent, then, were these books successful in helping to translate theory into practice? Captain John Smith's advice was still universally true at the beginning of the eighteenth century, and four of the books on his list were advertised by Richard Mount at the beginning of his career. A stimulus to improvement came in 1714 when Parliament passed the Longitude Act offering the then prodigious prize of £20,000 for a prctival means of determining longitude at sea. The Act began to bear fruit in the 1760s when improved means and texts began to appear and found their way aboard the relatively few ships with masters sufficiently mathematically minded. Most observations and mathematical calculations involved in determining a ship's longitude, by the methods then practicable, proved too difficult or too expensive for most masters into the nineteenth century. In the last analysis, however, the most frequent use made of the now almost traditional navigation manuals and almanacs was probably found in the various tables, which functioned much as a computer does today in solving the nautical triangle problems of course and distance made good by each day's sailing, in order to establish the ship's position at noon.

If there are any lists of books that were standard equipment aboard naval or merchant vessels I do not know of them. The closest thing is the list of books and charts the Admiralty supplied for Captain Cook's third voyage (1716-80). Among them were three Mount and Page publications, *The Nautical Almanac*, Tobias Mayer's lunar tables and Haselden.[44] These were, however, intended for the use of the people taking scientific observations rather than those navigating the ship, who presumably had their own books and equipment for navigating.

More direct documentation about what happened to some of these books comes from surviving copies. Of the over 150 copies recorded in the *Handlist*, a remarkably large number have inscriptions and annotations by their owners. Frequently these are more than a simple signature, and include the date and place of purchase and sometimes the price. Blank leaves were used for memoranda, working out navigational problems, recording the position of the ship or just the plain doodling so characteristic of the way students treat their schoolbooks.

Thus, Stephen Curlin recorded in his 1713 edition of Colson that he purchased it on 16 September 1714, paying 6s. 6d. Two months later he records the birth of his son and in 1717 the birth of another son. One would assume that he was a ship's officer rather than an apprentice. In 1748 Silas Blaque records his ship's position in the West Indies in a 1747 edition of the same book. This is followed in 1755 by a note by Joseph Blaque that it had been given to him by his 'honoured mother Mary Blaque'. Captain James Brown of Providence, Rhode Island, wrote in his copy of the 1745 edition of *The English Pilot: The Fourth Book, Describing the West India Navigation* that he had bought it in Boston in August of 1748. Later, in another hand appears 'York in Virgeny Febery 15th 1750/1 Capt James Brown Died half a Oure Past 6½ at Nite'. These people must have felt an intimacy with the book to which they entrusted family records akin to their feeling for the Bible in which births and deaths were recorded. A copy of the 1741 Wakely has a note by Edward Carlen that he purchased it from William Beeker, master of the *Lorall of Whitby*, a possible confirmation that masters sold navigation books to their apprentices. A provenance which still needs further confirmation, but is too tempting to omit, is found in a copy of the 1766 Wakely in the New Bedford Whaling Museum. On the half-title is inscribed 'Presented to J. C. Parmenter by a native of Pitcairn's Island, 1833'.[45] One might wonder about a twenty-one-year-old book on the *Bounty* at the time of the mutiny, but such books were used over long periods of time. Cadet Robert E. Lee took the 1790 edition of James Atkinson's *Epitome of the Art of Navigation* out of the West Point Library on six separate occasions in 1828.[46] Individually these notes are incidental curiosities, but if enough were gathered with other demographic and social evidence they might reveal some interesting aspects of how navigation was practised.

V. A HISTORY OF THE PUBLICATIONS

In his early years, 1684 to 1689, Richard Mount was involved, usually with William Fisher, in the publication of eight titles. Then, from 1692, the year of Fisher's death, to 1701 he participated in the publication of twenty-seven well-established works, of virtually all of which he was ultimately to be the sole owner. Among them were seven titles which figure among the most prominent maritime books of the eighteenth century. The oldest was Norwood's *Seaman's Practice*, which had already gone through sixteen editions beginning in 1637. Mount and Page were to reprint it thirteen more times to 1732, which the firm continued to advertise it as late as 1776. The next oldest title was Wakely's *The Mariner's Compass Rectified*, first published in 1665; it was to become a mainstay of the firm's list with at least forty editions to 1796. The importance of Seller's *Practical Navigation* has already been noted. Mount acquired it in 1693. The date on the last edition published is 1739 but, like the Norwood, the firm continued to advertise it into the last quarter of the eighteenth century. According to James Atkinson's own account, his *Epitome of the Art of Navigation* first appeared in 1686. The earliest extant edition, however, is Richard Mount's 'Third Edition' of 1698 which he had advertised earlier in 1694. It joined the Wakely in popularity, being reprinted at least thirty-one times through 1790. In 1693 Mount also got control of the firm's most frequently reprinted publication, Nathaniel Colson's *The Mariner's New Kalendar*. First brought out by Fisher in 1676, it was probably intended to replace the first nautical almanac, *The Seaman's Kalendar*, begun in 1602 by John Tapp; it went through many editions and revisions and was still being published by Richard Mount as late as 1702. For a number of years the Colsons were legally considered to be almanacs and were printed on stamped paper. Also in 1693, Mount published his first completely original work, Greenville Collins's *Great Britain's Coasting Pilot*, which was last reprinted in 1792 after at least twenty-four editions.

Among the other well-established books he published during these years were: Captain John Smith's *The Seaman's Grammar and Dictionary*, dating from 1627; Henry Bond's *The Boate Swaine's Art*, from 1642; Thomas Miller's *The Compleat Modelist, or Art of Rigging*, from 1660; and Henry Gellibrand's *Epitome of Navigation*, from 1674. He also advertised, but did not reprint, nine titles inherited from Fisher, some of which continued to appear in his advertisements into the second quarter of the next century. Among them was Edward Wright's *Certaine Errors in Navigation*, the most important work on the theory and practice of navigation to have appeared anywhere up to that time. First printed in 1599, it went through four editions, the last in 1657. Wright's work is the key to D. W. Waters's statement that by the time of Captain John Smith's death in 1631, 'the English from being ignorant of the art of navigation had almost entirely through their own efforts transformed it into a science'.[47] The basic theoretical work had been done. The next step was the writing of the textbooks and manuals applying theory to the actual operation of ships. The 1630s, 1640s and 1650s actually saw comparatively little important activity in that direction. Notable exceptions were Henry Mainwaring's *The Seaman's Dictionary* (1644) and Edward Hayward's *The Size and Lengths of Rigging* (1655), but in both cases further editions did not appear until 1660 or later.

To what extent the Civil War was responsible for such reduced activity is not exactly clear, but the work of a number of mathematical practitioners was affected.[48] From the Restoration until the 1680s maritime publishing picked up again as William Fisher, Robert Boulter, Thomas Passenger (father and son), Benjamin Hurlock and Ralph Smith joined in bringing out new works. This generation began to disappear just as Richard Mount entered the trade. By 1700 there was only one book with maritime content with a long life that he did not control. This was William Mather's *The Young Man's Companion: Also some Secrets of Surveying, Astronomy, Dialling and Glazing, Navigation and Geography*, first printed in 1684 and reprinted frequently until 1775.

Without any business records it is impossible to document but it is reasonable to assume that the weakening of the Licensing Act in 1693 and its lapse in 1695 had some bearing on the speed with which Richard Mount acquired his monopoly. The Act had protected copyright ownership. Without it in force booksellers lost that protection.[49] This may well have made it easier for Mount to buy up shares owned by men, like Fisher, who were nearing the end of their careers. In any case, Mount gained his commanding position between 1693 and 1710 when the subsequent Copyright Act was passed.

In 1701 Richard Mount was forty-seven years old, half way through his career. He began the second half by taking Thomas Page into partnership. During the opening decades of the new century forty new titles were added which, together with reprints, amounted to more than five and a half publications a year. A distinctive feature of this period was the increase in the number of original works. Only nineteen of the forty new titles were acquired from other booksellers. All the rest were entirely new. Another interesting aspect of these years is that, despite having a partner, Richard Mount's name continued to appear alone in the imprints of many of the books right down to the time of his death. Apparently partnership did not necessarily include ownership. Thomas Page was able to add his name to only eleven titles, but three of them were *The English Pilots*. Another successful work in which he had a share was John Good's *Measuring Made Easy; or the Description and Use of Coggeshall's Rule* which, following its initial appearance in 1719, was reprinted in almost every decade until 1786.

During the thirty-eight years during which Richard Mount headed it, the firm published seventy maritime or related titles. About one third were original and two thirds were titles acquired from other booksellers. It is worth noting that there was one episode in maritime publishing history in which he might have been expected to be prominent, the spate of pamphlets offering solutions to the problem of longitude that were published immediately following the Act of 1714. At least twenty different proposals appeared, but he was involved in only one, Case Billingsley's scheme employing perpetual motion.

Thomas Page presided as the senior partner for only nine years. The most notable feature of those years was the regular republication of existing titles, but eight new ones were also added. Six were original, including the 1723 *System of Mathematics* by James Hodgson, Master of the Mathematical School at Christ's Hospital, which was not reprinted when it apparently went out of print fifteen years later. More successful was *Navigation New Modell'd* by Henry Wilson, which had first been published in 1715 by B. Pickard and W. Meadows. The firm became part-owners with the revised edition in 1723. In 1761, after eight more editions, they became the sole owners, and went on to issue five more through 1777. Thomas Page carried on Richard Mount's pattern but in a lower key. He averaged 1.2 new titles a year rather than Mount's 2, and 2.9 new editions per year as opposed to Mount's 3.3.

The many years during which William Mount, who succeeded Thomas Page in 1733, was senior partner saw a further increase in the number of books the firm reprinted and a decrease in the number of new works it issued to a little more than one every two years. The dominant factors in the improvement of navigation in the eighteenth century were the development of instruments, techniques and data for the application of theories.[50] The two best-known figures were John Hadley (1682-1744) and John Harrison (1693-1776). Hadley's quadrant, which he presented to the Royal Society in 1731, was a dramatic improvement over existing instruments for measuring altitude and was to make measuring lunar distances to determine longitude possible, but Harrison's marine clock, on which he began work in 1729, was ultimately to provide the most practical solution for the problem of longitude. Still another key figure was Nevil Maskelyne (1732-1811), the fifth Astronomer Royal, who developed lunar distances into a practical method for seamen to determine longitude, and was the author of the key publications, *The Nautical Almanac* and the *Tables Requisite* for their use issued by the Commissioners of Longitude, both of which Mount and Page published. Lunar tables, incidentally, continued to appear in *The Nautical Almanac* into the twentieth century. The problem of determining longitude at sea was the spur, and the firm, under William Mount and his son John, were the leaders in the publication of the fundamental books which enabled seamen to solve the problem. The manuals by Atkinson, Colson and Wakely, on the other hand, supplied 'the simple straightforward Rules and Tables which sufficed for the relatively uneducated shipmaster, who learned his trade by apprenticeship'.[51] The firm also brought out Edward Huxley's conventional *New and Complete System of Navigation* jointly with J. Hodges, and John Barrow's *Navigatio Britannica: or a Complete System of Navigation* of 1750, which included a description of the quadrant. Both books, however, appeared in only one edition. A more popular work was Archibald Patoun's *A Compleat Treatise of Practical Navigation*. It had first appeared in 1730 with the ownership shared among a number of other booksellers, but it was not until the fourth edition of 1751 that Mount and Page obtained such a share. After that, it went through five more editions with the last in 1770 shared by sixteen different firms. It was probably for this reason that Mount and Page never included it in their advertising lists.

The middle of the century saw a weakenening of Mount and Page's position. In 1754 John Nourse published John Robertson's *The Elements of Navigation*, a much more comprehensive textbook than anything that had appeared before. Frequently revised and enlarged, it appeared in six more editions by 1805. Robertson was Master of the Mathematical School at Christ's Hospital and went on to be the Librarian of the Royal Society; Nourse was to become the firm's principal rival. William Mount's years as senior partner spanned the transition from navigational texts derived from the seventeenth century to the newer ones that began to appear in the second half of the eighteenth century. Although some effort was made to keep their books up to date through revisions, the firm seems to have relied on the traditional reluctance of seamen to accept change as the basis for its sales.

After John Mount became the senior partner in 1763 he seems to have made an effort to improve the firm's situation. The average of new titles each year rose from one every two years to 1.4 every year. The average of new editions increased slightly from 5.1 to 5.5. However, unlike its practice in Richard Mount's time, few of the firm's new works were its sole property. Instead, the imprints show that they were shared with other booksellers, most frequently John Nourse. Further, most of the new works were not the sort that would have a wide demand and thus require frequent reprinting. Rather, they dealt with narrow and technical aspects of the development of navigation and were addressed to specialists. The major exception was *The Nautical Almanac and Astronomical Ephemeris*, first issued by the Commissioners of Longitude in 1766, in which Mount and Page shared the imprint with Nourse. Just as they failed to participate in the first major textbook of the eighteenth century, Robertson's, so they failed to invest in the second, John Hamilton Moore's *New Practical Navigator and Seaman's Daily Assistant*, which came out in 1772. By 1800 it had gone through twelve editions when it became the basis for Nathaniel Bowditch's *The New American Practical Navigator*, published in Newburyport, Massachusetts, in 1802.

Bowditch is an excellent example of a sailor's tendency to cling to familiar labels. It is still published in the United States by the Hydrographic Office in the Department of Defense. In 1941 my NROTC unit attempted to learn navigation from Bowditch because of shortage of copies of the Naval Academy's standard text, Benjamin Dutton's

Navigation and Nautical Astronomy. For me it was disastrous. Fortunately my unit was able to shift to Dutton, which had first appeared in 1926. The United States Naval Institute is still publishing it forty years later, giving it a status which equals many of Mount and Page's publications.

It was during John Mount's years that the firm's position as a leading chart publisher began to be threatened. The first important break came in 1775 when the firm of Sayer and Bennett, which had originated in 1720, obtained the rights to publish the results of Captain James Cook's survey of Newfoundland and the St Lawrence. This in turn led to their publication of the cartographical results of Cook's Pacific voyage. To improve the quality of their work they commissioned their own surveys. Sayer and Bennett became Laurie and Whittle in 1794 and continued to base their publications on up-to-date information. John Hamilton Moore entered the chart field in 1763, William Heather in 1765 and R. Steel in 1782.[52] Then in 1795 Alexander Dalrymple became the official Hydrographer to the Admiralty, marking the beginning of the modern Admiralty chart on which commercial chart makers were to depend in producing the Blue Backed charts of the nineteenth century.[53] The successors to the above firms merged in 1903 to become Imray, Laurie, Norie & Wilson Ltd. Mount and Page, on the other hand, made no effort to keep up but continued to re-use old plates which they attempted to revise from time to time.

The efforts to inject new activity into the firm ended with John Mount's retirement in 1781. His successors even lost, or gave up, participation in *The Nautical Almanac.* Although Mount and Page continued for another twenty years, probably almost entirely on momentum, their publications became less and less relevant. By the time the wars with France began in 1792 they possessed a comparatively small part of the market.

During the century and a quarter of their existence Mount and Page had helped to train the men who, during the eighteenth century, provided the foundation on which Great Britain's domination of the seas in the nineteenth century flourished. Richard Mount began publishing maritime books as Britain emerged as *a* major sea power. Mount and Page disappear just as Britain becomes *the* dominant sea power. In between, the books published by Mount and Page helped to educate and train the men who manned the ships during the century when this development took place; they also made it possible for two families to realize the perennial English ambition to retire from trade in the City to an estate in the country.

APPENDIX A

A SHORT-TITLE LIST OF THE BOOKS

PUBLISHED BY MOUNT AND PAGE

The inclusive dates of publication and the number of editions thus far identified are indicated. Books advertised but not published by the firm are not included, nor are earlier and later editions which they did not publish.[1]

Adams, John, *The Mathematician's Companion*, 1782-1796 (2)
Ainsworth, Robert, *An Abridgement of Ainsworth's Dictionary*, 1758 (1)
    Thesaurus Linguæ Latin ... or a Compendious Dictionary of the Latin Tongue, 1736-1761 (5)
Alingham, William, *Geometry Epitomiz'd*, 1701-1704 (2)
    A Short Account of the Nature and Use of Maps, 1698 (1)
Allen, Robert, *An Essay on the Nature and Methods of Carrying on a Trade to the South Sea*, 1712 (1)
Atkinson, James, *An Epitome of the Art of Navigation*, 1698-1790 (27)
Bamford, Philip, *Practical Gauger*, 1714-1725 (2)
Barrow, John, *Collection of Discoveries*, 1756 (1)
Barrow, John, *Navigatio Britannica: Or a Complete System of Navigation*, 1750 (1)
Bayly, William, *Original Astronomical Observations made in the Course of a Voyage to the Northern Pacific*, 1782 (1)
Bernoulli, Jean, *A Sexcentenary Table*, 1779 (1)
Bible. N. T., *The New Testament ... Translated out of the Latin Vulgat by John Wiclif*, 1731 (1)
Billingsley, Case, *A Letter to the Commissioners of Longitude Appointed by the Parliament ... for Discovering the Longitude at Sea, to further explain the late Proposal*, 1714 (1)
    Longitude at Sea, Not to be Found by Firing Guns ... or Watches ... but ... [by] Perpetual Motion, 1714 (1)
Binning, Thomas, *A Light to the Art of Gunnery*, 1689-1744 (4)
Bird, John, *The Method of Constructing Mural Quadrants*, 1768 (1)
    The Method of Dividing Astronomical Instruments, 1767 (1)
Bishop, John, *The Marrow of Astrology*, 1688 (1)
Blunt, John, *A True Account of the Payments made by Mr. John Blunt*, 1712 (1)
Bond, Henry, *The Boate Swaines Art*, 1695-1716 (3)
Brown, John, *Description and Use of a Joynt Rule*, 1686 (1)
    The Description and Use of the Carpenter's Rule, 1688-1704 (3)
Burton, John, *The Duty and Reward of Propagating Principles of Religion and Virtue ... A Sermon ... before the Trustees for Establishing the Colony of Georgia in America*, 1733 (1)

[1] I am grateful to the following people for making additions to this list: R. V. and P. J. Wallis for suggestions published with their review of my *Preliminary Hand-List* which appeared in *The Library* 6th Series, 1987, 9:303-9; Frances Woodward of the Special collections of the Library of the University of British Columbia who allowed me to use Coolie Verner's unpublished *The English Pilot ... A Preliminary Check list of Editions 1671 to 1803*; and Lars Bruzelius for pointing out the change in title in Bushnell's work and for the Hardingham edition in a library in Copenhagen.

Bushnell, Edmund, *The Compleat Ship-Wright*, 1699-1748 (4)
[Title changes to *Marine Architecture* with 1739 edition]
Butler, Nathaniel, *Colloquia Maritima; or Sea Dialogues*, 1688 (1)
Collins, Greenville, *Great Britain's Coasting Pilot*, 1693-1792 (24)
Collins, Hercules, *Three Books: I. The Scribe Instructed Unto the Kingdom of Heaven. II. Mountains of Brass... III. A Poem of our Lord and Savior*, 1696 (1)
Collins, John, *The Description and Use of Four Several Quadrants*, 1710-1750 (3)
Collins, Richard, *Country Gaugers Vade Mecum*, 1684 (1)
Colson, Nathaniel, *An Arithmetical Copy-Book*, 1710 (1)
  The Mariner's New Kalendar, 1693-1785 (66)
Desjeans, Jean Bernard Louis, Sieur de, *Expedition to Cartagena*, 1699 (1)
Ditton, Humphry, *The General Laws of Matter and Motion*, 1709 (1)
Donn, Benjamin, *The Description and Use of the Variation and Tide Instruments Improved*, 1766 (1)
  The Description and Use of Four New Instruments, 1772 (1)
Dixon, George, *The Navigator's Assistant*, 1791 (1)
Elements or Principles of Geometrie, 1684 (1)
The English Pilot, the First Book, Part I, Describing the Sea-Coasts in the Southern Navigation, 1701-1792 (35)
  The Second Part, Describing the Sea-Coasts ... in the Whole Northern Navigation, 1708-1785 (17)
  Part III. Describing the Sea-Coasts in the Whole Mediterranean Sea, 1703-1803 (18)
  The Sixth [i.e. Third] Book ... Oriental Navigation, 1701-1716 (11)
  The Fourth Book ... with all the West India Navigation, 1706-1794 (36)
  Part V ... Describing ... The West Coast of Africa, 1720-1780 (11)
Euclides, *An Epitome of Geometry ... by Willingham*, 1714 (1)
  Euclid's Elements ... Demonstrated by Mr. Isaac Barrow, 1714-1751 (5)
Flack, Nic. Ditleves, *The Ready Observer, or an Infallible Method for Determining Latitude at Sea*, 1778 (1)
Forster, Mark, *Arithmetical Trigonometry*, 1700 (1)
Gadbury, John, *Ephemeris of Celestial Motions*, 1709-1718, (2)
Gellibrand, Henry, *Epitomy of Navigation*, 1695-1735 (8)
Good, John, *Multum Parvo; or tables ... Teaching any Person ... to Draw a Sun Dial* (Title changed to *The Art of Shadows* with the 1731 edition), 1706-1731 (5)
  Measuring Made Easy, 1719-1786 (8)
A Grammar of the English Tongue (Attributed to J. Brightland), 1711 (1)
Gt. Brit., Commissioners of Excise, *Abstract of Cases and Decisions on Appeals Relating to the Tax on Servants*, 1781 (1)
  Appeals Relating to the Tax on Servants, 1781 (1)
Gt. Brit., Commissioners of Longitude, *The Nautical Almanac* (for the years 1767 to 1786), 1766-1781 (22)
  A Table of Proportional Logarithms, 1766 (1)
  Tables for Correcting the Apparent Distance of the Moon and a Star, 1772 (1)
  Tables Requisite to be Used with the Astronomical and Nautical Ephemeris, 1766-1781 (2)
Gt. Brit., General Acts, Selections, *An Abstract of all such Acts of Parliament, now in force, as Relate to the Admiralty and Navy of England*, 1715 (1)

An Abstract of the Several Acts of Parliament, Commission for Taking Subscriptions,
    Charter, and By Laws of the Honourable South-Sea Company, 1718 (1)
Greene, John, *The Privileges of the Lord Mayor and Aldermen of the City*, 1708 (1)
Greenwood, Nicholas, *Astronomia Anglicana ... Chiefly ... for the Use of ... Mariners*,
    1699 (1)
Guy's Hospital, *A List of the President and Governors*, 1708 (1)
Hardingham, John, *The Accomplish'd Ship-Wright*, 1709 (1)
Harrison, Edward, *Idea Longitudinis*, 1696 (1)
Harrison, John, *The Principles of Mr Harrison's Time-Keeper*, 1767 (1)
Harrison, Richard ed., *A New Sett of Logarithmic Solar Table*, 1759-1781 (5)
Haselden, Thomas, *The Seaman's Daily Assistant*, 1757-1800 (29)
Hatton, Edward, *Index to Interest*, 1711 (1)
    An Intire System of Arithmetic 1721 (1)
Hauxley, Edward, *Navigation Unveil'd*, 1743 (1)
Heyes, Samuel, *A Treatise of Trigonometry*, 1716-1725 (2)
Hodgkin, William, *A Short, New and East Method of Working the Rule of Practice in*
    Arithmetick, 1731 (1)
Hodgson, James, *The Doctrine of Fluxions*, 1736 (1)
    System of Mathematics, 1723 (1)
    The Theory of Jupiter's Satellites, 1749 (2)
    The Theory of Navigation Demonstrated, 1706-1738 (2)
Hunter, William, *The Out-Port Collector's Guide*, 1764 (1)
    The Tidesman's and Preventive Officer's Pocket Book, 1765 (1)
Hutton, Charles, *Tables of the Products and Powers of Numbers*, 1781 (1)
Instruction for Merchants, Ship-Owners, Ship-Masters, &c. Extracted and Digested from
    the Navigation, The Manifest, Newfoundland, and Wine Acts of Parliament, 1787 (1)
Jeake, Samuel, *Arithmetick Surveyed and Reviewed*, 1696 (1)
Jones, Willaim, *A New Epitome of the Art of Prctical Navigation*, 1706 (1)
Justice, Alexander, *A General Treatise of the Dominion and Laws of the Sea*, 1724 (1)
Kelly, Joshua, *The Modern Navigator's Compleat Tutor*, 1727-1733 (2)
Kersey, John, *Elements of that Mathematical Art Commonly Called Algebra*, 1717-1741
    (4)
Lewis, John, *A dissertation on the Antiquity and Use of Seals in England*, 1740 (1)
Leybourn, William, *Mathematical Institutions*, 1709 (1)
    The Seaman's New Kalendar, 1706 (1)
Lightbody, James, *The New Art of Gauging*, 1713 (1)
Mackenzie, Murdoch, *Nautical Descriptions of the West-Coasts of Ireland*, 1776 (1)
Malard, Michel, *The True French Grammar*, 1697 (1)
The Mariner's Jewel, or Pocket Companion, 1697 (1)
    [Attributed to James Love]
Maskelyne, Nevil, *An Account of the Going of Mr. John Harrison's Watch*, 1767 (1)
    The British Mariner's Guide, 1763 (1)
Mayer, Tobias, *Tabulæ Motuum Solis et Lunæ Novae Correctæ*, 1770 (1)
    Theoria Lunæ Juxta Systema Newtonianum, 1767 (1)
Michell, John, *A Treatise of Artificial Magnets*, 1750-1751 (2)
Michelot, Henry, *Directions for the Mediterranean Pilot*, 1767-1795 (2)
Miller, Thomas, *The Compleat Modelist, or Art of Rigging*, 1699-1700 (2)

Moore, Jonas, *A Mathematical Compendium*, 1693 (1)
Mountaine, William, *An Account of the Methods Used to Describe Lines on Dr. Halley's Chart of the Terraqueous Globe*, 1746-1758 (2)
The Practical Sea-Gunner's Companion, 1747-1781 (3)
The Seaman's Vade-Mecum and Defensive War by Sea, 1744-1783 (11)
Newhouse, Daniel, *The Whole Art of Navigation*, 1686-1727 (6)
Norwood, Matthew, *Norwood's System of Navigation*, 1692 (1)
Norwood, Richard, *Fortification; or Architecture Military*, 1694 (1)
Mr. Richard Norwood's Works, 1684 (1)
Norwood's Epitome. Being the Application of the Doctrine of Triangles, 1698-1721 (2)
The Seaman's Practice, 1692-1732 (12)
A Triangular Cannon of Logarithmicall: or Table of Artificial Sines, 1698 (1)
Park, Robert, *Defensive War by Sea*, 1703-1706 (3) [Title changes to *The Art of Sea Fighting* with 1706 edition]
Parsons, John, *Clavis Arithmeticae; or a Key to Arithmetick and Number and Species*, 1703-1705 (2)
Partridge, Seth, *The Description and Use of an Instrument, Called the Double Scale of Proportion*, 1692 (1)
Patoun, Archibald, *A Compleat Treatise of Practical Navigation*, 1747-1770 (6)
Phillippes, Henry, *Mathematical Manual*, 1683-1693 (2)
Povey, Francis, *The Sea-Gunner's Companion*, 1702-1703 (2)
Ramsden, Jesse, *Description of an Engine for Dividing Mathematical Instruments*, 1777 (1)
Description of an Engine for Dividing Strait Lines on Mathematical Instruments, 1779 (2)
Raphson, Joseph, *Historia Fluxionum*, 1715-1717 (2)
The History of Fluxions, 1715-1717 (2)
Rea, Roger, *The Sector and Plain Scale Compared*, 1727 (1)
Recalls of Ships in the Navy, 1698 (1)
Roper, William, *The Life and Death of Sir Thomas Moore* [sic], 1729 (1)
Russell, John, *A Sermon Preach'd ... November the 12th, 1695,* [1696?] (1)
A Sermon Preach'd ... June 28, 1697, 1697 (1)
Scamozzi, Vincenzo, *The Mirror of Architecture*, 1700 (1)
Seaman's Companion or Vademecum: Containing the Most Necessary things for Qualifying Seamen of all Ranks, by J. L., 1729 (1)
Seller, John, *Practical Navigation*, 1694-1739 (12)
A Sermon Preached at the Chappel Royal. By. J. D., 1695 (1)
Sharp, Abraham, *Geometry Improv'd*, 1717-1718 (2)
Sheperd, Anthony, *Tables for Correcting the Apparent Distance of the Moon and A Star from the Effects of Refraction and Parallax*, 1741 (1)
Sherwin, Henry, *Mathematical Tables*, 1706-1772 (10)
Smith, John, *The Sea-Man's Grammar and Dictionary*, 1699-1705 (2)
Stubbs, Philip, *God's Dominion over the Seas ... A Sermon Preached August 10th, 1701, on board ... The Royal Sovereign*, 1701-1706 (3)
Sturmy, Samuel, *The Mariner's Magazine*, 1684-1700 (2)
Sutherland, William, *The Ship Builder's Assistant*, 1711-1794 (6)
A Table of Logarithms, for Numbers Increasing in their Natural Order from a unit to 10000 ... Carefully Corrected by Sam. Heynes, 1717-1759 (3)

Tapp, John, *The Seaman's Kalendar*, 1696-1702 (2)

Taylor, John, *A Sexagesimal Table*, 1780 (1)

Waddington, Robert, *A Practical Method of Finding the Longitude and Latitude of a Ship*, 1763 (1)

Wakely, Andrew, *The Mariner's Compass Rectified*, 1694-1796 (44)

Wales, William, *The Original Astronomical Observations, Made in the Course of a Voyage Towards the South Pole*, 1777 (1)

Wastell, Thomas, *Application of a New Portable Scale*, 1700 (1)

Wilkinson, John, *Tutamen Nauticum; or, the Seaman's Preservation from Shipwreck, Diseases and other Calamities*, 1763-1764 (2)

Wilson, Henry, *Navigation New Modell'd*, 1723-1783 (17) [Title changed to *Wilson's Epitome* with 1783 edition]

Wright, Robert, *Letter of Advice to Navigators*, 1734 (1)

An Humble Address to the Right Honourable Lords ... Commissioners, Appointed ... to Judge all Performances Relating to Longitude, 1728 (1)

New And Correct Tables of Lunar Motions According to the Newtonian Theory, 1732 (1)

APPENDIX B

THE FORMS OF THE NAME OF THE FIRM

The dates include the years in which the form appeared in imprints. Under Richard Mount the previous form continued on some books after a new member joined.

W. Luggar	*c.* 1600-1656
W. Luggar & W. Fisher	1656-1658
W. Fisher	1657-1690
W. Fisher & R. Mount	1684-1689
R. Mount	1686-1722
R. Mount & T. Page	1701-1707
R. & W. Mount & T. Page	1709-1721
T. Page & W. Mount	1722
T. Page & W. & F. Mount	1723-1729
T. Page & W. Mount	1729-1732
W. Mount & T. Page	1733-1747
W. & J. Mount & T. Page	1747-1752
W. & J. Mount & T. & T. Page	1752-1762
W. & J. Mount & T. Page	1763-1775
J. Mount & T. Page & W. Mount	1775-1781
J. Mount & T. Page & W. Mount & T. Page	1780-1781
Mount & Page	1782-1789
Mount & Davidson	1790-1800
Smith & Venner	1801-1803
Samuel Smith	1803-1817
S. & F. Smith	1817-1824
S. Smith & Co.	1824-1826
Smith & Ebbs	1826-Present

Thomas R. Adams

NOTES

1 I want to thank Commander D. W. Waters for his many suggestions, additions and improvements. I frequently have simply used his wording in maritime and navigational statements. To have put everything he suggested in quotation marks would have made the text cumbersome. Without his help this paper would have had far less substance. Also my thanks to John Alden whose close reading of the text produced the usual rewarding improvements.

2 Fernand Braudel, *The Structures of Everyday Life*, New York, 1979, p. 385.

3 R. C. Anderson, 'Early Books on Shipbuilding and Rigging', *The Mariner's Mirror*, 1924 10, pp. 53-64; 'Eighteenth Century books on Shipbuilding Rigging and Seamanship', ibid., 1947, 33, pp. 218-25.

4 Lawrence C. Wroth, *The Way of a Ship: An Essay on the Literature of Navigation Science*, Portland, Maine, 1937.

5 E. G. R. Taylor, *The Mathematical Practitioners of Tudor and Stuart England*, Cambridge, 1954; *The Mathematical Practitioners of Hanoverian England*, Cambridge, 1966.

6 D. W. Waters, *The Art of Navigation in England in Elizabethan and Early Stuart Times*, New Haven, 1958

7 D. F. McKenzie, ed. *Stationers' Company Apprentices, 1641-1700*, Oxford, 1974; *Stationers' Company Apprentices, 1701-1800*, Oxford, 1978.

8 London, The Bibliographical Society, 1985, Occasional Paper, no. 1.

9 D. W. Waters, *English Navigation Books, 1528-1640: An Annotated Bibliography of Books on Navigation and Hydrography Printed in English down to 1640*, Greenwich, 1979, unpublished.

10 W. R. Chaplin, 'Seventeenth-Century Chart Publishers: Being an Account of the Present Firm of Smith & Ebbs Ltd.', *The American Neptune*, 1948, 8, pp. 302-24.

11 Wing B2934 lists a 1677 edition of Thomas Binning's *A Light of the Art of Gunnery*, with Mount's name in the imprint. The locations cited have all reported that their copy does not include his name. The Editor of the revised Wing believes it is a ghost.

12 The same list issued with Thomas Passenger appears in the 1694 Wakely. I am grateful to Ruth Wallis for calling this to my attention.

13 Chaplin, 'Seventeenth Century Chart Publishers', p. 310.

14 For an account of John Seller and his cartographical publications see Coolie Verner, 'John Seller and the Chart Trade in Seventeenth Century England', in *The Compleat Plattmaker*, ed. N. J. Thrower, Berkeley, 1978, pp. 127-57.

15 John Mount was freed by patrimony 1 November 1727, five years after his father's death. The only possible trace of his activity in the book trade is a pamphlet published in 1708 by 'J. Mount' entitled *The Arraignment, Tryal, and Conviction of Robert Feilding, Esq; for Felony, in marrying Her Grace the Duchess of Cleveland; his first Wife Mrs Mary Wadsworth, being then Alive*. It was a celebrated case involving an ageing Restoration rake but not the sort of thing the firm of Mount and Page would have been likely to publish.

16 John Dunton, *The Life and Errors of John Dunton*, London, 1818, p. 219. First published 1705.

17 *A Sermon Occasioned by the Death of Mr. Richard Mount, Who departed this Life June*

the 29th, the 67th Year of his Age; Preached at Slater's Hall, July 8, 1722, London: Printed in the Year MDCCXXII.
18 Taylor, *Hanoverian England*, p. 127, gives 1722 as the first printing. D. W. Waters, in a letter to me, 9 March 1987, points out that Professor Taylor was not entirely reliable on details such as this and suggests that she confused the work with Haselden's *Description and Use of the Most Excellent Invention commonly called Mercator's Chart* which was published the same year.
19 Based on an analysis of the list of Almon's publications in Deborah D. Rogers's *Bookseller as Rogue: John Almon and the Politics of Eighteenth Century Publishing*, New York, 1986.
20 *The Mariner's Mirror*, 1986, 72, pp. 479-80.
21 Coolie Verner, 'Copperplate Printing', in *Five Centuries of Map Printing*, Chicago & London, 1975, p. 71.
22 P. L. Richardson, 'Benjamin Franklin and Timothy Folger's first Chart of the Gulf Stream', *Science*, 1980, 207, pp. 643-5.
23 D. F. McKenzie, 'Printers of the Mind; Some Notes on Bibliographical Theories and Printing House Practices', *Studies in Bibliography*, 1969, 22, p. 75.
24 Letters to me, 16 May 1987 and 2 August 1987. He based his calculations on data from William Maitland's *The History of London from its Foundation to the Present Time*, London, 1756, and Ralph Davis's *The Rise of the English Shipping Industry in the 17th and 18th Centuries*, London, 1962. He also based his estimates on figures for Scottish populations kindly provided by Professor T. C. Smout, Professor of Scottish History, University of St Andrews, 28 July 1987, and on figures for British America derived from J. J. McKusker & R. R. Menard's *The Economy of British America, 1607-1789*, Chapel Hill & London, 1985. He is indebted to The Caird Fund Trustees, National Maritime Museum, Greenwich, for the fellowship under which he was able to provide these figures.
25 Lawrence C. Wroth, *Some American Contributions to the Art of Navigation*, Providence, 1947. A preprint from *The Proceedings of the Massachusetts Historical Society*, vol. 68.
26 For an account of Maury and American activity in the second quarter of the nineteenth century see Francis Leigh Williams, *Matthew Fontaine Maury, Scientist of the Sea*, New Brunswick, NJ, 1963.
27 The title Edward Wright gave to his English translation from the Dutch of Simon Stevin's *Hafenvinding*, both of which were printed in 1599.
28 Waters, *The Art of Navigation*, p. 500.
29 Based on an estimate of the dates of the working careers of all those biographies in Taylor, *Tudor and Stuart*.
30 N. Plumley, 'The Royal Mathematical School within Christ's Hospital, the Early Years – Its aims and achievements', *Vistas in Astronomy*, 1976, 20, pp. 51-9.
31 Daniel A. Baugh, The British Naval Administration in the Age of Walpole, Princeton, NJ, 1965, pp. 100-2.
32 *Dean's Doctrine of Naval Architecture, 1670*, ed. and introduced by Brian Lavery, London, 1981; Brian Lavery, *The Ship of the Line*, London, 1983, vol. 1, pp. 42-52.
33 F. B. Sullivan, 'The Naval Schoolmasters during the Eighteenth and Early Nineteenth Century', *The Mariner's Mirror*, 1976, 62, pp. 311-26.

34 Taylor, *Tudor & Stuart*, pp. 298 & 305. Davis, *English Shipping Industry*, pp. 124-5.

35 Baugh, *British Naval Administration*, pp. 99-100.

36 N. A. M. Rodger, *The Wooden World: An Anatomy of the Georgian Navy*, London, 1986, pp. 348-52.

37 Baugh, *British Naval Administration*, pp. 100-2.

38 Sullivan, 'Naval Schoolmasters', p. 312.

39 Quoted from a letter to me of 16 May 1987.

40 The original is in the National Maritime Museum, Greenwich. It is reproduced in Rodger, *Wooden World*, opposite p. 126.

41 Davis, *English Shipping Industry*, p. 126.

42 Ibid., pp. 117-21.

43 Rodger, *Wooden World*, pp. 47-54.

44 Derek Howse, 'The Principal Scientific Instruments taken on Captain Cook's Voyage of Exploration, 1768-80', *The Mariner's Mirror*, 1979, 65, p. 134.

45 On the half-title is the signature 'J. C. Parmenter'. Also on the half-title in another hand is 'This book was given to J. C. Parmenter by a native of Pitcairn's Island in 1833'. This is in the hand of William H. Taylor, a Deputy Collector of Customs in New Bedford to whom, another note says, Parmenter gave the book in 1835. James Taylor, apparently his son, gave it to The Old Dartmouth Historical Society, now better known as the New Bedford Whaling Museum, soon after it was founded early in this century.

   Based on research done by Virginia M. Adams, the Librarian of the Museum Library, we know that Jonathan C. Parmenter lived in New Bedford from at least 1836 (the year of the first city directory) to his death in 1838. We also know that two New England whaling ships called at Pitcairn's Island in 1833: the *Balance* of Bristol, Rhode Island, and the *Ploughboy* of Nantucket. While it is not yet possible to place Parmenter on board either of these vessels at the time they visited the island there is nothing about the book or its inscriptions to suggest that it is anything other than what it purports to be.

46 Douglas Southall Freeman, *R. E. Lee, a Biography*, New York, 1934, 1, p. 72-3.

47 Waters, *The Art of Navigation*, p. 500.

48 Taylor, *Tudor and Stuart*, pp. 84-98.

49 Raymond Astbury, 'The Renewal of the Licensing Act in 1693 and its Lapse in 1695', *The Library*, 5th series, 1978, 33, pp. 296-322; John Feather, 'The Book Trade in Politics: the making of the Copyright Act of 1710', *Publishing History*, 1980, 8, pp. 19-44.

50 Charles H. Cotter, 'The Navigational Revolution of the Eighteenth Century', *The Nautical Magazine*, 1963, 195, pp. 214-16.

51 I have not been able to locate where I found this quotation but it must have been in either Taylor, *Tudor and Stuart or Hanoveria*, n5, or Davis, *English Shipping Industry*, n24.

52 A. H. W. Robinson, *Maritime Cartography in Britain: A History of the Sea Chart to 1885*, Leicester, 1962, p. 119.

53 *The Story of the Blue Back Chart*, London, Imray, Laurie, Norie & Wilson, [1903?].

54 I am grateful to R. V. and P. J. Wallis for a number of suggestions and additions to this list which they published with their review of my Preliminary Hand-List

which appeared in *The Library*, 6th Series, 1987, 9, pp. 303-9. I am also under obligation to Frances Woodward in the Special collections of the Library of the University of British Colombia for allowing me to use Coolie Verner's unpublished *The English Pilot . . . A Preliminary Check list of Editions 1671 to 1803.*

LIBRARIES AND THE MIND OF MAN

Nicolas Barker

This topic, which originally provided an introduction to the 1986-7 series, must seem familiar to the point of banality. The book and its history must have been reviewed by countless authors from as many different points of view. What then is the point of yet another reprise of a familiar tale? What special view, what new angle, have we to offer? It is, briefly, this.

The book viewed as an historic artifact is, if not the oldest, at least as old as any other human construction. It is also the commonest; there are more books surviving for every period of the world's history than of all other objects put together. That is a large statement, which needs some justification. I have, perhaps, to stretch the meaning of the word book: by it I mean any vehicle conveying a message through the symbolic representation of language. There are, then, more cuneiform tablets than all the other Assyrian artifacts, from the great gates of Shalmaneser III's palace to the humblest pot (I except sherds); more Egyptian documents from inscriptions to papyri than pyramids to scarabs; more Greek and Roman inscriptions than temples, statues, lamps or pins; more medieval manuscripts than cathedrals, cups or clothes. Coins, themselves a form of document, are the only possible rival. I will not labour the point, but even if we go back to the prehistoric, or rather pre-literate, world of scrapers, arrowheads and firestones, we must remember that Stonehenge and the strange linear sites in Chile may be astronomical documents that we cannot read.

All these, taken both as documents and as artifacts, provide a wealth of evidence about the time which brought them into being – or times, since the text may predate its vehicle and the contrast implicit in that difference may itself be instructive. Such facts have engaged critical minds since the beginning of time, nor was such evidence about the past distinguished from the many other sources that, put together, provided the sum of what was known about it. That knowledge, the *Geisteswissenschaft* that linked the aesthete and archaeologist and the textual critic, Winckelmann and Wolf, the 'antiquity' that engaged Camden and Lambard, Humfrey Wanley and William Stukeley, was the ideal of these and many other great minds: it brought together Politian, Etienne Baluze, Olaus Magnus and the Abate Ficorini. 'A mere antiquarian is a rugged being', according to Dr Johnson (letter to Boswell, 23 April 1778),[1] but there was something admirable about the international comity of interest.

But about a century ago, a division of the ways took place: while the students of other artifacts changed from antiquarians to archaeologists (and thus achieved academic respectability so that there is now a faculty of archaeology in almost every university), those engaged with books took a different path, or rather paths. Librarians *pur sang*, following Cutter and Dewey, became numerologists: those interested in the history of books acquired the name of bibliographers, a word with many meanings, none very flattering. As bibliographers, anxious for a better fame, they sold themselves into slavery to the textual critic. Sir Walter Greg condemned those who 'regard bibliographers as a race of useful drudges *servi a bibliotheca* who are there to do for them some of the spade-work they are too lazy or too incompetent to do for themselves'.[2] But slaves they became, *servi a litteris* whose ultimate justification was the restriction of a text. This image was despatched by my friends David Foxon, in a lecture given in Los Angeles in 1970, *Thoughts on the Future and History of Bibliographical Description*, and Don McKenzie, in a memorable paper in *Studies in Bibliography* called 'Printers of the Mind'.[3]

The 'bibliographers', thus released, did not grasp their new liberty: instead, they are in danger of acquiring new chains. 'The History of the Book' – what book? – has become a flag of convenience for the social historian. The wealth of evidence offered by books – all those hundreds of millions of books devoutly catalogued and analyzed over the last five hundred years – is temptingly available. It is so much larger, so delightfully accessible, when compared with census returns, state papers, parish registers, all the other material from which the social historian derives evidence of adult literacy, religious observance, economic and political allegiance. Some historians treat it with respectful caution, others with generous enthusiasm, but all have an axe to grind. To them, the history of books is a means to an end, not an end in itself.

Milton, who had seen the written and printed word transcend the place, no trivial one, assigned it by society, had seen it, too, effortlessly break the bounds set by a repressive government, knew better. He saw in books 'a potencie of life'[4] that brooked no restraint and escaped easy definition. The purpose of this series is, then, twofold. It seeks to establish, or re-establish, the place of the book, the communicated word, as an independent and essential part of the framework of society, not just a symptom of other, presumably more essential, forces. It also aims to show that the sheer quantity of books, which has caused them to be neglected, cut down, under the name of texts, to a passive rather than active role, in fact makes them the best mirror of society. The evidence that they offer is not restricted to the texts they carry, though that may prove on inspection to be more important than received opinion allows. It is implicit in the physical constituents, the paper, script, printing types, layout and binding; in the evidence of transmission not only of the text but of every individual copy of it; in the concept of authorship and the structure of the book trade. These are the factors that justify the study of books as a subject in its own right, not an ancillary discipline.

It is clearly too much to demand of history both bulk and detail: the history of books seen as the sum of all the copies of all the books in the world and all the processes that brought them into being and brought them where they are would be unimaginably vast. It needs summary, selection and grouping; in this the history of libraries has a special place. The structure and decoration of libraries, the means by which the books in them are amassed, recorded and preserved, at different times from antiquity to the present day, tell us a great deal about the view of the function of the book taken by society at each period. If I concentrate now on these aspects, rather than the better-recorded details of the growth and function of libraries *per se* – their role in society, the separate functions of public and private libraries, the change from monastic to collegiate to institutional libraries, the growth of subscription and lending libraries – it is because the physical details, like the physical details of books, have tended to be neglected. What I hope to show here is that both are closely related, that neither can be considered in isolation from the other, and that together they form a body of information about the function of books in society that tells us much about both.[5]

I go back to that golden age of books and libraries, 'when the kings of Pergamon and Alexandria, rivalling one another in the magnificence and copiousness of their libraries, gave great rates for any treatises that carried the names of celebrated authors'.[6] The words are Bentley's in his *Dissertation on the Epistles of Phalaris*, and he goes on to point out that this 'was an invitation to Scribes and Copiers of those times to enhance the price of their wares, by ascribing them to men of fame and reputation'.

Nothing changes: the prodigality of American private collectors in the nineteenth century, and the Humanities Research Center at the University of Texas in our time, bred forgery just as it did when Attalus and Ptolemy were outbidding each other. Forgery, however, need not engage us today. What matters is the desire of the kings of Pergamon and Alexandria to acquire the works of famous men. The burning of the library at Alexandria was one of the great tragedies of the ancient world: if the destruction of Troy stood at one end of recorded civilization, the Caliph Omar's order to destroy all but the works of Aristotle, an order that kept the bath houses fuelled for six months, stood at the other end. Not even the foundations can be identified certainly.[7]

Fate has been kinder at Pergamon. A range of rooms to the north side of the cloister attached to the Temple of Athena were the traditional site of its library. When this was excavated between 1870 and 1886, the German archaeologists made an interesting discovery:

The foundations of a narrow platform or bench extended along the eastern, northern and western sides, and in the centre of the northern side there was a mass of stone-work which had evidently formed the base for a statue. The discovery of a torso of a statue of Athena in this very room indicated what statue had occupied this commanding position, and also what had probably been the use of the room.

This theory was confirmed by the discovery in the northern wall of two rows of holes in the stone-work, one above the other, which had evidently been made for the reception of brackets, or battens, or other supports for shelves, or some piece of furniture. The lower of these two rows was carried along the east wall as well as along the north wall. Further, stones were found bearing the names of Herodotus, Alcaeus, Timotheus of Miletus, and Homer, evidently the designations of portrait-busts or portrait-medallions; and also, two titles of comedies.[8]

Two salient features about this account will recur as we explore further, the evidence for the existence of shelves and the presence of the names and titles of books. And note, further, the statue of the genius loci, Athena herself.

At Rome there was no public library until the Empire: Caesar's intention to found one, for which he had engaged the great Varro as librarian, was frustrated by his assassination. It was left to C. Asinius Pollio, the patron of Virgil and Horace, to devote the spoils of his Illyrian campaign in 39 BC to this purpose. The Library that he built, in Pliny's striking phrase 'ingenia hominum rempublicam fecit'[9] – something more perhaps than 'made genius public property', a literal translation – did Pollio create the republic of letters out of the mind of man by building that library? It contained all the major works in Greek and Latin, together with busts of their authors, the living excluded except for Varro himself.

It was Augustus who established the first permanent public library at Rome, the Opera Octaviae, which may have been based on the model of the library at Pergamon. It too contained relief portraits of authors, and generous space for those who consulted it to meet and circulate.

But, then as now, private libraries were as distinctive and useful a part of the literary landscape as public. Lucullus owned a famous library, which he opened freely. Those who know him only as an epicure will be struck by Plutarch's vivid description: 'He collected fine copies in large numbers; and if he was splendid in the acquisition of his books he was more so in their use,'[10] a phrase which recalls Gibbon's memorable record of the Emperor Gordian II:

His manners were less pure, but his character was equally amiable with that of his father. Twenty-two acknowledged concubines, and a library of 62,000 volumes, attested the variety of his inclinations; and from the productions which he left behind him, it appears that both the one and the other were designed for use rather than for ostentation.

Gibbon adds a footnote: 'By each of his concubines the younger Gordian left three or four children. His literary productions, though less numerous, were by no means contemptible.'[11] After these instances it is, perhaps, otiose to call in evidence the strictures of that old prig, Seneca, on the evil consequences of excessive indulgence in bibliophily, but they have not only a certain uncomfortable familiarity but also a vivid evidential value.

Outlay upon studies, best of all outlays, is reasonable so long only as it is kept within certain limits. What is the use of books and libraries innumerable, if scarce in a lifetime the master reads the titles? A student is burdened by a crowd of authors, not instructed; and it is far better to devote yourself to a few, than to lose your way among a multitude.

Forty thousand books were burnt at Alexandria. I leave others to praise this splendid amount of royal opulence, as for example Livy, who regards it as 'a noble work of royal taste and royal thoughtfulness.' It was not taste, it was not thoughtfulness, it was learned extravagance – nay, not even learned, for they had bought their books for the sake of show, not for the sake of learning – just as with many who are ignorant even of the lowest branches of learning books are not instruments of study, but ornaments of dining rooms. Procure then as many books as will suffice for use; but not a single one for show. You will reply: 'Outlay on such objects is preferable to extravagance of plate or paintings.' Excess in all directions is bad. Why should you excuse a man who wishes to possess book-presses inlaid with *arbor vitae* wood or ivory; who gathers together masses of authors either unknown or discredited; who yawns among his thousands of books; and who derives his chief delight from their edges and their tickets?

You will find them in the libraries of the most arrant idlers all that orators or historians have written – book-cases built up as high as the ceiling. Nowadays a library takes rank with a bathroom as a necessary ornament to a house. I could forgive such ideas, if they were due to extravagant desire for learning. As it is, these productions of men whose genius we revere, paid for at high price, with their portraits ranged in a line above them, are got together to adorn and beautify a wall.[12]

Book presses (*armaria*) were a regular feature of the Roman library: they were inlaid with *arbor vitae* (cedarwood) which provided an oil that gave the rolls a pleasing yellow colour and protected them against mould and other pests. When Winckelmann visited Herculaneum in 1758, he found the calcined remains of one there, complete with rolls wrapped in their cases, *capsae*. The shape of the *armarium* did not alter when the codex began to supersede the roll. The jurist Ulpian, who died in 228, discussing the legal definition of the word 'book', *liber*, noted that it included *codices* as well as *volumina*. The first depiction of an *armarium*, standing on four legs, with a pedimented top, can be seen in the mosaic decoration of the tomb of Galla Placidia (d. 450) at Ravenna: on its shelves lie four codices, marked with the names of the evangelists. The miniature of the prophet Ezra in the Codex Amiatinus (mid sixth century) shows an exactly similar *armarium*: the nine codices on its shelves, each decorated with a diamond pattern (tooled or painted on the cover) have their titles neatly lettered on the foredge, which faces the spectator: together they make up the text of the Bible, complete up to the Acts. Ezra, in the foreground, sits with his writing instruments around him, writing in a tenth codex which rests on his knee.[13]

The Rule of St Benedict, which slightly predates the Codex Amiatinus, lays down precise instructions for the provision of books and the reading of monks of the order, and the rules of the Cistercian and Carthusian orders, which followed it, laid down further their rules for the custody of books. The customs of the Augustinian Priory at Barnwell, near Cambridge, provide the most detailed instruction of all:

Books which are to be kept at hand for daily use, whether for singing or reading, ought to be in some common place, to which all the brethren can have easy access for inspection, and selection of anything which seems to them suitable. The books, therefore, ought not to be carried away into chambers, or into corners outside the Cloister or the Church. The Librarian ought frequently to dust the books carefully, to repair them, and to point them, lest brethren should find any error or hindrance in the daily service of the church, whether in singing or in reading. No other brother ought to erase or change anything in the books unless he have obtained the consent of the Librarian ...

The press in which the books are kept ought to be lined inside with wood, that the damp of the walls may not moisten or stain the books. This press should be divided vertically as well as horizontally by sundry shelves on which the books may be ranged so as to be separated from one another; for fear they be packed so close as to injure each other or delay those who want them.

Further, as the books ought to be mended, pointed, and taken care of by the Librarian, so ought they to be properly bound by him.[14]

Each book was bound to be a fortress of knowledge, within or without a library chest. Like libraries, they bear instructions. One, at Montecassino, is inscribed: 'Quisquis quem tetigerit sit illi lota manus' – wash your hands before you touch it.[15] Others bear the familiar anathema against theft. Thomas à Kempis, more touchingly, adjures 'take thou a book into thine hands as Simeon the Just took the Child Jesus'.[16] These books were first kept in an *armarium* like Ezra's, in the cloister. This in turn grew to become a room, adjoining or built out of the cloister. Next to it, or part of the cloister, came, by the thirteenth century, carrels, the individual reading rooms for a single monk, which have become a familiar feature of twentieth-century libraries. Those at Westminster contained separate *armaria* for the use of senior monks. Inventories record that books were thus distributed in a number of places. The inconvenience of this resulted in the construction of a single room to house the complete collection of books. The earliest English examples of these, at Durham, Lincoln, and Salisbury, are fifteenth-century, but Cistercian houses, in France and elsewhere, regularly included such a room, two or three centuries earlier.

The lending of books was controlled by the custody of the keys of the locked chest in which they were kept, and the earliest note of such loans is recorded in the thirteenth-century records of the Oxford University chest. The use of chains attaching books to the shelves of the armarium was a natural extension of this process. The choice of books to be generally accessible was made a matter of annual selection by the fellows of William of Wykeham's New College in 1398 and Henry Chichele's College of All Souls in 1443. The existence of a library room, in which books were to be made accessible to a community, suggested the next step, the invention of the communal reading desk. This was a two-sided desk, pitched at a height convenient for the readers who sat at benches on either side of it. The books rested on the desk when not in use. They were protected by a chain which was secured at one end to the top fore edge of the front board of the books and at the other to an iron bar that ran lengthwise along the desk at its apex. Books could thus be chained to both sides of it. The earliest library to preserve its desks, which jut out at right angles to the length of the room between the windows (which thus let in light on the reader and the page) is at Queens' College, Cambridge,

1448. The books are no longer chained there, but an exactly similar arrangement in the church library at Zutphen, dating from the 1560s, preserves all the original fittings, with the locks that held the bar in position, which, unlocked, enabled the books to be changed.

A natural progression led to the standing desk with the books shelved, foredge outwards, on a shelf beneath, as at Trinity College, Cambridge (1600), and thence to the complete book-press, 6'-8' high, with four to six shelves on each side, each shelf with its bar to which the books on it were chained, and a desk at sitting height on each side, sometimes hinged to the body of the press so that it could be folded flat against it. Although, as we shall see, larger institutions abolished chains for other security measures, compelled by the mass of books that poured in upon them in the sixteenth and seventeenth centuries, smaller libraries preserved them. The best-known example is at Hereford Cathedral, and I recently found one, more or less intact, dating from a bequest in 1652, in a small parish church in Lancashire.

In Italy, Germany and the Low Countries a similar development took place, although the chain was normally placed in the centre of the lower, or foot, edge of the board. A fine early example can be seen in the famous Biblioteca Malatestiana, at Cesena (1452). The bar ran beneath the desk, and the books, when not in use, lay on their sides, foredge out, on a shelf beneath. The comparable later development can be seen in the famous bird's-eye viewpoint of the University Library at Leiden (1600). Here the books are shelved upright, as at Trinity Hall, but above, now below, the desk, since the normal place for chain and bar was below, not above, the book.

There was, however, another method of securing the custody of books required by the great increase of books brought about by the invention of printing, which led to the abandonment of all this cumbrous tackle. This was the catalogue. Few people today think of the catalogue as a defensive measure, rather than as a means of access, but so it was. The first catalogues are inventories. When the first book-cases, as we know them, were built, a catalogue, in the form of a shelf list, was placed on a board at the outer edge of the press, so that it faced the reader as he walked down the central aisle. This arrangement lasted from Bishop Fox's Library at Corpus Christi College, Oxford (1516), to the shelves made for the accession of Bishop Moore's Library at Cambridge (1714). It was the product of a more stable society. In a lawless age, books had to be physically protected from violent theft. In a better-controlled community, the subtler method of catalogue, register of loans and fines for non-return was substituted.

And this too reflected a new view of the role of the book. The old codex, from the Codex Sinaiticus to the Gutenberg Bible, was made to last far beyond the lifetime of the men who made it. Like the medieval cathedrals that took centuries to build, books reflected a theocentric view of the universe. Proof against human onslaught, and uncommonly difficult to read, they were meant to last God's good time. The invention of printing, gradually not immediately, reflects a change to books made for men. Paper substituted for vellum, binding in lightweight boards, unencumbered by chains, might only last a man's lifetime, but what men had made other men could replace. It reflects a new view of the function of books and learning. It was not left for each book to fend for itself. Instead, the cumulative mass of books, changing as new wisdom replaced old, grew to reflect a view of universality, rather than individuality, of creation. The library became not a repository for the individual book, but a monument to the unity of learning. The universal church was made of men, souls united in worship of God and combined in his majesty. So the books in a library combined in the majesty of a universal learning. The library, once a goal, now became a temple.

Something of this can be seen in the famous print of Leiden University Library. The serried ranks of books are labelled with their subjects, from theology to medicine. Globes on the table, maps and views of different places, depict the world known to man. Portraits of king and founder are flanked by those of the wise men who wrote the books or adorned the university. The locked presses at the end were for manuscripts; that in the foreground right is labelled 'Legatum Josephi Scaligeri'. The legacy of the great Scaliger, who had died the year before (1609), was honoured by separate safe-keeping. Every rare-book librarian will recognize an arrangement close to present day layout, in practice if not in detail.

It is, however, a prosaic vision, woefully short of decoration. It lacks beauty. The organization, intellectually comprehensible and practical, if clumsy, has no sense of unity. Something of this can, however, be seen in the marquetry that adorns the otherwise plain Biblioteca Malatestiana at Cesena. It is more apparent in the Biblioteca Laurenziana at Florence, begun in 1521, where in Masson's words, 'the genius of Michelangelo broke the medieval mould'[17] and built a room in which unity of design and decoration coordinate everything from the stained glass windows to the book-desks, an improvement on the Malatestiana not only in decoration but functional design (Michelangelo's sketch, complete with seated figure, for these still survives).

But greater than all these, the greatest of all the world's libraries, if not in size, in antiquity and the value of its contents, is the Vatican. Nicolas V, Tommaso Parentucelli, Pope 1447-55, was the first to give the university of learning practical form by drawing a list of the works that such a library should contain, and setting in hand their acquisition (some of the copies made for this purpose still remain). It was Sixtus IV, Pope from 1471, who formally inaugurated the Library by appointing Bartolommeo Platina as librarian and creating a special building for it. Although, alas, the set of four rooms overlooking the Corte del Belvedere no longer exists as such, the famous picture by Melozzo da Forli of Platina kneeling before the pope that faced the reader as he entered still survives. Part of the frescoes in the spandrels of the vaulted ceiling, by Melozzo and the brothers Ghirlandaio, have recently been recovered; they show that above the stalls, arranged as in the Malatestiana, was a frieze like a balcony from which figures representing prophets, doctors of the church, philosophers, looked down, each pagan faced by a Christian opposite. The four rooms, each opening off the other, contained, in order from the door that admitted the reader, the Libraries of Latin, then Greek books, the Bibliotheca Secreta, containing rare and out-of-the-way books, and the Bibliotheca Pontificia where the greatest treasures were kept, among them 'Virgilius antiquis litteris majusculis', which must be the famous fourth-century Codex Vaticanus of Vergil. It too contained a map, framed in 1478, and globes for which sheepskin covers were supplied in 1477.[18]

This was the intellectual foundation of what is still perhaps the greatest of all library rooms, the creation of another Sixtus, Sixtus V, who transformed not only the Vatican but all Rome in the brief four and a half years of his papacy beginning in 1585. The pillared hall that spans the Corte del Belvedere from east to west, $184' \times 57'$, is not immediately recognizable to us as a library, since the books are all in closed presses set round the piers and between the windows. In fact, however, it is, in structure, decoration and function, at once a purely classical and completely modern library. The decoration of the pillars shows the discoverers of letters, Adam, Mercury, Cadmus, Evander and the rest; on the walls are pictured the great libraries of past and present learning, from Moses and Ezra above the Bibliotheca Hebraea, Ptolemy and the authors of the Septuagint above the Bibliotheca Alexandria, Tarquin and Augustus above the Bibliotheca Romana, to St Peter, ordering the preservation of the scriptures, and his successors above the Bibliothecae Apostolorum and Pontificum. On the facing wall are scenes depicting the Councils of the Church, and on the side walls allegories of the virtues inculcated by books, the whole typified by the pictures of the monuments of Sixtine Rome, the restored Lateran, obelisks, fountains, so that the whole city becomes an allegory of the learning enclosed in the library.[19]

If all this unites the glories of the Augustan libraries with the revelation of the Christian faith in a way that perfectly echoes the classical library, it is also thoroughly modern in dividing the storage of books from the needs of readers. The hall served, as did the classical library, as a meeting place; the decoration inspired discourse and directed the choice of reading that was done elsewhere. Just how influential this great model was can be seen from the Escorial, which must strike us as a more obvious model of the modern library. Its single vault, 212′ × 36′, has open bookshelves against the walls, with floor space punctuated only with a line of narrow presses and globes. But its decoration, though almost contemporary with the Sixtine library, must derive from it. There are personifications of Philosophy, Theology and the other subjects, the First Nicene Council, facing the School of Athens (like Raphael's in the Sala della Signatura), Solomon, Cicero, David, Orpheus, and so on. The Biblioteca Ambrosiana (1603-11) adds a gallery to this basic pattern. It became immensely influential throughout Europe. Sir Thomas Bodley, whose original library built in 1598 was on the medieval pattern with shelves and desks at right angles to the walls, was engaged in diplomatic missions on the continent in the first decade of the seventeenth century. On his return he added two extensions at each end, wall-shelved, with a gallery, and a frieze incorporating pictures of books and scrolls, inkwells, and globes, together with two hundred portraits of classical authors, the Fathers of the Church, English writers and contemporary scholars. The evidence of the new system inaugurated by Sixtus V could hardly be clearer.

Bodley may be the model for the Langley Marish Library, a magical little room in a country parish church, whose shelves are covered by doors, inlaid on the exterior with portraits and coats of arms, and on the inside with trompe l'oeil pictures of open books, while the frieze depicts landscapes and the virtues. This miniature library leads us to an even smaller library. The portable library of Sir Julius Caesar, as familiar to visitors to the British Museum in London as the Ellesmere library at Huntington Library is to Californians, is modern in its matched white vellum bindings, ancient in its panelled catalogue, but above all architectural in design. Samuel Pepys's elegant book-cases are the cabinet equivalent of the wall-shelf system. The 'steps' he had made to equalize the height of his books again emphasize the decorative quality of books, now chainless and turned *spine* out, with the title lettered on the spine. This arrangement suggests that the book itself has come to be the image of its content, not the great pictures which served the same purpose in the great institutional libraries.

At this point, it is instructive to recall the publication, within a few years of each other, of two manuals for the making of libraries, Gabriel Naudé's *Advis pour dresser une bibliotheque* (1627) and Claude Clément's *Musaei sive bibliothecae extructio, instructio, cura, usus* (1635), the one in limpid French, the other in florid Latin. At first sight Naudé, with his clear instructions on the choice of books, the construction and use of a catalogue, and above all his insistence that its resources should be available to all mankind, seems the first of the modern unitary theorists, just as the Bibliothèque Mazarin, the library that he made for Cardinal Mazarin that exemplifies his theories, is the first modern library. Yet Clément, who also made an exemplary library at Dole (now refurbished in an elegant eighteenth-century style that makes it hard to regret the loss of Clément's decor), was the more influential. This insistence on an integrated decor, shelves topped with appropriate busts, his enchanting combination of mottos with figures, all combining in a pyramid with Christ and the Virgin at its apex, supported by the Doctors of the Church whose feet rest on the pagan writers or press down the oppressed figures of heretics, was to be given splendid reality in the great baroque and rococo libraries. Coimbra, built by John V of Portugal between 1716 and 1723, shows a series of triumphal arches to learning. Fischer von Erlach's Hofbibliothek at Vienna uses *trompe l'oeil* in every medium to fuse the books in a decor that recalls Clément's vision. At Admont, Altomonte's paintings and Stammel's sculpture actually give physical form to his theological mythology.

But Clément's most lasting contributions to library structure were not to be realized by architects and artists. First, and too easily forgotten, is his insistence on the importance of site. Clément never forgot his reader, not Naudé's generous but generalized vision of mankind, but an individual, selected by natural sympathy, seated between the shelves, surrounded by inspiring imagery within, but looking out of a window from time to time on a landscape with high mountains or an expanse of fields, the clear waters of a river or verdant forests; or, if that is not possible, a garden or orchard, *tantula animi et oculorum relaxatio* – some little relief to mind and eyes.[20]

Secondly, there was his painstaking and laborious construction of a subject catalogue, like his mythological imagery a pyramid, with theology its apex and every branch of human learning arranged in dependent sequence beneath. To Clément these two pyramids, or personified and intellectual learning, were two visions of a single whole, each repeating, rather than complementing each other. The wild reality of baroque decor, in one direction, and the great 'Tableau', the diagrammatic summary of human knowledge in Diderot and D'Alembert's *Encyclopédie* (which derives from Clément), in the other direction, split author and subject catalogues apart. Peignot's *Dictionnaire raisonné de bibliologie* (1802-4) gave the 'Tableau' bibliothecal form. Brunet's *Manuel* canonized both it and the alphabetical author catalogue.

Before exploring this divide, pause for a moment to recall one specifically British contribution to library architecture. Both the medieval right-angle press and the renaissance wall-system had their merits. By typically British compromise it was left to Sir Christopher Wren to combine the two, forming alcoves, enclosing a table with a revolving lectern at which a reader might sit, within a glorified carrel whose walls were books. Wren built three great libraries, at Lincoln and St Paul's Cathedrals, and, greatest of all, Trinity College, Cambridge, where his final solution can be seen within a structure whose great windows are divided by Ionic pilasters and the whole supported on a cloister of Doric pillars. Sansovino's Marciana was the immediate model but behind it lay Michelangelo's Laurenziana. Its classic restraint, with its natural evolution from its medieval and renaissance predecessors, give it a combination of elegance and utility that is timeless.

After Wren's Trinity, the two great nineteenth-century library rooms of the British Museum, the long King's Library (1823-8) and the revolutionary round Reading Room (1853-7), are perhaps the greatest British contributions to library architecture. Between the building of the two, Anthony Panizzi, the greatest of all Principal Librarians, fought and won a battle whose consequences had great and sinister consequences on library structure. The Trustees wanted a subject catalogue; Panizzi was convinced that an author catalogue (properly cross-indexed) was superior. It took him ten years, and the cost was a library shelved in a subject order.

This concession led to the belief that the dual system, alphabetic catalogue and subject-shelving, was an ideal arrangement. Subject shelving with a subject catalogue (or shelf-list) in the old way, was a practical model for a closed library. For libraries contending with a rapidly increasing intake, it has proved disastrous. Watts's 'elastic system', the fruit of Panizzi's compromise, was canonized in the numerical systems of

Cutter and Dewey. While Dewey sufficed for the public library, with fixed shelf-space but variable content, the Library of Congress system, embracing both subject and author, was required for libraries with a content invariable save for the factor of constant growth. The inevitable result has been an overwhelming concentration on the appalling logistical problems of building a container – *any* container – that will allow growth within the Library of Congress procrustean bed. All this, besides the complexities of modern building and reader's needs, make the new edition of Keyes Metcalfe's a large as well as admirable book. But there is not much in it about matters other than logistical: design and decoration are briefly and – one splendid indiscretion apart – guardedly dealt with.

An academic or research library, as much as any building, should express human dignity and assert the centrality of books for an informed civilization, the timelessness of materials therein which record human thoughts, successes, failures, theorems, dreams,

> 'The New York Public Library is not … one great confusion of ornamental episodes. Anyone who looks even hurriedly at the New York Public Library can hardly fail to be aware of an order in the disposition of its parts. A central pavilion pierced with three deep arches anchors the building to the fine terrace upon which it stands; from this pavilion two peristyles march equal distances right and left and end in identical little temples; and the blithe ornament dances across the marble walls in rhythmical ecstasies. The intention of the architect was clearly so to relate all of these that taken together they would present a unity; and if we are persuaded of that unity, finding it complete and without adventitious parts or discordances, it may happen that we will find in such unity a mode of beauty.'

Opinions of course change (see fig. 4.1).[21]

(Fig. 4.1 is a particularly sober and eminently recognizable view of the Fifth Avenue façade.) There is, however, much sound sense in a small compass here, and one observation in particular deserves our notice here. 'Traditionally library buildings have tended to be monumental in character. … Because of the long-term inertia derived from the desire for monumentality, the impact of such a design should be clearly understood … the cost of monumentality is high [and can] add cost that may limit the ability to provide a facility that meets the programmed operational needs.'

We all recognize the symptoms. There are notable modern exceptions, the Beinecke Library at Yale with its interior column of indirectly lit books in a shell of translucent marble, the irregular hexagon of Fisher Library at Toronto, with its interior walls also indirectly lit. Using light *off* books as illumination has also transformed the Herzog August Bibliothek. But the costs in all three cases were, in Metcalfe's phrase, 'high':

is there no way out? Is the modern library architect to be left only the outside of the building to signal its purpose, the inside to be left as 'functional' (a euphemistic pejorative) as an office or an airport?

Perhaps relief may be seen in an unexpected quarter, in – I hardly dare breathe the word – the computer. Computers, we have learnt, are all very well for compiling or retrieving, but not for *being* books. The human mind is a thing of wayward impulse, unpredictable (as yet) by mechanical means. A page of a book, as developed over the centuries, has become its convenient frame. No concatenation of CRT and computer is so agile that it can answer these impulses. But it can tell you where to find books, what is in them, and much else, that books have been forced, against their nature (try reading the back of today's title-pages), to tell us themselves. Let the computer do this: what then? The books can be in random order. If order is needed, let it be, like Samuel Pepys's, order of height; it looks well and is better for the books. If anyone complains that this will destroy the pleasure of browsing – well, the secret of successful browsing is its serendipity. Must a library be all books to all people? May it not have a character of its own, a character imposed as well as described by its physical surroundings?

All the libraries I have mentioned have, and were planned to have, a character of their own. Many of their characteristics are to be found within and without the walls of the William Andrews Clark Library: shelves that merge with the interior walls; emblematic paintings that reflect the founder's purpose and interests, add to and illuminate the contents; above all, an exterior and surroundings that make it, for me, the prettiest building in California. Will the computer, of all unlikely allies, by doing away with the constraints that have squeezed human imagination out of library design, let it back in again? If books deserve, as suggested at the beginning, to be treated as objects of study in themselves, not just as means towards the study of something else, may not books, not the real or imagined needs of systems and administrators and users (who I take to be different from readers) – may not books suggest, even dictate, the company they keep and the structure best fitted to hold them?

NOTES

1 Letter to Boswell, 23 April 1778 (*Life of Johnson*), ed. G. Birkbeck Hill and L. F. Powell, Oxford, 1934, III, p. 278.
2 W. W. Greg, 'Bibliography – a Retrospect', in the Bibliographical Society's *Studies in Retrospect*, Oxford, 1942, p. 24.

3 D. F. McKenzie, 'Printers of the Mind', *Studies in Bibliography*, 22, 1969, pp. 1-76; David F. Foxon, *Thoughts on the History and Theory of Bibliographical Description*, Los Angeles, 1970.

4 John Milton, *Areopagitica and Of Education*, ed. K. M. Lea, Oxford, 1973, p. 6.

5 The view of the history and function of libraries taken here owes much to J. W. Clark's *The Care of Books*, Cambridge, 1901, still the best and most humane account of the subject.

6 Richard Bentley, *A Dissertation upon the Epistles of Phalaris*, London, 1699, p. 9. The copy cited (BL 1088.m.9) is heavily annotated by Thomas Warton.

7 But see P. M. Fraser, *Ptolemaic Alexandria*, Oxford, 1972, I, pp. 334-5, II, pp. 479-80, 493-4.

8 Clark, *Care of Books*, p. 11.

9 Pliny, *Historia naturalis*, VII, 30.

10 Plutarch, *Lucullus* c.xlii, cit. Clark, *Care of Books*, pp. 21-2.

11 Edward Gibbon, *The Decline and Fall of the Roman Empire*, ed. J. B. Bury, New York, 1946, p. 139.

12 *De tranquillitate animae*, c.IX; quoted by Clark, *Care of Books*, p. 21.

13 Clark, *Care of Books*, pp. 39-40.

14 Clark, *Care of Books*, p. 71.

15 Clark, *Care of Books*, p. 76.

16 Clark, *Care of Books*, p. 77.

17 André Masson, *Le Décor des Bibliothèques du Moyen Age à la Révolution*, Paris, 1972, p. 69.

18 Clark, *Care of Books*, pp. 208-32.

19 Clark, *Care of Books*, pp. 49-60; J. A. F. Orbaan, *Sixtine Rome*, London, 1911, pp. 75-129.

20 C. Clement, *Musaei, sive bibliothecae tam privatae quam publicae extractio instructio, dura, usus*, Paris, 1635.

21 Keyes DeWitt Metcalfe, *Planning academic and research Buildings*, 2nd edn, ed. Philip D. Leighton and David C. Weber, Chicago, 1986, p. 59; the quotation is from J. Hudnut, *Architecture and the Spirit of Man*, Cambridge, 1949, p. 5.

INTENTIONALITY AND
RECEPTION THEORY

SINCE a large part of the thesis advanced in 'A New Model for the Study of the Book' depends upon the intentions of the author, publisher and others involved in launching books into the world, and the other intentions of those who have, in one way or another, preserved them since, and also upon the reception of books, whether expressed by purchase or loan, reading or familiarity at second hand, it is only appropriate to reflect on what has been written about 'intentionality' and 'reception theory', two topics much discussed over the last thirty years. These discussions have, it is true, little bearing on our 'new model', but their course indicates, yet again, why books have not been studied in the way that we suggest.

Intentionality, 'the quality or fact of being intentional',[1] is a word that has crept into the vocabulary of bibliography in all the mass of critical writing on editorial theory and practice that has followed Greg's 'The Rationale of Copy-Text'.[2] It relates specifically to the author's intentions towards his text, as reflected (rightly or wrongly) in the documentary witnesses of it, and the editor's principles and practice in recognizing and restoring these intentions. The problems thus presented are complex, and justify not only the mass of case-law that has accumulated round them, but also the series of theoretical essays that followed Greg's, notably those of Fredson Bowers and G. Thomas Tanselle.[3] The specific question of intentionality was addressed by Tanselle in 1976 in 'The Editorial Problem of Final Authorial Intention',[4] to which James McLaverty made a thoughtful rejoinder, 'The Concept of Authorial Intention in Textual Criticism' (1984):[5] the theme was addressed again by Tanselle in 'Historicism and Critical Editing' (1986).[6]

All these, and others in the same genre, relate to one set of intentions only, the author's, and are mostly taken up with the specific issue of editorial treatment of authorial intent. As such, they would seem to have little to do with our theme. However, a number of topics raised by this line of enquiry have served to broaden it. McLaverty, for instance, rightly distinguishes the need to define intention, and in particular points to the misconstruction that has been put on the views of the leading literary theorist who has addressed the problem, E. D. Hirsch, on the relationship between motive and intention. Motive is different from intention: motive is a state of mind peculiar to the author, strictly irrelevant from intention. Intention, as the editor may interpret it, is an objective in which the author's motives are only a partial factor:

While the editor is not morally free to alter his author's work or misconstrue it (unless, perhaps, he announces joint authorship), he is free to choose any version he wishes. The act of publication (subject to copyright laws) bestows such freedom on him.[7]

This has led to an exploration of the wider area in which the editor is free, and, in consequence, to a revision of the boundaries that separate (less and less absolutely) the functions of the textual or literary critic, the editor or bibliographer, the literary and social historian. From the editor's point of view the spectrum has widened to two extreme points: 'the view that literature is social and collaborative in nature and therefore that the historical forms in which a work was presented to the public are of primary significance; and, at the other end of the spectrum, the view that literary works are the products of discrete private acts of creation and therefore that their essential forms do not include alterations by others nor even later revisions by the authors themselves'.[8] The former view, without any sense of editorial *ukase*, was suggested by D. F. McKenzie and the present writer at a symposium at the Herzog August Bibliothek, Wolfenbüttel in 1977,[9] and has subsequently been enlarged and explored by McKenzie.[10] Its application to the editor's task, seen as a branch of historial scholarship, has been reinforced by Jerome McGann.[11] Randall McLeod, in a series of articles, has emphasized the importance of physical form in interpreting intention.[12]

The evidence, then, of the intention not merely of authors, but of compositors, printers, binders, publishers, booksellers (new and second-hand), of the owners and editors of journals and of circulating libraries, are factors not merely in the editor's world, although that is where they have been most carefully weighed. It is too much to assert, as McGann does, that the editor's task is not complete without them:

The dynamic social relations which always exist in literary production – the dialectic between the historically located individual author and the historically developing institutions of literary production – tends to become obscured in criticism. Authors lose their lives as they gain such critical identities, and their works suffer a similar fate by being divorced from the social relationships which gave them their lives (including their 'textual' lives) in the first place, and which sustain them through their future life in society.[13]

Editorial criticism is not the agent of demolition: rather, it is a strand, a creative and fruitful element, in our new model for the study of the book. How that strand can be interwoven with the broader web of social history without loss to itself can be seen in Peter Shillingsburg's *Scholarly editing in the computer age* (Athens, 1986). The value of collaborative work, embracing textual, critical and historical methods and views, has been stressed by both Tanselle and the present writer.[14]

The reception of any bibliographical document is obviously a process complementary to the intention that set it in motion. Here again critical theory has tended to take priority over the accumulation of fact, let alone historical analysis. Even a work like H. S. Bennett's *English books and readers*, covering the period 1475 to 1640, though admirably thorough in its scope, suffers from the fact that it is written from the point of view of the modern student of early English literature. A sociologist like Leo Löwenthal could note, as early as 1932:

It is sociologically interesting that a task like the study of the effect of literary works, which is so important and central for research, has been almost entirely ignored, even though there exists in journals and newspapers, in letters and memoirs, an infinite amount of material that would teach us about the reception of literature in specific social groups and by individuals.[16]

This call for action has yet to be answered. Reader-response criticism has preferred to develop its own theories of reaction, whether from the point of view of linguistics (Saussure), Russian formalism (Shklovskii and Jakobson), Prague structuralism (Mukhařovský), phenomenology (Ingarden), hermeneutics (Gadamer) or sociology. It was the last that provided the 'Constance School' (Jauss and Iser) with the basis on which to construct a reception theory, although other critics, Norman Holland, Jonathon Culler, Stanley Eugene Fish, have pursued similar paths from the stand point of literary criticism.[17] The author's intention anticipates a response, which it may or may not obtain; this counterpoint was ingeniously displayed in Fish's *Surprised by sin: the reader in 'Paradise Lost'* (1967).

Reception theory itself, however, is the result of 'a more cohesive, conscious, and collective undertaking',[18] in Germany, both West and East. It originates in the need to make a new start, in literature and scholarship as in socio-political matters, *geistliche* as well as *weltliche*. If *Geistesgeschichte* was no longer a satisfactory solution, the harder approach of the 'Constance School', involving a distinction between *Rezeption* and

Wirkung (roughly speaking, between the reader's and the author's idea of what has taken or will take place), has presented its own problems. The 'conversion' of past masterpieces (and not only masterpieces but trivia) to serve present needs requires the reinstatement of history as central not merely to literary studies, but to the understanding of society and its artifacts, on exchange of hermeneutics for a new aesthetic approach.

This is not the place to summarize Jauss's work, set out at magisterial length in *Aesthetische Erfahrung und literarische Hermeneutik* (1977, revised and enlarged edition 1982); it involves three different kinds of aesthetic experience (*poiesis, aisthesis, katharsis*) through five different modes of identification (associative, admiring, sympathetic, cathartic and ironic). Each of these is illuminated by case-studies, involve myths (The Fall, Faust), different treatments of the same theme (Goethe and Valéry, Racine and Goethe's 'Iphigenia'), the contrast of Enlightenment and *Sturm und Drang* in *La nouvelle Héloïse* and *Werther*, and, under the title of 'La Douceur du Foyer', a suggestive analysis of the interpretation of French poetical texts in the magic year 1857.[19] This is a substantial broadening of the horizon (Husserl's word) or reception, a denial of Adorno's negative view of pleasure as escapism, a re-assertion of *Genuss* as the primary aesthetic experience, central to communication as a social activity. All this takes us a long way from our model for tracing the impact of bibliographic documents, nor does the phenomenological approach of Wolfgang Iser to the interaction of text and reader bring us any closer. The debate between Iser and Fish on determinacy, and the 'communication aesthetics' of Günter Waldmann, involve reception at a philosophical rather than practical level.[20]

You cannot reject, as Jauss did, the traditional Marxist view of the function of literature as social response (Marx specifically opposed the value of aesthetic pleasure), without eliciting a response from Marx's intellectual heirs. The theory of corporate response to a literary tradition as the yardstick by which to measure reception was linked with a re-definition of a literary 'heritage'. All this was set out in the introductory section, by Dietrich Sommer, of *Funktion und Wirkung: soziologische Untersuchungen zur Literatur und kunst* (Weimar, 1978), themes worked out in subsequent essays by Sommer, Dietrich Löffler, Achim Walter and Eva Maria Scherf. The contrary directions of *Rezeption* and *Wirkung* are resolved in terms of Marxian 'exchange', and the whole illustrated with a series of diagrams and tables on the reading habits, including book ownership, of 1794 interviewees in Halle and Leipzig (42% male, 57% female; 44% workers, 30% housewives, 13% managerial, 9% students), who responded to a questionnaire of 66 fixed questions. This was followed by a still broader survey, *Leseerfahrung, Lebenserfahrung* (1983), based on 21 fixed and 2 open questions put to 1424 interviewees, industrial employees and local inhabitants in Querfurt.

At first sight, such exhaustive analysis, based on carefully planned and analysed sampling, seems to offer a more practical approach. But the nature of the questions, the purely literary texts discussed, the strongly Marxist sociological base of the interpretation and the lack of any sense of historic movement deprive it of any real value as a study of reading habits, as well as limiting its effect as a response to the 'Constance School', which becomes progressively more self-regarding.[21] Nor is current writing in English more encouraging. A final essay by Jane P. Tompkins in a survey of reader-response criticism, which seems to offer a sense of reception as historic, proves to be jejune.[22] Other recent studies by Cathy Davidson and Janice Radway show an equal absence of any feeling for the documents of contemporary or subsequent response.[23] Only Catherine M. Bauschutz, in a study of Montaigne's concept of reading,[24] is aware of the vast spectrum of change in ways of reading, as well as in subject matter and volume, that these records reveal. The dangers of applying ahistorical criteria to historic facts about meaning and interpretation have been emphasized by Fish.[25]

Why, it may well be asked, expect more of literary criticism than it pretends to offer? The answer lies in the extension of the concept of 'intentionality'. Finding out the meaning of the text is the oldest, the most critical, of human responses to it. While it is restricted to finding out what the author meant, it can be limited, so to speak, to the traditional functions of textual and literary criticism. If the concept of meaning is no longer personal, if intention is indeed to be taken as a corporate or abstract aspect of the text, then the facts of reception need to be studied with the same thoroughness and intensity as those of meaning, before a theory of reception can be erected that can be compared with the theory of intention.

It is difficult not to regard the theorizing, the controversy, the construction of elaborate models of response, as activities detached from the texts to which they have been applied. What has caused this alienation? Is it not perhaps itself a response, an instinctive social reaction, to the terrible disruption of society in the first half of the century, the disturbance of accepted canons about human behaviour as well as about the function of the arts in general and texts in particular? If so, no doubt this reaction will find its own response. It will have served a useful purpose if it returns attention to the need to study the facts about intention and reception, the object of our new model for the study of the history of the book.

The plain fact of the matter, common to both intention and reception, is that they are abstractions, or, rather, that neither can be discussed or understood without reference to the fact of transmission, without which neither has any substance. Transmission is the essence of our new model, which links intention and reception, and converts them into a historic process. Transmission gives intention a practical sense, because it constitutes the meaning of a text at a particular moment in time. Reception similarly can only be recorded by gathering together the facts of the transmission of the text; their sum represents its reception. The process is one of Darwinian selection and survival: of all the different intentions involved, those of writer, editor or compositor, publisher, bookseller or reviewer, reader at first or second hand, or of those still further removed, only some survive to form that part of the general reception (and onward transmission) of the text. It is thus that it is subsumed in the study of the history of the book.   N.J.B.

NOTES

1   O.E.D., 2nd ed., s.v., which gives no special usage in this context: 'Observe the consciousness and intentionality of his wit' (Coleridge, 1834).
2   *Studies in Bibliography* 3 (1950-1), 19-36.
3   Collected in, respectively, *Essays in bibliography, text, and editing* (Charlottesville, 1975) and *Selected studies in bibliography* (Charlottesville, 1979).
4   *Studies in bibliography* 29 (1976), 167-211.
5   *The Library*, 5th ser., 6 (1984), 121-38.
6   *Studies in bibliography* 39 (1986), 1-46.
7   McLaverty, loc. cit. n.5, p. 130.
8   Tanselle, loc. cit. n.6, pp. 3-4.
9   *Buch und Buchhandel in Europa im achtzehnten Jahrhundert*, ed. G. Barber and B. Fabian (Wolfenbüttel, 1981), 81-165.
10 'The Sociology of a text: orality, literacy and print in early New Zealand', *The Library*, 6th ser., 6 (1984), 333-65, and *Bibliography and the sociology of texts* (London, 1986).
11 'The Monks and the Giants: textual and bibliographical studies and the interpretation of literary works', *Textual criticism and literary interpretation*, ed. McGann (Chicago, 1985), 180-99.
12 'Spellbound: typography and the concept of old-spelling editions', *Renaissance and Reformation*, n.s., 3 (1979) 50-65; 'The marriage of good and bad quartos', *Shakespeare Quarterly* 33 (1982), 421-31; and elsewhere.
13 Jerome McGann, *A critique of modern textual criticism* (Chicago, 1983), p. 81.

Appendix

14 G. Thomas Tanselle, *The history of books as a field of study* (Chapel Hill, 1981); N. Barker, 'Reflections on the history of the book', *The Book Collector* 39 (1990), 9-26.

15 H. S. Bennett, *English books and readers*; I, 1475-1537; II, 1558-1603; III, 1603-1640 (Cambridge, 1952-70).

16 L. Löwenthal, *Erzählkunst und Gesellschaft: die Gesellschafts problematik in der deutschen Literatur des neunzehnstens Jahrhundert* (Neuwied, 1971), 39; cited by R. Holub, *Reception theory: a critical introduction* (Methuen, 1984), 45.

17 I have drawn heavily on Holub, op. cit., for the antecedents of reception theory.

18 Holub, xiii.

19 H. Jauss, *Aesthetische Erfahrung und literarische Hermeneutik* (1982), 377-653, 704-49, and especially 777-86.

20 See W. Iser, *The act of reading* (Baltimore, 1978); *Diacritics* 11 (1981), 2-13, 82-7; G. Waldmann, *Kommunikationsaesthetik; 1. Die Ideologie der Erzählform* (Munich, 1976).

21 H. Jauss, *Die Theorie der Rezeption: Rückschau auf ihre unerkannte Vorgeschichte* (Konstanz, 1987), contains a section on Christian and Jewish *receptio* in the Middle Ages, as well as reflections on later attitudes from Montaigne to Borges, but the framework remains that of modern *Rezeption-Theorie*.

22 'The Reader in History: the changing shape of literary response', Jane P. Tompkins (ed.), *Reader-response criticism: from formalism to post-structuralism* (Baltimore, 1980), 201-31).

23 Cathy N. Davidson, *Revolution and the word: the rise of the novel in America* (Oxford, 1980); (ed.) Susanna Haswell Thompson, *Charlotte Temple* (Oxford, 1986).

24 'Montaigne's Conception of Reading in the Context of Renaissance Poetics and Modern Criticism', Susan R. Suleiman and Inge Crosman (eds.), *The reader in the text: essays on audience and interpretation* (Princeton, 1980), 264-91.

25 S. Fish, *Doing what comes naturally: change, rhetoric, and the practice of theory in literary and legal studies* (Durham, Duke University Press, 1989), in particular 'Going down the Anti-Formalist Road' (1-33) and 'Why No One's Afraid of Wolfgang Iser' (68-86); see also pp. 246-51 and 351-5.

INDEX